Praise for
Coach Anyone About Anything Volume 2

"We believe peak performance comes from providing responsibility, learning, recognition, and joy. This book will help you deliver all four."
— KEVIN ROBERTS, CEO Worldwide Saatchi & Saatchi

"I have spent several hours with this book, and I am truly fascinated by it. There is so much in it—so many good things. This book causes us to question our basic assumptions about how we view people, time, and how we can positively influence others. It is loaded with practical tools, tips, and stories that drive home critical points and make them come alive. *Coach Anyone About Anything Volume 2* is a powerful guide to effective coaching for managers, executives—anyone who wants to help others reach their goals."
— DAVE DOWNEY, PhD, Executive Director
Center for Food and Agricultural Business, Purdue University

"*Coach Anyone About Anything Volume 2* is full of insightful aha moments! Germaine and Jed have such clear and engaging voices, they kept my attention. Through personal examples and stories, I was able to make fast and meaningful connections to how what they teach will be useful for me. The distinctions between coaching and mentoring will make a significant change in the way I approach and listen to people. I love how there are applications for all roles and perspectives—be it as a manager, executive, coach or just as a helper—helping others who want to succeed. It's easy to tell or teach; what's important is that readers learn and are motivated to apply what they learned. *Coach Anyone About Anything Volume 2* is a real motivator—from those who read it to those who get the benefit of someone reading it."
— BOBBI DEPORTER
President, Quantum Learning Network, SuperCamp / QL Education
Author of *Quantum Learning, Quantum Business, Quantum Success*

"Coach Anyone About Anything Volume 2 is one of the few books I have found that offers entertaining insights to develop and empower others while providing real-life tools that can be immediately applied to any business situation."

> —STACEY SCHETZSLE, PhD
> Assistant Professor of Marketing and Management
> Ball State University

"In today's business environment more than ever, it is people who provide the competitive advantage for business to succeed. This book provides leaders with the insight and toolkit to develop and maximize that resource; to the benefit of the organization, the coach, and the player!"
—MICHAEL GROJEAN, PhD, Professor in the Practice of Management
Director of Custom Programs, Executive Education
Jesse H. Jones Graduate School of Business, Rice University

"Jed and Germaine's approach to coaching is filled with humor, conviction, wisdom, and the clear passion they have for a subject over which they have true mastery and many years of top-level experience. Anyone in any area of life and work will benefit from this book."

> —TERRY TRUEMAN, MFA, MS
> Printz Honor Author of *Stuck in Neutral*

"Germaine and Jed apply their wisdom and insight from years of consulting experience into this example-laced coaching road map packed with easily applied tools. I highly recommend *Coach Anyone About Anything Volume 2* to any leader looking to instill a coaching style within managers or to build a coaching culture within their organization."
—BRAD DICKSON, Chief Marketing Officer, Dresser-Rand Company

"This is not the same ol' ideas repackaged. This book is a gift to those who have studied time management, high performance, sales, and success their whole life and who realize if you stop getting better, you stop being good! This book will make you better!"

> —THEODORE J. ZOUZOUNIS, CLU
> President D|A Financial Group of California, Inc.

"A must read for the small-business owner trying to move to the next level. Chapter 9, *Business by Accident or by Design?*, was a big eye-opener for my partners and me. It illuminated our company's strengths, opportunities to leverage for growth, and best next actions. And typically small-business owners are the worst managers/coaches/mentors for lack of time. *Coach Anyone About Anything* gives us easy-to-learn methods to help us improve in those roles rapidly. If this book doesn't energize you, you aren't paying attention!"

  —LARRY A. WATTERS, Managing Director, Taggart Global, LLC

"Coach Anyone About Anything Volume 2 is a concise, yet excellent treasure chest of proven methods to empower your direct reports and high-impact teams. You will want to keep this valuable reference guide handy and a permanent part of your business library."

  —DIANA MORALES TAYLOR, CEO, YWCA Houston, TX

"I have had the opportunity to read many, many books on coaching—probably far too many. Rarely have I found a book as thoughtful, replete with practical examples, and written in such an engaging style as Jed and Germaine's *Coach Anyone About Anything*. Their perspective, built on years of experience, is refreshing. In today's business environment, few competencies are more important for leaders, whether CEOs or supervisors, than the ability to coach people and teams to peak performance. This book provides much needed clarity for leaders pursuing this agenda."

  —D. BRENT SMITH, PhD
    Associate Dean for Executive Education
    Associate Professor of Management and Psychology
    Jones Graduate School of Business
    Rice University

COACH
ANYONE
ABOUT
ANYTHING

VOLUME 2

COACH ANYONE ABOUT ANYTHING

How to Empower Leaders and High-Performance Teams

VOLUME 2

BY GERMAINE PORCHÉ AND JED NIEDERER

Edited by Jacquelyn Landis

The
Eagle's View®
Company

The Eagle's View Company
P. O. Box 6154
Kingwood, TX 77325

Printed in the United States of America

Cover and interior design: Robert Aulicino/www.aulicinodesign.com
Edited by Jacquelyn Landis / http://jackielandis.wordpress.com

"The Paradoxical Commandments" are reprinted with the permission of the author.
© Copyright Kent M. Keith 1968, renewed 2001.

Porché, Germaine
> Coach anyone about anything : how to empower leaders
> > and high performance teams Volume 2/ by Germaine Porché
> > and Jed Niederer - 1st. ed.
> > p. cm.
> > Includes bibliographical references and index.
> > ISBN: 978-0-9826604-1-6
> > Library of Congress Control Number: 2010911734

ACKNOWLEDGMENTS

We are thankful for God's guidance in writing this book.
Countless people have contributed to
Coach Anyone About Anything Volume 2.
Attempting to display a list with every contributor's name here is
madness and is an entirely insufficient acknowledgment.
We offer in its place our sincere appreciation and thanks to each
and every individual who has touched our lives and helped
make this book happen.

Epigraph

"Peak Performance calls for love and passion.
Peak performers love what they do.
Love doing what they do better.
And doing it better than anyone else.
Dissatisfaction never gives way to complacency.
Characteristically, peak performers dream it, then they do it.
And then they aim for a higher peak."
—Kevin Roberts,
CEO Worldwide Saatchi & Saatchi

Coach Anyone About Anything
Volume 2

CONTENTS

Foreword	xv
Introduction	xvii

Chapter 1
Who Dat? — 1

Chapter 2
Do You Hear What I Hear? — 15

Chapter 3
Coaching Conversations — 29

Chapter 4
And the Band Played On — 43

Chapter 5
Environment and Action — 51

Chapter 6
Why Things Bog Down — 65

Chapter 7
It's About Time — 73

Chapter 8
The Magic of Generating Time — 87

Chapter 9
Business by Accident or by Design? — 95

Chapter 10
Building a World-Class Coaching Culture — 111

Chapter 11
Coaching Dynamics and Delivery Scenarios ———————— 121

Chapter 12
Sales Coaching and Getting an Eagle's View———————— 127

Chapter 13
Five Great Tools for Your Coaching Tool Kit———————— 143

Chapter 14
Make Planning Fun and Effective———————— 161

Chapter 15
Games Worth Playing ———————— 169

Chapter 16
How to Be Disorganized, Guilt-Free ———————— 181

Chapter 17
The Value of the Coach———————— 197

Chapter 18
Gutsy Coaching Moments———————— 203

Addenda———————— 253

Index———————— 263

Biographies ———————— 271

FOREWORD

People are the lifeblood of any organization. While products and technology help define an organization, it is the people who create the success. Germaine and Jed have worked extensively with National Oilwell Varco over the past 16 years to help nurture a culture of empowering teams and individuals in the company to settle for nothing less than the best performance possible. They have helped to coach and teach our employees to create an environment that constantly strives to be the best.

In *Coach Anyone About Anything, Volume 2: How to Empower Leaders and High Performance Teams,* Germaine and Jed share many of the proven tools and techniques that lead to high-powered performance in an organization. Just as Volume 1 has become an indispensible tool for all levels of management at NOV, I believe Volume 2 will be invaluable to personnel at all levels striving to help their organizations create an environment of empowerment and learning.

Germaine and Jed have created a book based upon their shared successes in their careers, and I believe you will enjoy reading this book and will continue to use it to further the success of yourself and others in your organization.

—M. A. (Pete) Miller, Jr.
Chairman, President and CEO National Oilwell Varco.

INTRODUCTION

"No matter what accomplishments you make,
somebody helped you."
—Althea Gibson, tennis champion, first Black American to win
Wimbledon, the French Open, Australian doubles, and the U.S. Open

coach´-ing: facilitating people in their own commitment and
enthusiasm to accomplish their objectives.

We wrote this book for people like you—people who want to help
others succeed. This book will benefit anyone interested in discovering
new methods with which to coach others to realize their dreams.

It's been nine years since the release of our first book, *Coach Anyone
About Anything*. During those nine years, it's been a privilege to share our
work with many of you around the world. Thank you for all your stories
and contributions as you applied many of the models and methodology.
The chapter "Gutsy Coaching Moments" highlights some of those stories.
This Volume 2 book builds on the work presented in Volume 1.

In Volume 1, the focus is on the individual and equipping you with
tools to help your clients succeed, as well as growing your knowledge and
confidence in the world of coaching. Volume 2 addresses an additional
and different perspective of coaching: coaching within the organization.
You can still apply all the tools personally; however, the tools contained
herein will help you to bridge your work from an individual to an organizational context.

Who is this book for?

- For managers who want to have their employees improve their
  performance. It will help supervisors save time through coaching
  to develop their people, not just train them.
- For executives committed to expanding their direct reports' ability to take on extraordinary business objectives and win. It's for

chief executives looking to create and sustain a coaching culture to help guarantee continued success and increase shareholder value. And this book will assist mentors who want to do more for their protégés than merely "orient" them to their organization's traditions and customs.

- For professional coaches on the hunt for proven tools and techniques to help their clients make more money. Coaches desiring new, straightforward ways to contribute to their clients will find this volume a gold mine of fresh approaches.
- For coaches seeking easy-to-implement performance models to enable their players/clients to increase their revenues and profits. By the way, throughout the book we will refer to persons being coached in any industry as players. And every coaching approach we share with you can be applied to teams as well as individual players.
- For people who would love to learn how to coach themselves to achieve their goals.

In these pages you will discover models and lenses to help give your players an eagle's view of their organizations in order to illuminate the pluses and minuses. You'll discover a process to help players uncover the things they have in place that drive high performance and those things that dampen it. This methodology includes helping your clients to invent ways to redesign their business processes to generate greater results.

Sales coaching has become a hot topic today in many enterprises since the Sales Executive Council published these revelations:

1. Average producing salespeople improve their performance 19 percent when receiving effective sales coaching.
2. Poor sales coaching drives sales results down and is actually worse than no sales coaching at all.

We offer you unique tools and proven techniques to coach salespeople effectively. We will also dismantle the notion that sales coaching is merely a new trendy term for sales management or sales training—common misconceptions.

Coaching is a conversation, and effective listening is critical, of course. But did you know that players can be coached in the appropriate way to listen to different speakers? That's right; players are more successful when they listen differently to coaching, mentoring, leading, and managing. You'll learn about these frameworks for listening to different roles and identify reasons why the responses you receive from players sometimes don't fit the situation.

Have you ever wondered how coaching differs from mentoring? Many people use the terms interchangeably. Well, we offer a set of principles that distinguish the two and increase the power of each. In addition, we differentiate coaching and mentoring from management and leadership.

Are there things you've dreamt about but haven't found the time? In these pages, we deliver a new pathway for you and your players to realize your dreams. Contrasting outcome management with traditional time management is bound to challenge your thinking and supply new openings for achievement. This pathway could well transform your experience of time from a constraint to an opening. In the process you may find yourself giving up the bankrupt paradigm for time you inherited that has plagued you since you were born.

A word about our writing style . . . we have always been committed to ending sexism in the workplace and promoting diversity everywhere we go. However, attempting to remove or include everyone's gender in our writing can often produce some extremely awkward reading. Therefore, in order to smooth out your reading experience, please forgive us for using he alone or she alone instead of the cumbersome *he/she or s/he or she/he or him/her*. And rest assured that whenever we might use a designation like *salesman*, we mean to include sales professionals of both sexes.

Something else worth noting ... the examples and cases we present are from genuine situations—that is, they really happened. And, consistent with our commitment to maintain client confidentiality, names, titles, and company names have been changed or omitted in some instances.

We sincerely hope you enjoy the read and acquire new ways to help people succeed.

— Germaine Porché and Jed Niederer

CHAPTER 1

"You cannot hope to build a better world without improving the individuals. To that end each of us must work for our own improvement and, at the same time, share a general responsibility for all humanity, our particular duty being to aid those to whom we think we can be most useful."
—Marie Curie
Pioneer in researching radioactivity, and
the first person to receive two Nobel Prizes

WHO DAT?

Distinguishing Who Is Speaking
and Who Is Listening

Figure 1.1

Outcomes for this chapter:

- Distinguish Coaching, Mentoring, Leadership, and Management.
- Discover how to coach your players' listening.
- Appreciate the value of being clear with your listeners; which "speaking hat" you are wearing.

Fortune magazine, July 2009, had an article titled "The Best Advice I Ever Got," which included interviews of several well-known influential leaders, including Bill Gates Jr. and Sr.; Lauren Zalaznick, president, Women & Lifestyle Entertainment Networks at NBC Universal; and others. These people shared advice that they received from mentors who impacted their lives and careers. In reading the article, the advice from these mentors occurred in environments from living at home with Mom and Dad to a formal setting in the office. Mentors ranged from parents to coworkers to bosses. The bottom line is that these "mentors" gave advice from their experiences in life and on the job that made a positive difference for their protégés.

Bill Gates shared that the best advice he ever got from his parents was their encouragement to participate in things that he wasn't good at, like sports. According to Bill, ". . . it ended up really exposing me to leadership opportunities and showing me that I wasn't good at a lot of things, instead of sticking to things that I was comfortable with."

Since the writing of our first book, we've been frequently asked, "How does mentoring compare to coaching?" We refer to the coaching scope as the landscape of roles from expert to facilitation. According to the dictionary definition below, mentoring falls under the expert side of the coaching scope.

Encarta Dictionary: English (North America):
men•tor (noun) 1. Experienced adviser and supporter: somebody, usually older and more experienced, who advises and guides a younger, less experienced person 2. trainer: a senior or experienced person in a company or organization who gives guidance and training to a junior colleague

People often use the coaching and mentoring terms interchangeably. In the *Fortune* magazine article, chairman and CEO of Google, Eric Schmidt,

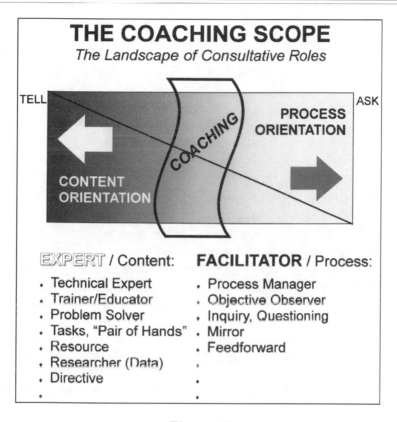

Figure 1.2

shared that the advice that stuck with him was to have a coach. Schmidt, interestingly, draws a distinction about coaching. His first reaction was how could a coach advise him if he (Schmidt) is best at doing what he does? He continues to explain that a coach doesn't have to play the game as well as the player, but in observing the player, offers different perspectives, discusses different approaches, and sees things that the player may not see. This fits well into our definition of coaching—facilitating a person in his own commitment and enthusiasm to accomplish his goals.

You may be thinking that mentors don't always *just tell* and, like coaching, listening is a big part of mentoring. Can't mentors use coaching skills? Absolutely, mentors can implement coaching skills. We think that's where the confusion starts. Many mentors will offer suggestions and are not accountable for the outcomes of their mentees or protégés. They don't manage the protégé, so there are some similarities with the coaching role. The key difference is, as a mentor, people expect you to be experienced in a specific area and be willing to give expert advice in how best to succeed. The expectations of a coach are to help you accomplish your goals and seldom to tell you what to do or how to do it.

Referring again to that article in Fortune magazine, Lauren Zalaznick shared that the best advice she ever got was to listen. At her first TV job at VH1, her boss, Jeff Gaspin told her, "Lauren, you're very smart. You're ten steps ahead of people. Don't cut them off."

Some organizations have mentoring programs for employees to help them with their careers. Many of our clients have mentoring programs called *onboarding* for new employees to help them acclimate to the organizational culture. One of the goals of the program is to give the new employee some direction in "how things work around here" and to acquaint them with programs and opportunities available to them.

Similarly, new people are sometimes encouraged in organizations to seek out mentors who can help them further their career aspirations. One of our clients, Mary Cunningham, shares that she's frequently asked by young managers to mentor them in their careers. These managers are inspired by Mary's leadership and want to obtain the confidence and respect that Mary possesses. They're looking for the golden nugget of advice that will help them move up the corporate ladder.

> *"… Help you I can, yes.*
> *Always two there are, no more, no less:*
> *a master and an apprentice.*
> *Already know you that which you need."*
> —Yoda, *Star Wars*

Mentors Light the Way . . .

Germaine was asked to participate with a panel of speakers to share about the mentors in her life at an American Business Women's conference held in The Woodlands, Texas. "While organizing my speech, I realized that along the way, many people have contributed to my life. I don't recall having any formal mentoring relationships; rather, I remembered moments of mentoring that stuck with me," Germaine reports. In the book *Balcony People,* by Joyce Landorf Heatherley, the author writes, "Balcony people listen and then, instead of tearing down others, they build them up." Below is Germaine's speech acknowledging the mentors or balcony people in her life.

Mentoring Moments

1. My parents have been wonderful to me. In addition to being great parents, they've been great mentors. Whenever I was faced with new challenges or obstacles, I can remember them saying, "You can do it—you can do anything you set your mind to." *Mentors light the way . . .*

2. My husband, Jed, is also my business partner. When we once worked at another consulting firm, I was assigned to be the lead consultant on a three-day intervention for the president and the top 100 people of a Fortune 500 organization. My consulting team included one of the partners of our consulting firm. This was my first time leading this sort of intervention, and I was the one in charge. Can you sense my anxiety? Of course, I knew I would mess things up! I shared my trepidation and feelings of anxiety with Jed. He said, "Whenever you think that way, you're insulting the partners in the firm and everyone else who knows you and trusts that you can do the job." From that moment on, I stopped insulting people. *Mentors light the way . . .*

3. Raise your hand if you can remember someone impacting your career with words of wisdom. I'll never forget one of the most powerful things someone told me. This was a consultant who worked mainly with CEOs of Fortune 500 companies. Bill Broussard told me that really good consultants can work with ambiguity. That's right, ambiguity. A good consultant can work with not knowing all the answers and can allow the process to unfold and guide it along the way. Ambiguity became my friend. *Mentors light the way . . .*

4. I was sharing about this mentoring panel with one of my clients, Vicki Aucoin. She told me that she wanted to attend the conference to hear me speak. Not only is she attending the conference today, she's also a sponsor. She gave me the boost and confidence that I didn't know I needed. *Mentors light the way ...*

5. When I was 13, June and Ralph, my relatives in California, started sending for me every year to spend the summers with them in Los Angeles. They opened my eyes to a larger world than living in Lafayette, LA. At the age of 26, they trusted me to manage an account of $200,000 and supervise the contracting and building of a home. That launched my real estate career, which they encouraged me to pursue. *Mentors light the way...*

6. Another mentoring moment is when David Fisher helped me with public speaking. I had only worked in my position as marketing manager for a couple of weeks. We were preparing for a special event with 300 people expected to attend. I found out only that morning that I would introduce the keynote speaker—David. Raise your hand if you ever felt butterflies in your stomach at the thought of public speaking. I made up my mind that someone more experienced should introduce David. When David walked into the office, I ran up to him and explained how someone more experienced would do a much better job than I would. David called me into the lunchroom, and as he ate his sandwich asked me to share with him my personal experience of how my life was impacted by the program he would be sharing that evening. With butterflies fluttering around, I must've started my story at least three times trying to get it perfect. David smiled and told me to just tell my story—I was doing great—it didn't need to be perfect. So, I told it again. He said, "You're the one, Germaine! You're going to introduce me. Just keep being yourself and being authentic." I took his advice—be yourself and be authentic. *Mentors light the way ...*

7. A few years ago, I was traveling with some colleagues. The person I happen to be sitting next to asked me what I did for a living. I fumbled with words, explaining the type of work that I do. Has that ever happened to any of you? I overheard my colleague, Mike King, answering the same question with the person whom he was sitting next to. Mike's answer was so eloquent that his response led to a much livelier conversation than the one I became engaged in. Later, when we were waiting for our luggage, I looked at Mike and complimented him on how powerful his response was when he was asked what he did for a living. Mike said, "It ought to be good—I've been saying the same thing for twenty years. And

every so often I get more than a pleasant flight home and some-times a new client." His advice to me was to have a crisp, com-pelling, short response no longer than 20 seconds. I took his advice, and now I have a quick, professional 20-second commercial. *Mentors light the way . . .*

8. Jed and I have a really great marriage and business partnership as well. Raise your hand if you ever felt like you or your partner has taken the other for granted. As creative as Jed and I are with our marriage, at one point it felt like all we did was work. Then Iris Hatfield came along and reminded us of the importance of drawing boundaries and honoring them. Now Jed and I do not dis-cuss business in the bedroom. When we're at home, we ask each other for permission to discuss business or are free to say that we don't want to talk business at that moment. We respect the boundaries that we've created. And you know what? It works! *Mentors light the way . . .*

Now let's take one more look at distinguishing mentoring from coach-ing. Below are the definitions that we use.

men'tor•ing: providing instruction and orientation about an organiza-tion's culture, people, products, services and systems.
coach'ing: facilitating people in their own commitment and enthusiasm to accomplish their objectives.

Graphic Contrast of Coaching with Mentoring

The following is a graphic displaying some of the contrasting charac-teristics of coaching and mentoring that we have observed. Please bear in mind that these contrasts are not hard-and-fast. They are offered here as a tool for you to "think with" rather than "think as the rule." Certainly, some mentors receive training to mentor, for example, but with the majority of mentoring situations it is estimated that little or no training is provided, nor is it sought.

Contrasting Coaching with Mentoring

Mentor		Coach
Learning & Orientation	←——→	Accomplish Player's Objectives & Goals
Low priority	←——→	High priority
Career advancement	←——→	Results acceleration
Mentor neophytes	←——→	Coach anyone
Give Advice	←——→	Offer Possibilities
Expert	←——→	Facilitate
Give Information	←——→	Ask Questions
Convince	←——→	Inquire into
Sell	←——→	Enroll
Help	←——→	Assist
Tell	←——→	Ask
Force	←——→	Allow
Assigned	←——→	Chosen
Teach & train	←——→	Facilitate learning
Unstructured	←——→	Structured
Determined	←——→	Committed
"You must…!"	←——→	"Would you consider…?"
Authority	←——→	Influence
Untrained to mentor	←——→	Trained to coach
Industry expert	←——→	People expert
Unconscious about Player's style	←——→	Adapting to Player's behavioral style

Figure 1.3

Okay, Now Let's Talk About Leadership and Management

"Great leaders tap into the needs and fears we all share. Great managers, by contrast, perform their magic by discovering, developing, and celebrating what's different about each person who works for them."
—Marcus Buckingham, author

lead'er•ship: declaring a future and enrolling people into making that future happen.

man'age•ment: coordinating people and materials to accomplish specific milestones and objectives, which will make the declared future happen.

Leadership and management differ in many regards. The above are simple working definitions that have helped our clients distinguish which type of conversation or "hat" to wear to produce the outcomes they want to produce with people. Different outcomes often require different hats. For example, we ask our clients to first define the outcomes to be produced with the person they want to develop. Then we invite them to look backward from the outcome to the hats or roles and judge which one will have the best chance or be most appropriate to achieve the outcome. Sometimes it's neither leading nor managing. Sometimes their answer is coaching or mentoring. But whatever their choice, it's a choice made from four different approaches, which overall will be more effective than being stuck in one approach all the time.

> *"You may be really good with a hammer. But to fell a tree, there just might be a better tool."*
> —Porché/Niederer

How to Listen to Coaches, Mentors, Managers, and Leaders
Tuning Your Player's Listening

Listening is a very powerful tool, as you will discover in the next chapter. Consider the chart below. These are four very different levels of conversations. We endeavor here to illustrate effective ways to participate in those conversations, given our definitions for those roles. Look at the four possible roles. How does each speak? What does each listen for? Here are some examples: Leaders speak and listen to members of the organization they lead to find out if they are on board with the leader's vision. Managers speak and listen to their direct reports to determine whether they are clear on instructions given. Coaches speak and listen to their player/clients to understand what actions will be taken to accomplish their goals. And mentors speak and listen to their protégés to determine if they are making progress in understanding how to best navigate through their organization to get their job done.

Leading –

Speaking vision for the future, intended outcomes and time frames. The strategy to get there. The context or Being. Challenge. Assessments of the current state and insights. Acknowledgment and appreciation.

Listening For enrollment and alignment. Strategic understanding, declarations and promises. Accountability, integrity and results. Stepping up, taking a stand.

Being Led –

Listening For the vision of the desired future and intended outcomes. The strategy and how it relates to one's accountabilities. The context or Being. Insights into the current state in order to move forward in achieving the desired future.

Speaking questions to help align with accountabilities and the declared future. Questions to clarify vision and strategy. Declared alignment or honest grappling and questioning to bring oneself into alignment. Commitment for results. Results reporting.

Managing –

Speaking the mission and intended outcomes. Instructions on what to do and how to do it - tactics. Delegation. Providing details and parameters. Asking questions to ascertain whether directions are understood and to monitor progress. Appraisals and assessments. Acknowledgment and appreciation.

Listening For Compliance and questions to fulfill requests/directives. Promises. Integrity. Customer needs/wants. Planning. Progress reports, completion, requests for resources and help. Teamwork. Urgency. Results. Accountability.

Being Managed –

Listening For tactical information. Necessary, specific, detailed "how to's", to fulfill requests and directives. Conditions for fulfillment of requests and how to achieve them. Critical assessments and feedforward. Empowerment, trust and confidence. Context or Being. Collaborative resources.

Speaking questions on how to fulfill requests and directives (what to do and how to do it). Providing progress updates. Customer wants/needs. Asking for resources, further instruction or clarification. Plans. Promises to deliver. Communicating obstacles, results, completions and accomplishments. Career ambitions.

Coaching –

Speaking commitment to the Player's success. Questions: What, Why, How, Who, When? Offering possibilities, fresh perspectives, tips, experiences, expertise. Feedforward. Encouragement. Challenge. Acknowledgment and appreciation.

Listening For new openings for action, freedom to be, promises for action. Urgency and false urgency. Results. Debriefing actions. Creativity and development. Enthusiasm, inspiration, confidence and false confidence. Context or Being.

Being Coached –

Listening For new openings for high-value actions, and freedom to be. Empowerment in the face of circumstances and risks. Encouragement. Assessments, feedforward. Questions to ground possibilities in reality. New perspectives and new possibilities. Invitations to take action. Context or Being.

Speaking vision for Player's future, intended outcomes and commitments. Completion on promised actions and outcomes. Results. Reporting obstacles and breakdowns. Requests for coaching. New promised coordinated actions and promised outcomes.

Mentoring –

Speaking descriptions of organizational structure and dynamics. Introductions to persons to help the protégé succeed. Assign small tasks to assist protégé to learn how things work. Ask questions to monitor progress. Assessment, acknowledgment.

Listening For grasping the workings of the organization and appreciation for the culture. Questions for understanding systems and procedures. Progress reports. Protégé requesting introductions and help. Evidence of belonging, becoming part of "the team". Career plans and ambitions.

Being Mentored –

Listening For how to move through the organization to make things happen. Discover key influencers with whom to collaborate & essential processes. Career progression – what to do and what to avoid. Critical assessments, feedforward and encouragement. Suggestions for improvement. Mentor's trust and confidence.

Speaking questions on how to best approach fulfilling job accountabilities in the organization. Progress on discovery tasks. Asking for introductions to people resources. Requests for instruction or clarification of vital organizational systems and processes. Disclosing obstacles and missing abilities. Career insights, objectives and possible achievement pathways.

Figure 1.4

The way someone listens to you can be coached. Someone's listening can be tuned, like to a station on your radio. How should your player listen to you when you are coaching him? Check out the chart above, the unshaded quartile, third from the top. See if those attributes describe how you would like your players to listen to you when you are coaching. Isn't that something like the kind of listening you intend? And when you look at the players' Speaking portion, won't that give you clues as to how they are listening to you?

Now please take a few moments and read through the entire *Speaking-Listening For* chart above for understanding. See that? We just tuned your listening. We didn't ask you to study the chart or memorize it; we asked you to just read through ... for understanding. Get it?

Managing –

Speaking the mission and intended outcomes. Instructions on what to do and how to do it - tactics. Delegation. Providing details and parameters. Asking questions to ascertain whether directions are understood and to monitor progress. Appraisals and assessments. Acknowledgment and appreciation.

Listening For Compliance and questions to fulfill requests/directives. Promises. Integrity. Customer needs/wants. Planning. Progress reports, completion, requests for resources and help. Teamwork. Urgency. Results. Accountability.

Coaching –

Speaking commitment to the Player's success. Questions: What, Why, How, Who, When? Offering possibilities, fresh perspectives, tips, experiences, expertise. Feedforward. Encouragement. Challenge. Acknowledgment and appreciation.

Listening For new openings for action, freedom to be, promises for action. Urgency and false urgency. Results. Debriefing actions. Creativity and development. Enthusiasm, inspiration, confidence and false confidence. Context or Being.

Being Managed –

Listening For tactical information. Necessary, specific, detailed "how to's", to fulfill requests and directives. Conditions for fulfillment of requests and how to achieve them. Critical assessments and feedforward. Empowerment, trust and confidence. Context or Being. Collaborative resources.

Speaking questions on how to fulfill requests and directives (what to do and how to do it). Providing progress updates. Customer wants/needs. Asking for resources, further instruction or clarification. Plans. Promises to deliver. Communicating obstacles, results, completions and accomplishments. Career ambitions.

Being Coached –

Listening For new openings for high-value actions, and freedom to be. Empowerment in the face of circumstances and risks. Encouragement. Assessments, feedforward. Questions to ground possibilities in reality. New perspectives and new possibilities. Invitations to take action. Context or Being.

Speaking vision for Player's future, intended outcomes and commitments. Completion on promised actions and outcomes. Results. Reporting obstacles and breakdowns. Requests for coaching. New promised coordinated actions and promised outcomes.

Figure 1.5

Examine the chart above. Notice how the coach's speaking is being listened or received as though he were managing him, instead of coaching him. The player is bound to be disappointed because, in this illustration, he is listening for specific, detailed instructions and how-to's. And the coach probably won't be too pleased, either, because he is waiting for the player's creativity to come forth in his speaking—he's waiting for the player to invent his own answers for accomplishing his objectives.

Surely you have experienced or can imagine other ways people can get their wires crossed in a conversation. For example, when a leader speaks, what if she were being listened to as though she were managing? The member of the organization listening would be waiting for her to tell him the specific actions he should take to fulfill her requests. The listener is destined to be dissatisfied. Leaders' speaking, as we defined earlier, is declaring a future and enrolling people into making that future happen, not giving specific instructions as to how to fulfill their employees' accountabilities to realize the vision. That's the manager's job.

At a large dinner meeting in New Hampshire, the chief executive officer was speaking to a group of about a hundred executives and managers. The purpose of the dinner was to launch a reengineering program across their five business units.

The CEO, Dave Klingenbacher, gave a rousing and inspiring speech about the objectives he asked people to meet: a 30 percent reduction in fixed costs across the board. At the end he asked for questions. Remarkably, the first question he got was from a new manager, Rick Everly. Rick stood up and addressed the CEO, "This is clearly an important companywide undertaking. What is this going to do to my scheduled vacation?"

The room went still. A hush permeated the room except for soft disapproving whispers here and there. Most of the hundred people seated at their tables were shocked by the low level of Rick's question. Surprised at the level of question himself, the CEO thought for a moment before answering.

Then Dave leaned over the podium in Rick's direction and, grinning, he replied, "Yes, sir, you understand this initiative perfectly, Rick. And thank you for being so committed to its objectives that you are even willing to rearrange your life to get them accomplished. Good for you!" Then the room broke out in applause.

Now that's a savvy CEO. He translated Rick's speaking into the appropriate level for everyone, spoke it, and literally saved the evening's luster.

"There are two ways of spreading light: To be the candle or the mirror that reflects it."
—Edith Wharton, author

Conclusions

- Know which hat you are wearing when you speak, or which role you are assuming.
- If appropriate, tell the listener the role you are taking before you speak. Tune their listening.
- Know which hat the speaker is wearing before you listen. (Ask if you aren't certain.)
- After you have listened, respond appropriately to the speaker's capacity, level, or role.

We want to leave you with an important inquiry: leader, manager, mentor, or coach? Who do you need to be in order to make happen what you want to have happen? Which role do you need to play? Which hat should you wear?

The Spandex Story

The following is an excerpt from the book *Balcony People*, describing the author's experience of Spandex when purchasing her first pair of designer jeans.

"So that's it!" I shouted. "Spandex! Five percent Spandex is what makes the difference. That stretching flexibility given to the threads makes it possible for the jeans to go in where I go in, and to go out where I go out." The jeans were perfect! And suddenly I knew why we have such a problem listening to others and making allowances for them. We don't have 5 percent Spandex in our attitudes. Affirmers, balcony people who love and listen from their heart, do so with much Spandex; and, consequently, they hear between the words."
—Joyce Landorf Heatherley
Bestselling author, Christian communicator, and speaker

Consider for a moment, that the affirmers, or balcony people, could be leaders, managers, mentors, or coaches. Do you have at least 5 percent Spandex when working with others?

Summary

In this chapter, we distinguished mentoring, coaching, managing, and leading to empower you and your players to use appropriate tools to accomplish their objectives. Knowing the differences inherent in these roles and conversations can be the difference between communicating effectively and experiencing frustrating disconnects.

In the next chapter … wait a moment. Do you hear what I hear?

CHAPTER 2

"If we treat people as they ought to be, we help them become what they are capable of becoming."
—Johann Wolfgang von Goethe

DO YOU HEAR WHAT I HEAR?

Outcomes for this chapter:
- Reinforce that hearing is not always accompanied by listening.
- Discover that how we listen can profoundly impact others' behavior. Learn new techniques to help you listen more powerfully.
- Capture how to steer dialogue of low-value activity toward high-value action.
- Uncover easy ways to sharpen your listening skills fast.

Have you ever walked away from speaking to someone feeling that he didn't listen to you? During the conversation, the other person looked interested in what you were saying, he even nodded his head and contributed an occasional "hmmm . . ." or "oh" or a "that's interesting" remark. Yet as you walk away or end the conversation, there's this nagging feeling that you were talking into a black hole or to an impenetrable wall. You may have asked yourself, What's all that about? This may even happen more frequently now during these times when it seems that everyone is multi-tasking and rushing to meet deadlines with fewer hands to help. Let's examine perhaps the most important coaching skill of all: listening—the skill that even the best coaches can become complacent about.

What's That? Did You Say Listen?

There are many different ways that we can listen to others. Depending on the person with whom you're interacting, there may be history or baggage you carry about him that shapes how you listen to him and colors the communication you receive.

It's different listening to your supervisor, who has an impact on whether you receive a paycheck. And how you may listen to a coworker with whom you enjoy working varies markedly from how you listen to one who has annoyed you in the past.

What about when you meet someone for the first time? How about when you are really interested in the person romantically or intellectually? Don't you hang onto every word he says, especially if the relationship is new? If you have children, how do you listen to them? Depending on the situation, aren't there times when you listen more intently than other times?

People listen in many different ways. The following examples are things we might be "listening with" as people speak to us—internal thoughts that color and shape any message we receive:

"Get to the punch line, will ya?"
"Yeah, okay, and let me tell you my story."
"This is what you ought to do."
"If you would just be quiet I'll tell you."
"You're so talented; this is very interesting."
"I've heard this before. Here we go again."
"I'm just not good enough to be your partner in this. How can I tell you?"
"Enough whining already."
"Are you still here?"

Now, you may be thinking, Yeah, it's obvious that my listening varies depending on whom I'm speaking with. So what? Well, if you knew that how you listen to others can impact their actions profoundly, would that alter how you listen to what they have to say?

Let's start with the context for how we listen to our players. As coaches, we believe it is our job to be an opening or clearing for others' speaking. Listening from a clean slate provides our players the opportunity to freely communicate. We want to be able to listen without judging them. Of course, we don't literally mean a clean slate. It's impossible to listen without having some thoughts in our minds as people speak. Our coaching philosophy begins with the premise that people are intelligent, able, capable, and know their business.

What context shapes how you listen to people? What is your premise before your players speak? Is it one that empowers them and you? We invite you to invent a powerful context or philosophy for listening and coaching others. Players can hear it by the way you listen to them.

We've noticed that coaching from the premise that *people are intelligent, able, capable, and know their business* helps remove arrogance on our part and deepens the respect we have for our players' speaking. It also reminds us not to listen like a know-it-all and keeps us from interrupting too soon with our infinite wisdom. We don't have to have all the answers or solutions to our players' problems or challenges. No one does. We are their strategic partners in having them discover the answers for themselves to be more effective in their lives. And the longer we listen generously, the more viable answers our players create.

The Coaching Scope—The Landscape of Possible Coaching Roles

This model distinguishes the coach's role from expert to process facilitator. People usually hire an expert to tell them the answer or answers, and a process facilitator/coach monitors the process and asks questions to move things forward. (See Figure 1.2 page 3)

We say that coaching is all over the landscape of possible roles you could play or tracks you might take to get the job done with your player. And we have observed that the most successful coaches land sort of in the middle, with a leaning toward asking questions. Of course, if you happen to be an expert in your client's business, it's perfectly acceptable to give him a nudge toward the answers to save him some time and money.

Here is a critical element in this discussion: Are you ready? The degree to which you tell people what to do is the degree to which you rob them of their power and responsibility. And if you provide all the answers, the moment something goes wrong, who do you think they're going to blame? You, of course! "Well, you told me what to do, didn't you? And it didn't work."

As a coach, your objective isn't to continually direct players, and it certainly isn't to have your clients become dependent upon you. Your job is to facilitate them in their own commitment and enthusiasm to accomplish their objectives.

Consider the possibility that the more you tell people what to do and how to do it, the more you contribute to the type of atmosphere in which they become victims or adopt a victim mentality. How do you recognize a victim mentality? Here are some clues: When you observe a person acting helpless, not taking responsibility for his actions, or witnessing him busily blaming others for his unwelcome situation, you may have a victim. According to the Encarta Dictionary, this is the definition of a victim:

Vic•tim (noun) 1. somebody hurt or killed; 2. somebody or something harmed: somebody who or something that is adversely affected by an action or circumstance; 3. somebody duped: somebody who is tricked or exploited; 4. living being used for sacrifice; 5. helpless person: somebody who experiences misfortune and feels helpless to remedy it

So, how do you work your client out of a victim mentality? You start with a lot of patience, friend, a lot of patience. One way is to give her back the problem she tried to get you to solve. Ask her for her possible solutions. Patiently wait for her to think and give you her suggestions. Sometimes we have to listen and wait for a long while before some clients respond with their own possible solutions. But it's usually worth the wait.

> *"We are all faced with great possibilities brilliantly*
> *disguised as impossible situations."*
> —Sarah Doherty,
> First one-legged person to climb Mt. McKinley

Sometimes a client feels helpless to get something done in his organization. Find out if he may need to make a request for action. He may not realize that all there is to do is go to the person with the authority to help him fulfill his request. You may have to continue working with your client to draw out possible solutions or actions for him to take. Please keep in mind that this is something for the client to work through—your job is to only facilitate him through the process, not do it for him. This next sentence is important—trust us. You do not want to be drawn into organizational politics or become the person who has to speak up for your client with his management. If you do, you've just removed yourself from the coach's role and have become a pair of hands doing his job. You've also robbed your client of his responsibility and power. Let your players do their work. Be patient.

When Jed was 20 years old and learning to fly, he encountered an impatient coach—his first flight instructor, Eric Hansen.

Things went pretty well for Jed the first couple of lessons. Then after three or four hours of instruction, it seemed to Jed that he just couldn't work the airplane's controls fast enough to satisfy Eric. He would ask Jed to perform a maneuver, but before Jed could reach for the throttle or push the pedals, Eric would do it for him. Although Jed knew what to do, he had no opportunity to do it. Before Jed could reach to cut the throttle, for example, Eric would push it in and say, "Why didn't you cut the throttle? C'mon, kid." The instructor was just too impatient.

Similar instances occurred time after time until Jed finally just gave up. Jed became a victim. He vividly recalls when it happened and the thoughts he had. Jed literally thought, Fine. If that's the way you're going to play, then you fly the plane.

The next day, when Jed arrived at Renton Aviation for his next flying lesson, Eric met him in the lobby of the flight school as usual. But on this occasion, instead of immediately turning around and heading out to the Cessna 150 trainer, Eric whispered, "We have a meeting with the boss, kid." And Eric escorted Jed into the flight school owner's office and shut the door behind them.

After the greetings and handshakes, owner-manager George Senter asked Eric and Jed to be seated. Looking across his desk with his hands folded, George said, "Jed, Eric tells me that he's worried you aren't going to be able to solo on time. He says you just aren't progressing at the speed you should be. What do you have to say about that?"

Jed sighed and then told George the truth—that he had "sort of given up" and why he had.

Eric's jaw dropped as he listened to Jed, and he soon interrupted with, "Why in the world would you think that, kid? That's crazy!"

"Never mind, Eric," George Senter said calmly. "Jed, I am assigning you to a new instructor today. His name is Ed Stiller. Let's go meet him right now, shall we?" Mr. Senter said, smiling.

Mr. Senter walked Jed out of the office, through the lobby, and toward the airplanes docked just outside. There they found Ed Stiller walking around the tail of a bright red-and-white two-seater Cessna. After they were introduced, Ed asked Jed to run the preflight checklist on the same airplane before they went up for the lesson.

Ed watched Jed carefully inspect the plane. Without saying a word, he observed Jed. When he had completed the preflight, his new instructor said, "Okay, Jed, let's take her up. Show me what you can do."

They swiftly leaped into the cockpit. "We don't see many days this clear in Seattle. Let's get going." Ed said as he briskly rubbed his hands together. Ed allowed Jed to do everything while he observed him. Jed taxied out onto the runway, communicated with the tower, and within a minute or two they took off.

Ed said very little on the flight and didn't touch the controls. Well, now, this is different, Jed thought. After they were airborne and a safe distance from the airport, Ed asked Jed to perform several maneuvers and asked him some questions. Ed never touched the controls. Then, after about twenty minutes, Ed said, "Okay, Jed. Take her back in." Jed wondered what Ed was thinking, but he was afraid to ask. Most lessons lasted a full hour. Jed landed the plane smoothly and taxied back up the side of the gray runway toward the red Renton Aviation building. As they neared the office, still on the runway, Ed said, "Just let me out here."

"Okay, I'll go park it" Jed replied a little disappointed.

"No, sir. It's about time you soloed, don't you think?" Jed's new instructor opened his door to step out. As he walked away from Jed's airplane, Ed shouted over the sound of the engine. "It's all yours, Jed. Have fun and I'll see you when you get back."

Jed had gone from being a problem student pilot to a confident pilot, earning his solo certificate in less than an hour. How could that happen? It happened because Ed Stiller got out of the way. It happened because Jed's new instructor/coach believed he was intelligent, able, capable, could fly the plane, and Ed Stiller had the patience to let him prove it.

"A coach is someone who tells you what you don't want to hear, who has you see what you don't want to see, so you can be who you have always known you could be."
—Tom Landry, Dallas Cowboys Head Coach, coached the Cowboys to win two Super Bowls and 20 consecutive winning seasons—the longest in NFL history

Ya Gotta Have Style
Lots and Lots and Lotsa Style!

In the film *Million Dollar Baby*, Maggie (played by Hillary Swank) wasn't doing well against the current British boxing champion. Back in her corner between rounds, she asked Frankie (Clint Eastwood), her manager, "What's happening, boss?"

Frankie replied, "Well, she's faster and stronger than you. She's a better boxer and more experienced than you are. Now, what are you going to do about it?" Maggie then got up from her stool, moved out into the ring, and knocked out her opponent.

In the story, Frankie just stated facts to Maggie. He didn't tell her what she should do. Frankie's coaching style worked for Maggie because she knocked out her opponent. What is the style that you rely on when coaching people?

Experience has shown us that most human beings are telling machines. We love to tell our stories or tell people what to do, how and when to do it, etc. This is quite obvious when you examine most people's speaking. It is fraught with "you have to," "you must," "you need to," "you should," and "you had better." These phrases signal an expert way of being—having the answer. It puts you at the extreme side of the content-orientation part of the coaching scope.

We have demonstrated this human telling tendency with hundreds of folks from Houston to Moscow. In a simple exercise we call TELL versus ASK, people experience it for themselves. Naturally, we have to help the exercise along by giving participants exact phrases with which to begin their sentences: You must . . . , You need to . . . , You have to . . . , You should . . . , You'd better . . . , and If you don't. . . .

Then we coach them to rephrase the same statements and information into questions: Have you considered . . . ? Did you know . . . ? In my experience . . . , You might consider . . . , Would you consider the possibility of . . . ? Have you thought about . . . ? How would you feel about . . . ?

The results of the exercise are expressed the same way wherever we go: "I didn't realize how much I lean toward telling"; "I wanted to just get away from her telling me what to do"; "I felt so acknowledged when he asked me what my ideas were, how I felt, and what I thought"; "I felt my body tighten up, and I was cringing from all his telling me what I should think and how I should act. Arrrgh!"

There have been a few who were comfortable telling people what to do and a handful comfortable with being told what to do. But everyone realizes their automatic drift toward telling and agrees that better player results are possible through *asking*.

This *telling* posture seems to be a phenomenon embedded in the culture of human beings, and we have all inherited it. Look at the contrasts in the two-columned chart below, and you will begin to see the nature of the modern coaching way of being as contrasted with the inherited telling tenor. This is not to say that the modern coach doesn't ever use the approaches of the left-hand column. These are legitimate tactics available to any coach when appropriate. It is their predominate use and overuse that we invite you to manage in your coaching expeditions.

Contrasting Coaching Styles or Ways of Being

Traditional or Old Paradigm	Coaching or New Paradigm
Give Advice	Offer Possibilities
Convince	Inquire
Make Accountable	Invite Accountability
Sell	Enroll
Rescue	Assist
Sympathy	Empathy
Tell	Ask
Force	Allow, Empower
Expert	Facilitate
Mandatory	Discretionary
Toward Outcomes	From Outcomes
Activity	Action
Problem solving	Future building
Driving	Forwarding Action
Control	Freedom
Determined	Committed
Hard Work	Adventure
Push	Challenge
"You have to..."	"You might consider..."
Passive Listening	Active Listening
Authority	Influence
Manipulate	Inspire
Feedback	Feedforward
Demand	Invite, Request

Figure 2.1

Last June we were working with a small group of sales managers in Norway. They were accustomed to telling their direct reports what to do. We had them do the TELL versus ASK exercise to see how well they changed statements into questions. It was a tough chore for them to do because they were so accustomed to just telling their salespeople what to do and how to do it. The CoachLab workshop we conducted was a rare opportunity for these sales managers to learn and practice new coaching skills: asking and listening. The sales managers clearly saw the possibility of their direct reports becoming more responsible for their actions, so they were quite eager to master these new skills. They shared that their salespeople always looked to them for the answers to how to best serve their customers—what to do, how to do it, and when to do it. They were worn out having their employees be so totally dependent on them. Learning the art of crafting and asking questions helped free these managers to successfully coach and empower their sales personnel.

Feedforward: It's All in How You Listen

During a coaching session with an executive named Jodie, Germaine patiently listened as she described recent conversations with her staff. The feedback that Jodie's staff gave to her went something like this: "You're hard to communicate with." "I don't feel empowered when you speak to me." "You sound impatient when you speak to me." "You make me feel stupid."

Does this scenario sound familiar to you? Do you know people or have clients who have ever felt helpless when it comes to communicating with their staff? What is a person to do with this type of feedback? Can you guess that this executive spent her entire weekend getting information and coaching from people closest to her after that feedback?

Jodie said, "It felt like being hit with a fire hose full of bad news, Germaine." She even went out and bought some self-help books and began investigating possible workshops she could attend. She was determined to better herself to take care of all her staff's woes.

After surfing the Internet for communication seminars, Germaine was next on Jodie's list. Their coaching session was first thing Monday morning, and after listening to Jodie's story and her decisions, Germaine asked one simple question:

"Jodie, where were your actions coming from?" Of course, she asked for clarification of that question, so Germaine went into more detail. "Are your actions coming from the results you're committed to accomplishing, or are they coming from 'What's wrong with me?'" The cloud that had been hanging above Jodie's head began to lift as they discussed the difference between the feedback that she was given and transforming it all into *feedforward*.

The feedback that Jodie received left her feeling dumped on and sent her on a wild goose chase trying to fix herself. What exactly do we mean by feedforward? Feedforward is not merely a coaching term we use instead of the term feedback. Our friend, Jerry Gauche, shared this valuable distinction with us during one of our CoachLab courses. He uses feedforward to distinguish giving assessments (what we would normally call feedback) to someone, plus suggestions to forward the player to the next level. Feedback is usually only a report about the past with some evaluation. Feedforward, on the other hand, acknowledges the past with a keen eye toward the future—a future made up of possible actions the player may take to improve her results.

The distinction of feedforward helps us to tune players' listening to concentrate on capturing ways they might improve in the future rather than dwell on what didn't work in the past. Feedback is often merely opinion, judgment, or evaluation without any intention or conversation to enable the player to move ahead—just as Jodie felt stuck with the bad news from her staff.

Feedforward is intended to help players design a way forward *and*, at the same time, provide them with an honest report on how they have performed up to now.

Now, let's get back to Jodie. In designing a way forward, we used the Activity Versus Action model. The words *action* and *activity* are commonly thought to be different words used to describe the same phenomenon. They are often used interchangeably in ordinary conversation. Actually, action and activity are poles apart. Once you recognize their distinction, you may have a thunderbolt (a personal insight or ah-ha). It's been an enlightening experience for many people with whom we have worked. (Refer to the full explanation in the Addenda.)

Jodie's thunderbolt was realizing that she was caught up in the muck and mire of activity. She was determined to fix herself so that she could be the best boss in the world. Her only problem was that she didn't know what to fix. It's hard to try to fix others' perceptions. Jodie now realized that she was on the downward spiral of activity. And she had been thinking about taking a course to help her conduct the "right" kind of meeting with her staff—at least one they might like.

If a player wants to reach her desired future or intended results, it is critical that she develop a bias for outcomes and a bias toward actions correlated to those outcomes. Once a player envisions the desired intended outcomes, then the possible actions the player may take to accomplish the results will begin to bubble up automatically. The intended results or desired future naturally begins to shape thoughts and generate actions to fulfill the vision.

When Jodie looked into the future and saw her desired outcomes associated with having an outrageous year in her business and having the staff aligned on the results of the company, she began to think about last week's dump-on-Jodie session differently. She put aside the what's-wrong-with-me conversation and focused on designing a way forward. With a little planning, Jodie decided to have a meeting where everyone was free to communicate in a way that moved the action forward. She wasn't going to suppress negative feedback, but rather transform it into feedforward that would assist them all in accomplishing their aligned-upon company objectives.

As a coach, distinguishing activity from action assists your player in determining where his actions and motivation come from. *Action* is always related to a high-value outcome. *Activity* isn't—it's just handling little urgencies or scrambling just to stay above water. In his book *The 80/20 Principle*, Richard Koch explains Pareto's rule that 80 percent of your productivity comes from 20 percent of your actions.

> *"Most activity, en masse and individually, is a waste of time. It will not contribute materially to desired results."*
> —Richard Koch

An effective way to coach your player to accomplish her intended results is to have her make a conscious contextual shift toward having a bias for outcomes and away from a bias for activity. One way to do this is simply asking your player to identify the driver of her actions: activity or action. This opens the opportunity for you to share what you mean by those terms. We suggest you inquire with her as Germaine did with Jodie until your player realizes her actions are activity-driven. Upon realizing this, she is free to choose to shift to outcomes.

At this point in our conversation, Jodie felt renewed and invigorated. Her enthusiasm to share her insights with her staff was bubbling over— she could hardly wait. Germaine ended their phone call with Jodie scheduling a strategy session with her staff later that week.

The following Monday, Germaine received another call from Jodie. There was a striking difference with this conversation. Jodie was enthusiastically describing the *feedforward* she enjoyed from her team. Her staff's conversation switched to how they could do things differently to achieve the business outcomes that they had designed. Way to go, Jodie!

Great Coaches Listen Well
Now, Aren't You Glad It's Easy?

Now that we've shared with you some things that can drive the way we listen to each other, it's time to provide some simple techniques to enhance your listening skills. Did you know that there just isn't a whole lot you have to do to be a good listener?

That's right. It's just not very difficult. The first and most important step we have found is to give up the notion that you are not a good listener. Just do that, and your ability to listen effectively to your players will increase instantly. After you do that, coupled with being conscious of your internal dialogue, there isn't really very much to do to improve your listening.

The organizational effectiveness research team of Lombardo and Eichinger (Lominger) has published a superb book titled *FYI: For Your Improvement*. They've identified 67 competencies that any employee might need to get his job done in any one of today's modern organizations. And, of course, one of those 67 competencies is *listening*. For each competency, they list the attributes of a person who would be considered skilled in the area and the attributes of someone unskilled. They go on to recommend remedies for the unskilled in each competency as well.

Below is an excerpt from the *FYI* book listing the three skilled and eight unskilled attributes for *listening*.

The Listening Competency

Skilled

- Practices attentive and active listening
- Has the patience to hear people out
- Can accurately restate the opinions of others even when he/she disagrees

Unskilled

- Cuts people off and finishes their sentences if they hesitate
- Interrupts to make a pronouncement or render a solution or decision
- Doesn't learn much from interactions with others
- Appears not to listen or is too busy constructing his/her own response
- Many times misses the point the other is trying to make
- May appear arrogant, impatient or uninterested
- May listen to some groups/people but not others
- Inaccurate restating the case of others

Source: *For Your Improvement*, Lombardo & Eichinger

Figure 2.2

Now, how about that? There are eight things you can do to be a poor listener and only three things you have to do to be a skilled listener. Looks to us like being a good listener is a whole lot easier than all the things people do to become really bad listeners. We think *FYI* is an excellent guide and reference book for any coach or manager committed to developing people.

We have used the FYI book ourselves to great advantage on numerous occasions. But we do think the authors missed one unskilled listening behavior: frequent yawning and an inability to keep one's head from falling and hitting desk. (Sorry, we just couldn't help ourselves.)

The *FYI* distinguishes competence, not necessarily excellence. We know that great coaches do other things to be the extraordinary coaches that they are. One attribute of what makes an extraordinary listener and a great coach is the ability to distinguish what the player actually says from what the chatterbox in the coach's head may add or subtract.

Listen to your own chatterbox. What is it saying to you right now? Well, if you can tell the difference between what we wrote on this page and the chatter in your head about what we wrote, you are an extraordinary listener or well on your way to becoming one.

Summary

Throughout this chapter, we have shared how coaches can be a clearing or opening for effective coaching through uncommon listening. And we suggested ways to use questions to help players invent their own solutions to their unique problems, rather than telling them what to do.

It all comes down to our ability to tune the listening of our players-like finding the perfect radio station to reach them. Continue to scan the channels or turn the dial until you find the best reception. By tuning the listening of your players, they will know what to expect from you and hopefully will find themselves ready to engage you as their strategic partner. Stay tuned, friend, stay tuned.

It may sound paradoxical, but it is nevertheless true: Your coaching philosophy, premise, or context speaks loudly through the listening you provide for your players.

Our dear friend and colleague, Mike Straw, shared the following quote with us:

"I have come to the frightening conclusion that I am the decisive element. It is my personal approach that creates the climate. It is my daily mood that makes the weather. I possess tremendous power to make life miserable or joyous. I can be a tool of torture or an instrument of inspiration;

I can humiliate or humor, hurt, or heal. In all situations, it is my response that decides whether a crisis is escalated or de-escalated, and a person humanized or de-humanized. If we treat people as they are, we make them worse. If we treat people as they ought to be, we help them become what they are capable of becoming."
—Johann Wolfgang von Goethe

In the next chapter we reveal the power of language to steer business results into pleasant and profitable waters or to send you crashing into jagged, destructive cliffs.

CHAPTER 3

"If you only give people what they already want, someone else will give them what they never dreamed possible."
—Anonymous

COACHING CONVERSATIONS

Outcomes for this chapter:
- Understand and learn how to manage the different coaching conversations.
- Gain a tool to help you describe the many possible benefits of being coached.
- Discover that preparation is the key to success in coaching conversations.

The Coaching Dialogue Process

Coaching is a conversation—a dialogue. The dialogue's purpose is to design a way forward. The coaching conversation is a dialogue directed at closing the distance between the current level of results and the player's intended outcomes. The fruits of the dialogue are promised actions to close the distance, followed by coordinated action and results.

You coach the dialogue in the pathway to the player's intended outcomes.

The Coaching RoadMap (see Addenda) displays a step-by-step process for effective coaching. The following is an in-depth explanation regarding the last "A" in RoadMap, the Action/Dialogue step. To expand further using this model, we've incorporated some of the many tools described in earlier chapters.

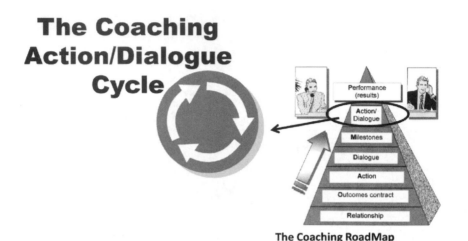

Figure 3.1

The Action/Dialogue stage is repetitive or iterative in nature, and that is why we call it a "cycle." Action/Dialogue is repeated over and over again during the coaching relationship. Let's look at the fundamentals of the various types of coaching dialogues that may occur during the Action/Dialogue stage. There are seven distinct conversation phases in the cycle.

The Case for the Lucky Seven

At the start of any coaching dialogue, we first ask permission to coach before attempting it. We have found that it shifts the player's listening and has the player be the cause for the coaching. Then, with permission, we proceed.

A colleague called us one day to thank us for the tool

"May I coach you?" Dick said, "It is a jewel! I just received some written feedback about my coaching that I've been doing with several individuals in the same company. Nearly every one of them said something on the order of, *I like that you ask permission before you try coaching me or giving me input."*

Look at All the Pretty Bubbles

The seven distinct phases of the coaching Action/Dialogue cycle are listed below. On the pitch, in the thick of the action, the shifts from one phase of the dialogue to another may be almost imperceptible to inexperienced listeners. In addition, the logical order of things presented may not be followed exactly, but rest assured, in a complete and fruitful coaching session, all the bases will be covered.

1. **Data & Observations**—Listening and noting what has been happening in the client's world since you last met. This includes the actions he has taken and not taken, and other specific measurable results, such as sales figures. Note results against promised actions/outcomes. Included in sales results are the he said-she said of particular sales calls. Also, notice how much story you're told versus the results produced.

2. **Listening/Discussion**—Listening carefully to our player's interpretations of the Data & Observations of what went on since the last coaching session and any obstacles that are being encountered. The coach ensures that some of the player's interpretations are not taken as facts. Useful tools in this regard are the quick orientation questions of Think or know? Believe or prove? Is the player on track to accomplish his major objectives?

3. **Facts Assessment**—Recognizing new opportunities, finding leverage points to move things forward, and encouraging high-value future actions distinguished from low-value activities. What small number of potent actions could yield huge payoffs, applying the 80/20 principle?

4. **Conclusions**—Given the facts and our assessment of the facts, what conclusions can we draw? What will be our basis for action?

5. **What's Possible? Possible Actions?**—Conduct an inquiry into possible appropriate outcomes (appropriate to both long-term objectives and immediate concerns) to be achieved between this coaching session and the next. What are possible actions to

take to accomplish those outcomes? (What outcomes/actions? Why those? How will you accomplish them? Who should take the actions, produce the outcomes? By when should they be accomplished?)

6. **Promised Actions**—Evaluate the possible actions and possible outcomes now identified. To which does the player commit to accomplish, both long- and short-term? By when will these be completed? For major, longer-term goals, conduct Best, Worst, Probable outcomes inquiry and adjust promised actions if called for. Record the player's specific promises with by when dates for review at the next coaching session.

7. **Execute Coordinated Actions**—Player/client goes to work, taking promised actions and producing promised outcomes. He may have to enroll other constituents to help him achieve his intended outcomes. The player makes proper adjustments to achieve the results, employing different methods than planned. Player contacts coach for coaching as needed. Player keeps track of results and insights. Player assembles the data and prepares for his next coaching session with his coach.

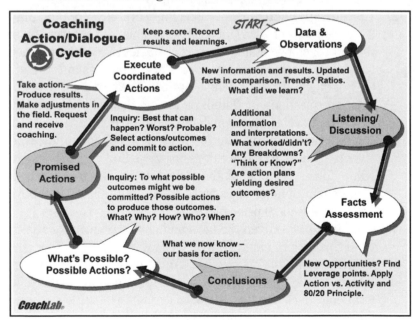

Figure 3.2

"It is the province of knowledge to speak, and it is the privilege of wisdom to listen."
—Oliver Wendell Holmes

What Is Written on Your Welcome Mat?

The best coaches are being an invitation or welcoming for some types of conversations and not an invitation for others. This invitation is analogous to an opening, like an open field. In this case an open, fertile field in which only certain kinds of seeds and plants are allowed to take root and grow. In the case of the coach, only certain types of conversations are welcome.

The best coaches are like farmers who help their player or team till the soil, plant the right seeds, fertilize, water, pluck the weeds, foil harmful insects, and harvest extraordinary results. The coach orchestrates the conversations to grow positive results like healthy produce.

The Fertile Field

- Optimism
- Possibility
- Creativity
- Self Expression
- Innovation
- Opportunity
- Commitment
- Requests
- Planning
- Action/Outcomes
- Urgency
- Courage

Figure 3.3

To close the distance between the current results and the player's intended outcomes, the best coaches listen for speaking from the player that will help close the gap, not widen it. For example, coaches listen for optimism, possibility, creativity, authentic self-expression, innovation, opportunity, commitment, requests, planning, and actions to be taken to produce specific outcomes.

Keep the Conversation out of the Weeds

Even the least experienced golfer on the course knows enough to try to keep the ball out of the weeds. The weeds in the coach's case are conversations that smack of pessimism, resignation, self-doubt, worry, victim, doom and gloom, sarcasm, gossip, mere activity, and disloyalty. Dwelling in any of these is a waste of breath if you want to achieve worthwhile objectives.

The Fertile Field

The Weeds

- Optimism
- Possibility
- Creativity
- Self Expression
- Innovation
- Opportunity
- Commitment
- Requests
- Planning
- Action/Outcomes
- Urgency
- Courage

- Pessimism
- Resignation
- Self Doubt
- Worry
- Victim
- Doom & Gloom
- Sarcasm
- Gossip
- Mere Activity
- Disloyalty
- Complacency
- False Urgency

Figure 3.4

The farmer doesn't go to market with his weeds when his trees bear no fruit. Sorry, stretching metaphors too far can get pretty ugly, can't it? We just thought we would demonstrate that for you.

"When we choose not to focus on what is missing from our lives but are grateful for the abundance that's present ...
we experience heaven on earth."
—Sarah Breathnach

How Change Happens

As coaches, we normally invest a good deal of time in cultivating and nurturing conversations for what's possible in the future. Conversely, we may spend little or no time discussing how bad things are. We all like to stay positive. But if the client/player is willing to put up with the status quo, our efforts to help them improve will be all for naught.

Here is a revealing perspective we adapted from a model originally conceived by David Gleicher and the late Richard Beckhard about how organizational change happens. They devised what they called a Formula for Change. The formula proposes that the combination of organizational dissatisfaction, vision for the future, and the possibility of immediate, tactical action must be stronger than the resistance within the organization in order for meaningful change to occur. The same is true, we have witnessed, for individuals, which makes sense given that an organization is always composed of individuals. (Our model differs slightly from the Gleicher-Beckhard original in that the F, First Steps, doesn't in practice act as a multiplier, but rather acts as an addition to Vision multiplied by Dissatisfaction.)

$$V \times D + F > R$$

V = **Vision** for the future, desired state, or condition
D = **Dissatisfaction** with the status quo or the present condition
F = Clearly defined **First Steps** to get you to the desired condition
R = Natural **Resistance** to change (including the environmental pull, or drift, toward business as usual)

So, the Vision, Dissatisfaction, and First Steps combined must be greater than people's Resistance to change. Said another way, the conversations for fulfilling the vision, dissatisfaction with the present level of results, and clear first steps to move toward fulfilling the vision all must outweigh the conversation for business as usual, or the current state.

As management consultants and coaches, it is to our advantage for us to remember to promote a conversation about what is intolerable right now, the D in the equation, so that it is vivid and real for the player/client. We want him to be so emotionally involved, or hooked, by how bad things are that he feverishly desires to change them for the better as rapidly as possible. Rich conversations for what's possible in the future, V, and actions to take now, F, coupled with a sufficient amount of D will drive change for the better.

When *the intolerable D* is undistinguished long enough and is put up with, it will eventually become tolerable, and complacency will set in. And when the unwanted condition does become visible for a moment, you will hear familiar comments such as, "Well, that's just the nature of this business" or "That's just how it is, you know? I've been around fifteen years now and I don't expect things will get any better during the next fifteen."

Terry Weingarten was plant manager for a large manufacturing company. At this particular time, when Germaine was coaching him, the back orders for his plant's product were vast. Terry was under considerable pressure from his customers (not to mention his upper management) to deliver what they had ordered.

But the reject rate was 22 percent, and these unacceptably flawed products coming off the machines delayed deliveries continually. The company's expert quality consultant, Charlie Everett, said, "I've analyzed everything, Terry. I don't find any way to improve your process or equipment. This is typical quality for this industry."

"Well, Charlie, I'm sorry, but that's just unacceptable," Terry told him.

Terry, unwilling to live with the status quo, declared the intolerable D to his direct reports. They formed a high-performance team to drive down the number of rejects that had been coming off the line. And within 60 days, they had driven down the reject rate to 2 percent-that's right, 2 percent!

We do our best to remember Terry's inspiration whenever we are confronted with conventional wisdom that says our clients cannot do something that needs doing.

"Don't listen to anyone who tells you that you can't do this or that. That's nonsense. Make up your mind ... then have a go at everything. Go to school, join in all the games you can. Go anywhere you want to. But never, never let them persuade you that things are too difficult or impossible."
—Douglas Bader, British WWII Pilot credited with shooting down 22 enemy aircraft despite being a double amputee, having lost both legs.

In Chapter 2 we shared with you contrasts between the old and new paradigms of coaching. To further distinguish the differences, take a look at Figure 3.5, Traditional & Coaching Dialogues. In Germaine's coaching example above with her client Terry Weingarten, the expert consultant, Charlie, was content to tell Terry what reject rate was typical in the industry and leave it at that. Look at the second set of contrasting conversations below. Charlie was seeking to explain. Terry was seeking to deliver—a world of difference.

Read the contrasting dialogues on page 38, and see if you aren't inspired by the possible coaching dialogues you can have from a modern coaching paradigm.

Dialogue, Dialogue—How Do We Prepare?

"If a man knows not what harbor he seeks, any wind is the right wind."
—Lucius Annaeus Seneca,
Roman Philosopher-Orator, 3 B.C.-65 A.D.

Up to this point, we've been talking about the coaching dialogue cycle. Now we're turning our attention to preparing clients for these coaching dialogues. Have you ever had your client come to his coaching session with you unprepared? If you have been a coach for even a little while, this has probably happened to you. And if you are a coach and it hasn't happened yet, it surely will.

Although in creating our relationship with a new client we impress upon them the importance of preparing for our sessions, from time to time our clients come to our coaching sessions unprepared. In the Addenda you will find 10 Ways to Get the Most From Your Coach. Number 9 on the list is prepare for each coaching session—to list their objectives and outcomes they intend for the session.

Traditional & Coaching Dialogue

■ Traditional dialogue succumbs to the prevailing mood and suffers the result.
▲ *Coaching dialogue **brings forth the appropriate mood** to deliver the desired result.*

■ Traditional dialogue seeks to explain.
▲ *Coaching dialogue **seeks to deliver**.*

■ Traditional dialogue is based upon ruthless and immediate judgment (right/wrong, true/false, like/don't like, good/bad, want/don't want, yes/no, agree/disagree).
▲ *Coaching dialogue **explores possibilities** interrupting the rush to judgment and **averting premature conclusion**.*

■ Traditional dialogue sets up false dichotomies and contradictions that stop action (want/but, either/or).
▲ *Coaching dialogue **embraces both sides** of a dichotomy or contradiction and **seeks to design a way forward**.*

■ Traditional dialogue believes that information and judgment are sufficient for decision making.
▲ *Coaching dialogue, in addition, deliberately **generates new thinking and new ideas**.*

■ Traditional dialogue asks what is wrong or lacking.
▲ *Coaching dialogue asks **what's missing** and **how to provide it**.*

■ Traditional dialogue seeks the right process.
▲ *Coaching dialogue **seeks the right result**.*

■ Traditional dialogue dwells in adversarial argument and refutation to explore a subject.
▲ *Coaching dialogue explores the subject **cooperatively with a willingness to be surprised**.*

■ Traditional dialogue is concerned with search and discovery.
▲ *Coaching dialogue, in addition, is concerned with **design and invention**.*

■ Traditional dialogue entertains reasons and excuses.
▲ *Coaching dialogue invites **declarations, proposals and promised actions**.*

■ Traditional dialogue drives for prediction and control.
▲ *Coaching dialogue inquires for **freedom to be** & **new openings for action**.*

■ Traditional dialogue merely describes and reports what is possible given the circumstances.
▲ *Coaching dialogue **distinguishes facts from interpretations** and **generates new possibilities** that reshape the circumstances **and provide new openings for action**.*

■ Traditional dialogue succumbs to urgent demands, abandons planning and ultimately swims in low-value activity.
▲ *Coaching dialogue **plans vigilantly**, to **manage interruptions** and **execute high-value actions**.*

■ Traditional dialogue discusses a problem dwelling upon what should & shouldn't be, who's right & who's wrong, eventually contemplating solutions.
▲ *Coaching dialogue assembles the facts, **inquires into possible resolutions**, and **generates promises & requests** to **produce specific outcomes** by **specific times**.*

Figure 3.5

Loafers, Beware!

Pilots, the kind who fly airplanes, would never consider taking off without performing a preflight checklist. It would be unthinkable. And it matters not how many times before the pilot has flown this particular aircraft. It is a new airplane every time to a top aviator. A good pilot maximizes his chances of a successful, uneventful flight by adding to his certainty about his equipment. The pilot's future, the pilot's very life is at stake. Why, then, would your players risk not preparing for their coaching session?

For one reason, they don't consider that their life is at stake. They don't consider the difference-making opportunity the coaching session is. Oh, there are those who do. And we are fortunate to have many of these. But even the best of these players forget. They too can become embroiled in their day-to-day activities and not carve out time to prepare for their sessions with us. They too can forget the difference a well-prepared-for coaching session can make for them in their lives.

Below is the Player's Preflight Checklist that we have developed and successfully used with our clients. It has, in some cases, appreciably reduced the instances of unprepared players for us. And although the questions on the checklist have worked well for some years now, feel free to tweak them for your use.

Player's Preflight Checklist

Strategic Thinking
- What dreams or ideas do you have that your coach might help you to transform into commitments, enthusiasm, and results?
- What future scenarios might you ask your coach to help you visualize? What constraints or apparent obstacles do you face that your coach might assist you in designing creative ways forward?
- What plans do you have that are not yet grounded in reality?
- What goals and objectives do you have that are not being realized or are not moving toward attainment?
- About what would you like a fresh perspective?
- What part of your business needs work or attention? What part of your life?

- What do you want your coach to know or what should your coach know?
- What has to happen this week to obtain your objectives? This month? This quarter?
- What important decisions do you have to make?
- Where have you been wasting energy on low-value activities?
- What high-value actions have you not been taking?
- What new opportunities or challenges might your coach help you to evaluate?
- How might your coach collaborate with you?
- What requests of your coach might you invent?
- List the outcomes you intend to accomplish in this coaching session.

Preparation Resources
1. Reread your Coaching Outcomes Contract.
2. Review the Ten Ways to Get the Most From Your Coach list. (Addendum)
3. Ask a colleague in what area you might request coaching.

You're Firing Me?
I'm Your Client!

Tony Fortunato, a business coach, was about to fire his client, Angelo D'Amico. Angelo owned a small chain of floor covering stores in Pittsburgh, Pennsylvania. Angelo continually came to his coaching conferences with Tony unprepared. This was frustrating to Tony, and although he did his best to coach Angelo successfully, he told us he felt "guilty about taking Angelo's money."

Tony had become one of our clients to help him build his coaching practice. We had been coaching Tony for about a year and a half by this time. We had been testing and developing the Player's Preflight Checklist but had not shared it with Tony yet. We didn't have to. Tony had never failed to come to his coaching sessions well-prepared. Tony, being a business coach himself, knew well the value of preparation.

"Tony, we have a new tool that Angelo might find useful in preparing for his coaching sessions with you," Jed said.

Tony replied, after glancing over the new checklist, "Frankly, Jed, I'm not sure even this will help. Angelo says he enjoys meeting with me and gets value out of our conversations, but he just won't set aside the time to get ready for our meetings. I know I could serve him so much better if he would just prepare. I think I'm just going to have to end the coaching relationship."

"Tony, I understand your frustration. But how would you feel about taking one more shot at Angelo using this tool?" Tony agreed to present the idea to Angelo at their next meeting.

Eureka!
There's Gold in Them Thar Hills

Two weeks later Tony called. "Angelo did his homework," Tony whispered. "He actually came to our last session prepared. I asked Angelo what happened, and he said the checklist was so easy to use, it made preparation effortless. He said the very first question got him started. You know what, Jed? I discovered Angelo was making 'preparation' really *significant*, and he actually didn't know where to start." Thunderbolt! Tony had been taking for granted that Angelo knew what to do to prepare. A simple tool like a Player's Preflight Checklist showed Angelo how.

The Player's Preflight Checklist is a great way to help manage the *value drift*, the phenomenon of the player taking you for granted over time and familiarity. The preflight checklist assists you in ensuring that your client will continue to receive maximum value from your coaching interactions.

Summary

In this chapter, we explored the seven steps of the coaching dialogue process. Each step of this process builds on the previous step that leads to actions. Actions enable change. The formula for change gives one focus in how to strategize to allow change to happen. In addition to asking for permission to coach as an effective tool to gain your client's receptivity to your coaching, the Player's Preflight Checklist promotes proactivity. This checklist enables your client to strategize and prepare for coaching calls.

"The will to win is important, but the will to prepare is vital."
—Joe Paterno, Head Football Coach, Penn State

In our next chapter we illustrate the power of language.

CHAPTER 4

"Don't mistake activity for accomplishment."
—John Wooden, UCLA coach of Ten NCAA
basketball championship teams

AND THE BAND PLAYED ON
But It Really Needed to Take a Break

Outcomes for this chapter:
* Distinguish the power of interpretation and how to stay grounded in the facts.
* Gain insight into what sometimes drives people's actions in the wrong direction.

You may remember the HBO film *And the Band Played On*[1] , starring Matthew Modine and Alan Alda. It is a docudrama about the process researchers experienced in their quest to discover the cause of a rapidly growing number of deaths from unexplained sources among men in Los Angeles, New York City, and San Francisco. The researchers were led in the early 1980s by Dr. Don Francis, played by Modine. In the end, they uncovered the source—a virus that has come to be known as HIV (Human Immunodeficiency Virus), which can result in AIDS (Acquired Immune Deficiency Syndrome). And what does this have to do with coaching? Glad you asked . . .

In addition to being a great film, portions of the screenplay are amazingly instructive in terms of how to conduct effective business meetings. The researchers, during their in-depth investigation of the possible caus-

---

[1]*And the Band Played On* is a 1993 American television film, winning Emmy, Golden Globe, and CableACE awards. It was directed by Roger Spottiswoode. The teleplay was written by Arnold Schulman, based on the best-selling 1987 nonfiction book, *And the Band Played On: Politics, People, and the AIDS Epidemic* by Randy Shilts.

es of the alarming death toll, had to come together frequently to share their findings.

As we watched the portrayal of these meetings in the movie, we were drawn into and even riveted to similar recurring interactions. For example, one of the researchers would begin to share his findings and then be interrupted abruptly by Dr. Francis who would ask sharply, "Think or know?"

The researcher would respond with something like, "Oh, this is just something *I think*—it's a theory for the moment. I can't prove it yet."

And then sometimes Dr. Francis or another researcher would interject, "Believe or prove?" This was meant to find out whether the researcher's statements or conclusions were things he *believed*, like a plausible but still theoretical explanation, or a hypothesis he could prove because he had collected sufficient evidence.

Those three-word sets, Think or know? and Believe or prove? were used frequently in those critical debriefings to orient everyone how to listen to the reports they were hearing. The researcher's response to those brief questions quickly satisfied for everyone: Am I listening to facts or interpretations without proof?

How critical do you think being clear about whether you are hearing facts or people's interpretations might be in your business meetings or coaching sessions? We think it's vital. We had been looking for a clarifying tool that wouldn't stop the action during discussions for our clients for years. This Hollywood film gave us a fast, easy method that we could apply during a conversation to distinguish facts from interpretations efficiently and effectively.

We never dreamed that we would find the perfect tool in an HBO made-for-TV movie one hot summer night after work. But as one of our favorite teachers, Werner Erhard, used to ask, "If you knew what you needed to do to produce the outcome you wanted was to kiss the garbage can, would you do it?" Would you?

Ready to Go, Boss

Jed was facilitating a session with the executive team for a Fortune 500 insurance company. As people were entering the conference room for this monthly results meeting, some were studying the most recent month's sales report they had all received earlier that afternoon. One executive said sourly, "Hmmm ... our auto insurance policy sales revenues are down-down by six percent." The meeting was underway now without any official announcement.

"Whew! Six percent—that's considerable, isn't it?" Zach replied.

At that moment, the president, Rick, looked up from his laptop computer toward Zach and pondered, "Yeah. I wonder, Zach; maybe our sales agents aren't properly motivated."

Susan chimed in, "You know, I was at lunch with Rob Moore from the Acme Insurance Group last week ... most of you know Rob. Anyway, they had a similar situation with their agents, and they ran a contest to motivate them. It was very successful he said."

"Great idea, Susan," Geoff, the VP of Sales said. "We'll run a contest. Why not? We could divide up the regions among us and each of us can visit them to kick off the contest. You know, give it that personal touch, and create a little competition among them. That will get our agents jazzed." And Susan asserted that she could design an even better contest than Acme had done.

Several other executives began nodding their approval, smiling, and one even did a drum roll with his hands on the conference table, signifying his enthusiastic support for the new, exciting sales contest.

Uplifted by people's enthusiasm, Rick asked, "How does everyone's schedule look this month? No, forget I asked that. This is urgent. Rearrange your schedules if you must. We've got to turn these revenue numbers around now! Let me get Jack in here to help us plan our travel," he said as he reached for the telephone in the middle of the table.

Then Jed asked, "Excuse me. Why are you launching a sales contest?"

Geoff replied quickly and in disbelief, "Jed, haven't you been listening? We want to motivate our sales representatives to improve their sales. Our sales have slipped six percent! That's a lot of premium dollars lost, my friend."

"And tell me again why you think they need to be motivated?" Jed asked Geoff.

Geoff sighed and said, "Because, well, because ..." Geoff's words began tapering off as he slowly recalled the recent discussion.

Rick jumped in, reminding everyone, "Because I said that maybe our agents weren't motivated enough, or something like that."

"Right, something like that. And, Rick, do you know for a fact that your salespeople lack motivation?" Jed probed.

Rick replied, "No. No, I do not. As a possible explanation for the downturn I wondered out loud whether our sales agents were motivated. That question turned into a speculation. And then, and then somehow my speculation morphed into a fact. And now here we are ready to book flights all over the country to launch a new sales contest. Well, that's annoying," Rick said softly. Then he added, "Annoying? Correction: That's downright infuriating."

Zach said, "You kind of warned us just last week about acting on opinions rather than facts didn't you, Jed?"

Some of the executives began to chuckle a little, while others looked down at the conference table and shook their heads in recognition, perhaps a little embarrassed. And soon nearly everyone was laughing out loud.

"Nothing is more terrible than activity without insight behind it. Behind the expenditures of the precious energy of life there must be the highest degree of wisdom."
—Thomas Carlyle, Leaves of Gold

Just the Facts, Mister, Just the Facts

This executive team, without distinguishing facts from speculation, had almost made an expensive mistake. They had leaped to a decision based upon a possible cause that was offered. In the conversation that ensued, that initial interpretation of the statistical fact, 6 percent down, without anyone noticing, almost instantly gained the dignity of a *probable cause*. And soon after, people began speaking as though it were a fact. In addition, that unintended transformation had the effect of derailing any further investigation into the actual cause of the dip in sales results.

Now, these were not stupid people. These executives were well-schooled, experienced, and successful businesspeople. So how could they have lost their way so easily in the conversation?

Because most of us were never taught, and few of us have become skilled at distinguishing facts from interpretations in any conversation. It's as though anything anyone ever says, any conjecture, any postulation, drifts automatically toward, and inevitably winds up in, the fact bucket. Unless we are awake enough to notice, interpretations are dealt with like facts. It's as if that invisible drift is always in the background, falsely shaping the direction of our thinking.

I Sure Hope There's a Pony Under All This Manure

So, what did they do about the 6 percent drop in new sales revenue? Well, after the meeting, real investigative work was begun, and they discovered that in some states, their competitors had lowered their prices for auto insurance policies. The 6 percent drop in sales results wasn't due to a lack of motivation after all; it was directly attributable to increased competition in certain states. So the company quickly adjusted its rates to support its agents. And, you guessed it, that action was indeed motivating to their sales representatives. Sales went back up the following month, and the company was getting back on track to meet its aggressive sales targets for the year.

Oh, What a Web We Weave

What a trap opinions and speculation can become when you hear them as facts. Distinguishing facts from interpretations is one of the most critical things you can do in any coaching conversation—in any coaching dialogue. We invite you to adopt the convention of Think or know? and Believe or prove? in your coaching conversations. One of our clients actually framed those two questions and hung them in every conference room in his building. We like to think that that company's astronomical growth had something to do with our client's adoption of those two questions to enhance his employees' ability to make wise, fact-based business decisions.

Two simple questions: Think or know? Believe or prove? They can help improve your coaching dialogue with your players significantly and perhaps increase your players' results substantially. These questions add just enough rigor to people's thinking so that their conversations are grounded in reality.

Don't Just Sit There!

The insurance company's executive team had failed to distinguish facts from interpretations and had found themselves ensnared in what John Kotter[2] calls *false urgency* in his latest book, *A Sense of Urgency*. We have all experienced false urgency—a frenzy of unfounded and uncoordinated reactionary activities to solve a problem. Have you ever been in a meeting and someone says, "Well, we can't just sit here; we need to do something. So, let's do something. *Anything!*" That will surely start the false urgency ball rolling if nothing else will.

"False urgency is built on a platform of anxiety and anger. Anxiety and anger drive behavior that can be highly energetic ... the energy can easily create activity, not productivity, and sometimes very destructive activity."
—John P. Kotter[2]

Similar to Kotter's observation is the Activity Versus Action model that we referred to in Chapter 2. Action is executing thoughtful, well-calculated, and coordinated actions to produce specific outcomes, while activity is furious, half-thought, knee-jerk reactions to problems or undesirable situations-a frenzy of unproductive activities. (For a full description of this model, please refer to the Addenda).

Help Me, I Think I'm Falling!

Here is another example of unproductive activity that was avoided through effective coaching. Fred Foster, one of Germaine's clients and a highly skilled engineer, once complained to her: "Germaine, I cannot figure out why my boss doesn't like me. She never asks my opinion about project designs she's working on. I've won industry awards for my engineering and project designs. Why doesn't she use me? You know what? I'm just going to have to ask her why she doesn't like me. Yep, that's what I'll do."

Germaine asked Fred, "May I coach you?" Fred said, "Sure. I guess that's why I mentioned it."

---

[2]John P. Kotter is the Konosuke Matsushita Professor of Leadership, Emeritus, at Harvard Business School.

Germaine continued, "Fred, your boss not liking you—is this something you *think*, or is this something you *know*?" In the coaching dialogue that followed, Fred had a realization: His manager Adrianna's not asking him for advice on her engineering projects didn't necessarily mean that she didn't like him. There could be all sorts of other reasons or interpretations behind her not seeking his counsel. Maybe she didn't need his help. Maybe she didn't want to bother him—after all, he had his own heavy workload. Maybe she felt threatened by his prestigious awards. Maybe she was too busy just getting the work out to take time to ask him. Maybe it never even occurred to her to ask him. Maybe it's just not her style to collaborate. Maybe this or maybe that ... until Fred finally saw that there might be an endless number of possible explanations for her behavior other than her not liking him personally.

This insight freed Fred up considerably. So much so that he gave up worrying about whether Adrianna liked him or not, and he just went back to doing his usual great work. And not long after, she began discussing her engineering projects with Fred and even asked him to coach one of her other direct reports.

Summary

Too often we are consumed in the moment with our reactions to situations or how we interpret what is happening. The rush to action could cost us, and our company, a lot of money without ever coming close to the types of results we're after. One fact can have several different interpretations depending on who is doing the interpreting. Take just a few minutes to examine the validity or to clarify the nature of what is being said by asking two simple questions: Think or Know? Believe or Prove? They add rigor while keeping us grounded in the realities of any conversation about a situation.

> *"Possibilities are like the wings of birds; they allow man to soar and climb to the heavens. And facts are like the atmosphere against which those wings must beat, and without which the soaring bird will surely plummet back to earth."*
> —Ivan Pavlov

"The environment that people live in is the environment that they learn to live in, respond to, and perpetuate. If the environment is good, so be it. But if it is poor, so is the quality of life within it."
—Ellen Swallow Richards, American chemist and ecologist

ENVIRONMENT AND ACTION

Outcomes for this chapter:
- Understand how you can coach your players to maximize their productivity by managing their environment.
- Learn the three main aspects of environment and ways to manage all three.
- Expand your ability to relieve stress for your clients.
- Uncover the awful truth about clutter that was buried under clutter.
- Examine the possibility of easily building physical pathways to productivity.

There is currently an influx of television programs that focus on improving your living environment, giving your home a facelift for very little money and, while you're at it, improving your appearance as well. According to many of these programs, an improved environment or enhancing one's appearance usually results in a better quality of life and increased confidence. What if they are right?

Take Stock of Your Environment

"Be careful the environment you choose for it will shape you; be careful the friends you choose for you will become like them."
—W. Clement Stone
1902-2002, author and businessman

What in your environment is there but not consciously there? What is there as part of the atmosphere, like air? And, like air, it is invisible, yet it affects you? We define environment as that which you put there *consciously*. Atmosphere is there and not consciously so.

Environment is both internal and external. The internal environment is what's going on inside of us—how we are feeling, what we are thinking, and what we do with those thoughts. The external environment is just that—everything that we experience as external, or outside of us.

People grossly underestimate the impact of the environment on their productivity. What are you reacting to or responding to in your environment? The environment includes your office, car, closet, music, radio—all of it.

"Most important, we've learned that we can change teens' behaviors and attitudes dramatically for the better with relatively modest, well-targeted efforts to change their environment."
—Joseph Allen, PhD and Claudia Worrell Allen, PhD
"Escaping the Endless Adolescence"

Let's begin with examining the three aspects or categories of our environment.

There's Stuff Everywhere!

"People tend to underestimate how much clutter contributes to their stress."
—Jan Jasper, productivity consultant, author

The first aspect of environment is *stuff*—the physical parts of your life. One study claims that, on average, people handle 300 pieces of paper and e-mails each day. Whew! Is that too much to imagine? Well, we've had a few personal experiences lately with our clients where they've validated that figure.

Ever notice how many times you might handle one piece of paper or read the same e-mail? We began to take note of this, and we were amazed. Sometimes we would read the same letter and put it in a file to handle later, then read it again only to place it somewhere else until we had more time to work with it. Research indicates that some of us will read a letter five times before we respond to it, pass it on, or just delete or discard it. Take an audit of how often you handle one piece of paper or an e-mail. You may have a rude awakening. Then again, you may discover that you move through the onslaught of these communications with ease and seldom retouch them indecisively. If that's the case—bravo!

By the way, you can find many tips on handling e-mail and reducing the number you receive by inserting "tips for e-mail" in your favorite Internet search engine. In a matter of seconds you'll find some tips that you can use immediately.

What other kind of stuff is there in your environment that gums up the works, squanders your time, and stops effective actions? Have you ever walked into your office (or any work area) and found stacks of paper piled high on your desk? Do you remember the instant energy drain it produced? Have you ever walked into a manufacturing area where the housekeeping and maintenance have been lax for some time? For some people, it gives rise to a feeling of almost hopelessness or low-grade despair. Environment plays a highly underrated, yet commanding role in our experience of available energy and morale.

Yikes! I'm Overwhelmed By My Environment. Help Me, Please!

Ellen DeLap, organizing consultant shared the following story with us.

"My client June called me to share what was happening in her office. She started tentatively, feeling insecure about asking for help from me. 'I was wondering just what do you do to help people in their offices?' I asked June to tell me a little bit about what was going on. A flood of words and emotion sprang out. 'It's my desk, under my desk, and it's my bookshelves, and just my whole office. It's totally out of control with paper everywhere. Every day I get more business cards as contacts, and I just have them everywhere. I try to work on new projects, but they are scattered around the room and I have no space on my desk to work on them. Can you help me?'

"June continued to share with me that she is a coach and needs immediate access to her files when her clients contact her. Knowing what was needed for easy access, we set up systems for her action items, ongoing projects, business cards, and reference materials. We moved her resources within arm's reach and eliminated all the extra magazines cluttering her shelves. Her desk now has only items on it that she uses every day.

"Once her system and structures were in place, June was able to set aside an hour in the morning and in the midafternoon as a power period to rejuvenate her energy, think, and become centered on creating new programs. Each evening June would clear her desk to the up-tempo strains of John Phillip Souza-her high-energy closure music.

"After two weeks I checked in with June. She exclaimed, 'I am a completely different person.' June was re-energized and thrilled to report that life was easier because she was more efficient and effective at work."

Talk, Talk, Talk
My, How People Do Talk

The second aspect of the environment is *talk*. Yes, talk. Many of us are not conscious that talk is part of our environment and has an impact on our productivity. The nature of the talk could be positive or negative. This talk includes our conversations with other people or when we happen to overhear someone's conversation. Listening to the radio or television are other forms of talk or conversation. How do these conversations impact you? Notice how some conversations can invigorate you and others can wind you up and tighten every joint in your body. As you take an eagle's view of your environment, become cognizant of the talk that is there from time to time.

"It is remarkable how much mediocrity we live with, surrounding ourselves with reminders that the average is acceptable. Our world suffers from terminal normality. Take a moment to assess all the things that keep you powerless to go beyond a 'limit' you arbitrarily set for yourself. The first step to having what you want is the removal of everything in your environment that represents mediocrity, removing things that are limiting. One way is to surround yourself with friends who ask more of you than you do."
—Stewart Emery, behavioral scientist, educator, author

You Know What They Say About People Who Talk to Themselves?

The third aspect of the environment is *self-talk*, or *thinking*. "People have 12,367 thoughts per day. Of those, ninety percent are automatic, and eighty-four percent of those are negative," according to our late friend, Walter Hailey, the behavioral scientist and sales and marketing consultant. Twelve thousand thoughts! That's a lot of talking going on. How do you think that might affect your environment, especially if 84 percent of the thoughts are negative? Manage your self-talk. You don't have to put up with it. You can infuse your thoughts with positivity and confidence.

Jerry Rice, former great wide receiver for the San Francisco 49ers professional football team, has caught more passes than anyone in NFL (National Football League) history. He has not only the reputation for being one of the greatest receivers of all time, but also a reputation for being one of the sharpest dressers of all time, on and off the field. But, don't all players just wear the standard issue uniform?

Taking Control of the Environment Self-Talk and All

Jerry Rice reported in an interview that he had to have everything about his uniform be just so, that is to say, impeccable. The only thing he wanted to stand out in his environment was catching the ball. He didn't want any distractions, not even a loose thread on his jersey. He says he keeps his car and his garage spotless, too.

Jerry found a way to quiet those more than 12,000 thoughts in his head when it comes to producing the result: catching the football. What can you do within your environment to quiet the noise in your head to allow you to fully focus on the task at hand?

Hunker Down and Get 'Er Done

You might say that to accomplish your dreams, it will take discipline. A common belief is that some of us have discipline and some of us just don't. Well, although we have witnessed that discipline can be developed, there might be an easier method to get yourself to do the things that you are committed to doing.

Instead, how about organizing your environment so that you don't need discipline? Replace discipline with a managed environment. For example, if you're committed to exercising and don't have time to go to the gym, how about placing a treadmill in front of your television set? Another good example of this is a scene from the motion picture *Awakenings*, starring Robin Williams and Robert DeNiro.

In the movie, Robin Williams plays Dr. Malcolm Sayer, a clinical doctor working with a number of patients all suffering from the same disease. The disease was a kind of waking sleep, and some of these patients hadn't been able to respond to or interact with other people for over 30 years. They were what one might describe as catatonic, or in kind of a stupor.

Robert DeNiro portrayed Leonard Lowe, one of those patients. By accident, Dr. Sayer witnessed Lucy, another patient, catching her eyeglasses before they hit the ground after they fell off a table. Sayer was stunned to see her quick reflexes. So he tried a tennis ball and found that Lucy could catch the ball easily when it was thrown to her. Every time!

Sayer tried the experiment with Leonard Lowe and the other patients. They too caught the ball with ease. Sayer observed that although these patients would not generate any action on their own, they could react easily and effectively to objects moving in their immediate environment.

When Sayer reported these findings to his colleagues, he said, "It's as if Lucy *borrows the will of the ball*." Now, consider for a moment that Lucy in effect did borrow the will of the ball and that that is precisely what called her to act. Isn't your environment like that? Doesn't it call you to action or, in a sense, pull for your actions? We suggest that it does. And we recommend that you organize your environment so that it calls you to take actions consistent with fulfilling your dreams. Why not borrow the will of your environment?

> *"Life is not about waiting for the storms to pass … it's about learning how to dance in the rain."*
> —Author unknown

Consider for a moment that our environment reflects the types of actions that we take. Yes, like Lucy's environment pulled her to certain actions, even if it was catching a ball or her eyeglasses before they hit the floor. Now, how is your environment set up? Is it set up to pull you to effective actions or to muddle in activity that leaves you in a state of chaos or being overwhelmed or stressed?

Activity Versus Action

The Activity Versus Action model has continued to prove to be an outstanding tool for sparking effective coaching conversations.

In fact, two of our corporate clients have been so struck by the model's value that they asked if we wouldn't mind if they built a physical representation. They both wanted to give models to their top managers and salespeople who would be attending their annual conferences from all over the world. Of course, we gave our consent and we were naturally gratified at their acknowledgment of our work. But that's not what excited us most.

Their intention was to have the Activity Versus Action model wind up on people's desks at all of their locations after the conference as a powerful reminder. Then, too, when people who had not attended the conference visited them in their offices, it might serve as a potent conversation starter to share the important concept of Activity Versus Action .

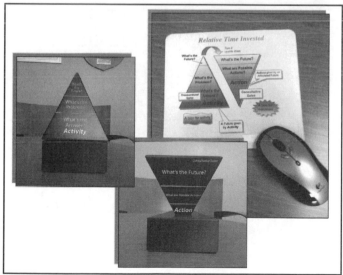

Figure 5.1

Figure 5.2

It worked, too. An employee who hadn't been to the conference would sit down across from the conference attendee at her desk. She would have the little model there on her desk, with the upside-down portion facing the visitor. The visitor would pick up the model's triangle from the base and start to turn it around to put the engraved message right-side up so that it was readable. The manager would say, "Oh, Simon that reminds me. Let me show you how this works and what it's all about. You may even find this enlightening."

And They'rrrre Off!

After that the conversation was off and running. Both clients had embraced our coaching to alter their environment—design their environment to call for the actions they wanted people to be taking.

One client even manufactured mouse pads with the Activity Versus Action concept imprinted on them in bright colors for all of their employees worldwide.

"First we shape our dwellings and then our dwellings shape us."
—Winston Churchill

Color Can Bring You Up or Down

There is a great deal of evidence that colors and temperature affect people's moods and energy. You may want to check this out for yourself by doing a little research.

In some parts of the world where it rains a good deal, some people become really depressed. Also, there are parts of the Earth where during certain times of the year there is very little daylight during a 24-hour period, and at other times it's almost always daylight. This can have a profound effect on people's moods as well as their ability to sleep. We recently found this to be the case while we were working in Norway in mid-June. The sun went down fully just before midnight and rose again around 3 a.m. We found it tough to get a good night's rest.

Have you ever noticed that your moods are just like the weather? They can change quite rapidly and frequently. Depending upon your mood, the types of results that you are producing can be positively or adversely affected. And environment has an enormous impact on your mood.

There are a myriad of topics concerning your environment that you can read about. You'll find everything from the ancient Chinese philosophy of feng shui (the art of placement) to the most recent studies of the effect color has on people's moods.

Take a Stand!

The fact that you are either seated or standing is also an important part of your environment.

"If you want employees to improve performance, ask them to work standing up. Or, at least get them to take stand-up-and-stretch breaks. Why: Research at the University of Southern California shows that people digest complex facts better and make quicker decisions when standing. Some absorbed information 40 percent faster when standing. Says Max Vercruyssen, who conducted the research: 'The more complex the information that has to be processed before making a decision, the more novel the thought, the greater the benefit.'" —USA Today

A similar study was done at Princeton University (Maya Braya) during the early '70s. It reported that people were 50 percent alert when lying down, 75 percent alert when sitting, and 90 percent alert when standing. Wouldn't you like to be 15 percent more alert while working or conducting an important telephone call? The next time you have an important decision to make or an important conference call, try standing up. Now, how can you use this information to coach your players?

One time, after leading a course in Spain, Germaine met with a team she was coaching, and for the first portion of the meeting, they all stood. Very quickly she noticed that people were more actively participating in the discussion and the team was making decisions much faster than they had been in previous meetings. Try having stand-up meetings and see if you don't experience improved results.

You Won't Work on What You Don't See
Building Physical Pathways to Productivity

You won't work on what you don't see, feel, hear, or somehow sense. If your work is outside those senses, it is hidden unless you happen to remember that it's in that drawer or file to be worked on.

Here are some ideas that we use in our environment, as well as coach our clients, to see it all with an eagle's view:

Try stand-up files. These can go on the floor, on the credenza, or any-place in your environment that will call you to work on them. Jed tells this story about one of his colleagues when he was in the insurance business. "Bob Albritton had client files around the room in stacks next to the walls," Jed shares. "All alphabetized: the A stack, B stack, etc.; these files surrounded him. Bob would sit in his swivel chair, spin around, and get an eagle's view of his clients. He didn't have to worry about what or whom he was dropping out, because everything was where he could see and get to it."

Ever lose your to-do list? Put today's to-do list or outcome list on a small easel on your desk, upright and visible, not buried under other work.

You can fold index cards, making tent-card reminders. We like to keep inspiring quotes on cards where we can see them throughout the day. You'll want to change them often and use different colors. This will keep you alert to what's different in your environment so that the cards don't disappear into the background with everything else you've stopped noticing.

Projects can also be displayed in the office for everyone to see by putting a progress board on a bulletin board on the wall. We use the progress board, as have many of our clients, to get an eagle's view of our entire business and plan the week's outcomes from it. The progress board was inspired by Walt Disney. He invented what he called a *briefing board* so that he could stay on top of what was happening in the many projects that were underway at any one time in his entertainment empire.

For each project and in each project's physical location or work area, he had people keep up-to-date information on a briefing board. This way he could see what was happening in each project without having to request a meeting to get reports from everyone.

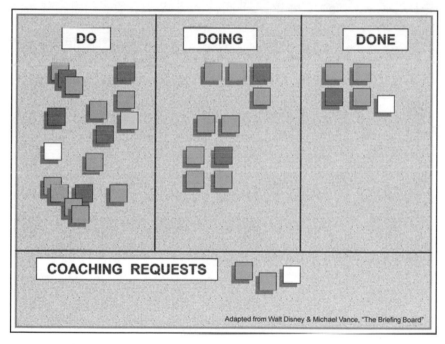

Figure 5.3

Here's how a progress board can work for your weekly planning and monitoring. Hang a large corkboard on an office wall. Your progress board ought to be about 36 inches tall by 48 inches wide. We've tried smaller boards and find they get too cramped for space. Make cards for labeling three main headings across the top of the board: **DO**, **DOING**, and **DONE**.

Underneath the DO heading, pin index cards that have written on them action items and outcomes that you plan to complete at some point, any point in time. The date for completion may or may not be written on the card in the DO category.

The cards in the DOING column indicate what you are currently working on, the date by when the outcome will be accomplished, and by whom.

When an item is completed, move the card to the DONE category. For example, if one of your outcomes for the week is to have a letter written, the card will indicate to whom the letter is to be written, the nature of the message, who will compose the letter, and by when. The card will be in the DOING column on the board before the accountable person performs the task and moves it to the DONE column.

Let's say that your partner, Cristin, is accountable for having this particular letter written by the end of the week. During the week, while you or other staff members are reviewing the board, they may write suggestions on the card about points to include in the body of the letter. Then when Cristin checks the board, she can receive the input or coaching feed-forward.

At the end of your week take stock of all that has been accomplished and celebrate appropriately. The progress board promotes participation in projects through displaying all the work in progress for others to see and to get their coaching on your task or project.

One guideline is that anyone is allowed to write suggestions and ideas on the cards. We have found the progress board to be a very effective way of managing all the different things that are happening at an office without necessarily having to interrupt people to speak about them or send an e-mail inquiry.

A progress board works very well for people working from one location. If people travel frequently, it's more difficult to keep it updated and managed. However, it is possible to have someone who is located where your board is located to update and move the cards along for you.

Our friend and client, Doug Upchurch, built his team's progress board electronically on his computer. "After an offsite with Germaine and Jed, we transferred all our intended outcomes to our Web site so that everyone could see them no matter where they were in the world," Doug reports, "and it made a remarkable improvement in our being in communication with each other."

Teamwork is enhanced when projects are vividly displayed. Because the progress board allows people to see every element to a project, when people keep it up-to-date, appropriate next actions are recognized easily. People begin to participate in the areas that they are skilled in or have experience in as well as others. The projects become a public conversation for the entire office rather than someone's private task list.

Remember, we're talking about altering your environment here, so be sure to put your progress board in a prominent place where everyone has access. We have found this to be good coaching if you make an electronic one, too.

Summary

Our environment on Earth is made up of just three things:
1. Stuff
2. Talk
3. Self-talk

These three things impact our actions and even our inactions. If we manage and become aware of these three things in our environment, we can be proactive in what shapes our actions. We can design our environment from the outcomes that we're committed to accomplishing and have our environment call us to effective action.

Next, we'll talk about procrastination …

CHAPTER 6

"There must be a beginning of any great matter, but the continuing unto the end until it be thoroughly finished yields the true glory."
—Sir Francis Drake

WHY THINGS BOG DOWN
How to Get Them Moving Again

Outcomes for this chapter:
- Discover how a little-recognized thought can slow even the most determined players to a halt.
- Learn how to overcome a little-known source of procrastination
- Acquire easy techniques to propel things forward.

Can you remember a time when you had an important project to complete, when things had to be perfect, but it moved slowly, bit by bit, until it came to a halt? Maybe your job depended on it or your family depended on you. Maybe this urgent project didn't even get off the ground. Or perhaps it was begun, and even though everyone involved agreed it was critical that the project be completed, the project had become bogged down quickly and forward progress stopped. Can you think of additional instances in your life when things stop moving forward with any kind of velocity?

We've not met anyone yet who hasn't had projects come to a grinding halt or slow to a snail's pace at some time in their life. How would you like to find out one of the most elusive secrets about why things bog down? It's a major discovery of ours that can immediately free you to act on those important projects you have that have been dragging along or have stopped altogether. You see, most people think there is something inherent in the project itself that makes it slow down. Or they think some person involved is the culprit. We'd like you to help us demonstrate the real source of a great many things bogging down.

Are You Talking to Me?

Take out a clean piece of paper, and take a few moments to write down all the things that you intend to accomplish in the next seven-day period. We don't mean for you to write down routine actions or activities. We're talking about important outcomes. We're talking about outcomes with a degree of priority or importance beyond a miscellaneous mission like picked up the laundry or a routine outcome like mowed the lawn. It's okay to include important pieces of a larger project you want to finish during the week. Okay, go ahead and make your list of next week's accomplishments. Take as much time as you like.

When you have completed your outcome list for the next seven-day period, look it over and make sure it includes everything you intend to accomplish between now and a week from today. Now, please, do the following:

1. Put an X next to every item that was on your list last week (or would have been if you'd made a list). That is to say, you have transferred it from last week's list to this next seven-day period lying ahead.
2. Put another X next to everything that was also on your list the week before that. This means you've transferred the item for two weeks in a row. Items may be marked more than once, even several times during this exercise. And include items you are bringing forward from weeks ago, when you didn't get them complete back then.
3. Now put a zero (O) next to any items that you probably won't finish or get to this week. You know, the stuff you're kidding yourself about really getting done this week. Tell the truth now.
4. Finally, look at all of next week's intended outcomes, and put a capital S next to all the ones that you would consider to be significant.

Chances are that you have put an S next to some of the same items that you X'd and zeroed. Among the thousands of people with whom we've done this experiment, it almost always turns out that way. Why? Because items that are transferred tend to be regarded as significant.

Significance in No Way Enhances Completion

"Knowledge is power; but enthusiasm pulls the switch!"
—Ivern Ball

At best, significance slows things down. How can that be, you ask? Well, think about it. How do you act and think about significant projects or outcomes? Most people reply with the following:

1. You are careful, tentative. (After all, it is significant. One should be cautious about significant tasks or projects, shouldn't one?)
2. The project is perceived as hard to accomplish. (Well, it should be hard; it's significant, after all.)
3. You try to avoid the risk of making a mistake because it's so significant, thus fostering your procrastination.
4. You *won't* start without sufficient:
    a. Time. (This is going to take significant amounts of time because significant things always take time.)
    b. People, the *right* people. (Oh, I have to wait until Anthony gets back from vacation because I really need his special expertise on this project.)
    c. Resources. *Enough* resources and the *right* resources.
5. Because it's so significant, you'd better do it perfectly. (I can't afford to mess this one up. So I'll slow down and take my time.)

Sound familiar? Do you recognize any of the above considerations or deliberations as ones you've made in the past that slowed a project or postponed a task? Let's see what the dictionary and thesaurus have to say about this phenomenon:

Significance: Importance. Great consequence.

Significant: Full of meaning. Important. Momentous. Major. Grand. Burden, weighty. Grave seriousness, gravity, solemnity. Pressure, urgency (a myth that we will dispel shortly in this chapter), stress. Huge, sizeable, hefty, substantial. Noteworthy, prominent, grand, and imposing.

Whew! *Momentous, prominent, grand,* and *imposing.* They might as well add frightening and intimidating, don't you think? That's how we start to feel reading those synonyms. How about you?

Time to Squash the Myth

The prevalent myth about significance is that it provides urgency to act. But its most common effect is to slow things down—just the opposite. Read points 1 through 5 above again. Do you find any urgency there?

Susan Gilbert studied to take the test to get her certification for the Human Resources designation. Susan partnered with another colleague, attended classes, and studied every night for this tough exam. This was really important to Susan because, upon passing and receiving the certification, Susan would also get a promotion.

Well, after taking the test three times and barely not passing due to missing by just a couple of points on her scores, Susan felt dejected and miserable. No surprise, right? Then she started making up reasons, as people often do: "I just can't take tests. It wasn't meant to be, that's all. The test is stupid—the questions are all convoluted and …"

Through Germaine's coaching, Susan let go of those disempowering thoughts and recognized the granddaddy of them all: the significance culprit. She decided then and there not to make the exam so significant anymore. She lightened up about it. Susan said, "The heck with it, Germaine. I'm not letting significance freeze me up again." She registered to sit for the exam a fourth time.

The morning of the HR exam, Susan was tired from the night before and felt more relaxed this time. She knew the material, now it was time for her to just do it. And that she did; Susan passed the test this time. There was much celebration after all those months of studying and worrying. I asked Susan what was different this time around. She answered, "I stopped making it so significant, and it freed me up not to worry and agonize about the test. It freed me up completely."

How was Susan able to change her point of view so quickly? How could she have turned around so very fast after having been so dug in before? Here is the secret. You see, there is no such thing as significance. It's all made up in thoughts. That is to say, its substance is only language. It isn't a solid object that you must contend with physically, like a brick wall. Significance is not a physical barrier blocking your way to completing the accomplishment or task. It is an interpretation arising solely in language, spoken or in your internal conversation. It's an interpretation that you are the author of. You spoke it, at the very least, in your mind.

You made it up, so why not make something up that's more empowering? Susan did, and her new attitude changed everything for her.

> *"There are no limitations to the mind except those we acknowledge; both poverty and riches are the offspring of thought."*
> —Napoleon Hill, *Think and Grow Rich*

Al Davidson CLU, a dear friend and one of the top life insurance professionals in the world, was asked to speak at the Provident Mutual's Leader's Club meeting a couple of years ago. One of the questions from the audience was, "How do you handle referred leads?"

Al said, "I call them." Well, the group roared with laughter. They had caught a glimpse of how significant they made things. Salespeople are notorious for looking for the magic way to do things, the silver bullet. It's a common form of significance and a great way to avoid work.

In the film *Pontiac Moon*, one of the characters befriends an 11-year-old boy who, from time to time, makes throwing a football rather significant. He's not very good at throwing the football, either. In one scene, the man is teaching the boy his version of the rules of life.

The boy is leaving with his father soon. So this man tells the boy, "Rule #1: Don't sweat the small stuff. Rule #2: It's all small stuff." As the boy's father drives them away in their Pontiac convertible, without thinking, the boy throws the football some distance—a perfect spiral and tight as a rope-straight to the wise coach.

Significance suppresses, constrains, and even kills creativity. It stops the action. Significance has the capacity to bring everything to a screeching halt—even the smallest and simplest things.

Here's another example. One Saturday morning after breakfast, Jed was concentrating on a number of note cards with drawings and lists. Germaine asked what they were for. He indicated that they were plans to build the latticework around the air-conditioning system behind their house.

Germaine inquired, "How long have you been planning this project?"

Jed looked at the date on his first card and replied, "Eight months."

"Eight months?" Germaine laughed, "Aren't you making this awfully significant?" Wham! She was absolutely right!

"Enough of that nonsense," Jed declared, and he jumped into their van and drove off to buy the supplies to build the long-awaited structure.

He left in such a hurry that he even forgot the precious note cards with the drawings and lists of materials required. Realizing this when he reached the hardware store and parked his car, Jed thought, I've got to go back home and get my cards. He began to back his car out, but then suddenly, in the next instant, he caught himself being significant about his note cards now. "Oh no," he whispered. "I'm not going to be 'slimed' by the snail of significance again today."

Jed reparked and walked into the hardware and lumber store. He bought what he could remember and what he figured he would need: lumber, screws, nails, hinges, etc. The job was done by early afternoon. First rate, too.

We recommend that you do a "significance scan" every time you make an outcomes list and at least once a week throughout your project display. This will go a long way to bust up the significance before it gets too costly.

The Significance Smasher

The Great Significance Smasher is to take immediate action. It's that simple and direct—and it's definitely not significant. This is one time when Do something; Anything! is not a bad prescription.

"You can't make footprints in the sands of time if you're sitting on your butt. And who wants to make buttprints in the sands of time, anyway?"
—Bob Moawad, author of *Whatever It Takes*

Option 1: Go back to your outcomes list now, and select one of the most *put-off items*. What one *thing*, no matter how small, can you do *right now* that will move that item forward?

PUT DOWN THIS BOOK
AND DO IT RIGHT NOW!

Option 2: Locate a major goal or desired accomplishment that you've made so significant that your progress toward its fulfillment has stopped entirely. Take a few moments now to plan completely the next first steps, no matter how small. This should not be an elaborate plan. Just the next few steps, thoughtfully laid out. Once you've finished your plan, put down this book and complete one of those steps *immediately!*

Can't decide which step you should tackle first? Here's a fun solution: A friend of ours, Gail Johnston, invented a significance smasher of her own with regard to housework. Housework isn't something she always finds appealing. In fact, it often is overwhelming and dreadful.

She says, "I just don't know where to start." When have you heard that before? So she invented a little game so that she could lighten up and take the significance out of housework. She takes out several index cards and writes on each one a separate chore to be completed. The cards in total represent finishing the whole job called "housework." One card might read *Vacuumed*; another might be *Washed Utility Room Floor*. When the cards contain all the housework outcomes to finish the whole job, Gail places the cards, face down, in a stack like a deck of playing cards. Then she shuffles them, fans them out with the writing facing away from her, and she picks one out at random. Then she goes to work on that outcome. When that's done, she picks another card. And in what seems like no time at all, the housework is finished. Brilliant! Thank you, Gail.

Try Gail's game whenever you find starting difficult.

"Sometimes you just have to take the leap, and build your wings on the way down."
—Kobi Yamada, author of *Be: Life Is Here and Life Is Now*

Summary

Making something significant to ensure that everything is done perfectly oftentimes has the opposite effect on people. Significance can slow us down and cause the disease of procrastination. To move beyond procrastination, we recommend you just start—start anyplace within the project—just get in action, start moving, do one small thing to break the hold of significance and procrastination. Try it—get up, put the book down, and do one thing that will get you closer to what you've made so ridiculously important.

In the next chapter, we share with you our breakthrough about time.

CHAPTER 7

*"Time is nature's way of making sure everything doesn't
happen all at once."*
—George Carlin

IT'S ABOUT TIME

Outcomes for this chapter:
- Conduct an inquiry into time as we know it.
- Reveal that what we have been taught regarding time is shaped
  by a bankrupt paradigm.
- Discover Time Transformation and new freedoms to enable you
  to realize your dreams.
- Shift from time as a constraint to time as an opening.
- Coach players from the context of Time Transformation.

*In 1989 we had a breakthrough with our relationship to time. In this
chapter, we will share with you that breakthrough and introduce a new way
of thinking in regard to time. We will inquire with you into the nature of
time—what we've been taught to believe about time and how we can
impact our thoughts and actions to realize our dreams.*

What Does Everyone Know About Time?

*"What then is time? If no one asks me, I know what it is. If I wish to
explain it to him who asks, I do not know."*
—Saint Augustine

What is this mysterious force that holds us captive despite phenome-
nal advances in science, psychology, and management practice? While we
may have revolutionized our workday, transformed our business culture,
enriched and deepened our personal relations, *why do we remain hopelessly
bound to an unworkable and restrictive experience of time?*

EXERCISE

What does everybody know about time? What comes to your mind? Take a few moments, right now, and jot down everything you can think of in answer to the question, "What does everybody know about time?" Don't try to get the right answer; that's not the point here. Don't censor yourself, either. Just write down everything that your mind offers in response to the question. No need to be creative, this is a mind dump, if you will. Simply jot down what comes to your mind. To assist you, we suggest that you keep the question in front of you as you write down your answers. Continue asking yourself this question until you've exhausted all the answers stored in your mind. When you have run out of answers, please move on to the responses below.

Here's a typical list of responses from our Eagle's View course participants.

• There's never enough time.
• You cannot save time.
• Time is money.
• Time is a state of mind.
• Time has no limits.
  I have all the time in the world
  (doesn't seem to help).
• Time is scarce.
• Time is an opportunity.
• Time waits for no one.
• No such thing as time
  (no help here, either).
	• There's only so much of it: 24
	  hours a day.
	• Time passes, it slips away, tick,
	  tick, tick …
	• Time flies.
	• Time is running out on me!
	• I'm running out of time.
	• Can't go back in time.
	• Time is the master.
	• Time is precious.
	• I wish I had more time.
	• You use it or lose it!
	• Everyone has the same amount
	  of time.

How does your list compare to the responses? Are there similarities? Now let's ask a different question:

Name That Tune

What is the name of the *paradigm* that shapes all of our responses?

You probably know that a paradigm is a point of view or a particular perspective about a subject, in this case, time. It's in the background, governing what we think. Paradigms limit our thoughts and behavior. Look at your list and the list above. What would you call the paradigm, or framework, within which we know and understand time? What is the primary theme behind all of our notions about time?

After many years of inquiring with people from all walks of life, and from several different countries and cultures, we have discovered that the vast majority of us share this dominant paradigm with regard to time: *time as a constraint.* Does time as a constraint sound fairly descriptive of *what's running the show* with you and time?

Consider that, each morning, we wake up to an environment where every moment must be carefully allocated and accounted for before it slips into eternity and is lost to us forever. We automatically, unwittingly encounter time as an inflexible constraint. Consider that we know time as a constraint.

"Relinquish your attachment to the known, step into the unknown, and you will step into the field of all possibilities."
—Deepak Chopra

An Abundance of Time Victims, a Shortage of Time

Time victims are everywhere: all of us who say that we cannot do, be, or have something because of time. "I can't take that vacation; there's never a good time." "I can't go back to school; there's too much going on at the office." "I'd love to go to my kid's soccer game, but I could never get off that early." "I wish I could host the family holidays this year; I just don't have the time."

Consider for a moment the following excerpt from Carlos Castenada's book, *Journey to Ixtlan: The Lessons of don Juan.*

"... He pointed out that everyone who comes into contact with a child is a teacher who incessantly describes the world to him, until the moment when the child is capable of perceiving the world as it is described ... From that moment on ... the child is a member.

He knows the description of the world; and his membership becomes full-fledged, I suppose, when he is capable of making all the proper perceptual interpretations which, by conforming to that description validate it."

We are all members of an inherited description of time.

Time holds us captive—to looming deadlines, unfinished projects, untapped opportunities, unexplored paths. Each time we give up on a project, compromise our commitments, sacrifice our relationships, abandon our dreams, we have once more capitulated to the relentless description of time: time as a constraint.

Stephen Hawking, author of *A Brief History of Time*, writes about an experiment that was done in 1962. *"A pair of very accurate clocks was mounted at the top and bottom of a water tower. The clock at the bottom, which was nearer the earth, was found to run slower, in exact agreement with general relativity."* Perhaps time is not fixed and unchangeable, as we've been led to believe.

A New Possibility

"All the possibilities of your human destiny are asleep in your soul. You are here to realize and honor these possibilities. Possibility is the secret heart of time."
—John O'Donohue, *Anam Cara: A Book of Celtic Wisdom*

But what if you lived in a world where time were not a constraint? What if you experienced time not as a boundary but as a vast horizon of possibility, a limitless expanse awaiting our unique touch to lend it order, unity, and direction? We propose a new view of time. We suggest approaching time as an *opening*. Viewing time as an opening can expand the realm of what's possible and transform time from a limited box in which we find ourselves to a window—an opening out onto a whole new landscape of opportunity.

If we look up definitions of the word *opening*, we find the following:

- an open space serving as a passageway or a clearing
- a favorable opportunity or chance
- the act of becoming open or being made to open
- the first period or stage; the first occasion

When one shifts her paradigm from time as a constraint to time as an opening, and stands in that opening, the opening pulls for the answer to the question, an opening for what? If time were an opening, what would you have in the opening? Read on.

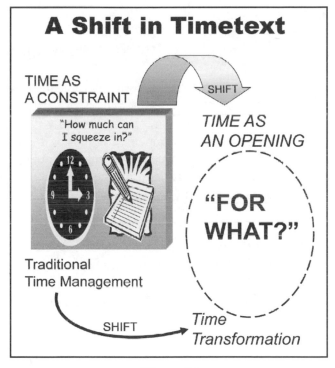

Figure 7.1

Conquering Time—You're Kidding, Right?

"Every new day begins with possibilities. It's up to us to fill it with the things that move us toward progress and peace."
—Ronald Reagan

Time transformation presents an inquiry into a view of time as an opening, not a constraint. It is a perceptual shift in the way we relate to time. Living time as a constraint, we are stiff, rigid, and careful about what we will allow ourselves to commit to accomplish or even dream about accomplishing. When we view time as an opening, our possibility for accomplishment is broader, wider, and deeper. Our dreams are brighter, more vivid, more real, and more likely to be fulfilled. Life is fun!

When Kevin, an executive and participant in our course, began living life from time as an opening, things began to change for him. He began coaching his daughter's soccer team and, not only that, he began playing the piano again!

A New Opening—With New Freedoms

As an opening, time would be transformed from an experience of being squeezed, or boxed in, to one of being pulled forward by the possibility of value and quality. Time as an opening literally draws you out into the opening called life. It is a compelling invitation for you to take action consistent with realizing your destiny. Time as an opening moves people from working to get more done to working to realize their dreams. Instead of being victimized by time, people begin to be energized and nurtured by the field of opportunity out in front of them.

> *"Walk with a purpose and you will collide with destiny."*
> —Bertice Berry, PhD, author and speaker

Putting Time as an Opening to Work

So, you may ask, how does this help me manage my time? I still have a limited number of hours. This new view might be intriguing, but I still have to make up my schedule, organize activities, and do all the stuff that comes with managing a limited amount of time. What about that?

First of all, time as an opening does not replace time management. However, instead of managing the sequential chunks called time, you start with your intentions and desired outcomes that you want to produce today. With time viewed as a constraint, however, we are stifled and strangled by even the best time-management principles.

Time as an opening brings a new way of relating to existing principles and ideas and opens the way to invent new ones. The result is striking! Old, dull time-management practices suddenly emerge in a new context and regain their effectiveness and power. Advances in time-management techniques are enhanced and enlivened.

Let's go back to the question: An opening for what? What would you have in the opening?

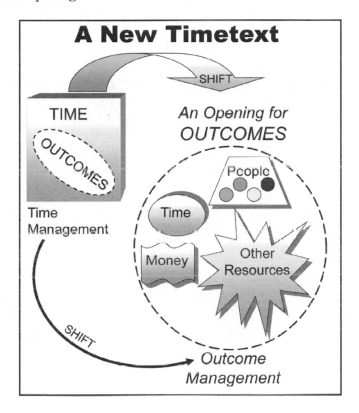

Figure 7.2

You shift from attempting to manage time to managing from outcomes. There is a shift from time management to outcome management, of which time management becomes a subset. Time is now just one of many resources like people, money, information, and circumstances. Time is no longer experienced as the constraining ceiling it once was.

This new approach to life, this shift in temporality, is invented in the face of the world's prevailing timetext. A timetext is a mental attitude, disposition, or perception that predetermines our responses to and interpretations of situations with regard to time. Timetext operates like a context or paradigm for time. It's the way we think about time.

"Time has been transformed and we have changed; it has advanced and set us in motion; it has unveiled its face, inspiring us with bewilderment and exhilaration."
—Kahlil Gibran

Time as a Constraint—a Smoke Screen

"The Wright brothers flew right through the smoke screen of impossibility."
—Charles F. Kettering

Time Transformation starts with the willingness to approach life from the point of view that time is an opening and not a constraint. It is an inquiry into the possibility that who you are, what you do, and what you have are not constrained by time.

To understand how a shift in timetext might work, we need look no further than the sports page in the newspaper. Why is it that some athletes are observably rattled by the pressure of the clock winding down, while others are calm, cool, and focused, and proceed to play their best game? Top professional athletes such as Tom Brady, NFL quarterback for the New England Patriots, have made sports history by slowing down and appearing to be completely relaxed with just seconds to play—and doing so with game-winning results. Is it possible that these last-second game-winners operate inside a different timetext during these moments? Any good Little League coach knows that by asking a batter to watch the seams of a spinning ball as it blazes toward him and home plate, the child's experience of the ball's speed is altered. A once small, blurry, threatening, speeding bullet is transformed into a large, white oval moving gently through space. The ball is quite simply more hittable, and that leads to home runs. Time as an opening can bring you that kind of focus.

Back to Business

Turning to the world of business, we may ask why one executive perceives herself as being fully engaged, turned on, and inspired while under pressure, while another feels boxed in, panicked, and experiences acute anxiety and stress. Is the latter's to-do list longer? Is her life expectancy shorter? Is she more ambitious than the former? Is her list of accomplishments longer to justify a pressure to excel? What if the answer to all those questions is negative? What's different for each? We suggest that the feelings associated with the demands of time are a function not of external demands, but of the attitudes we bring to those demands and the way we relate to the pressures at hand.

David, a vice president and general manager for an international consulting firm in Houston, Texas, reports that when he shifted his timetext from time as a constraint to time as an opening, his world changed immediately. David's new world began to pull for quality in his life, instead of mere quantity. The game he played was no longer how much could he get done in his day; but rather, what could he get done today? What could be done that would be consistent with the future outcomes he intended? These were outcomes for his company, himself, and his family. They were, in short, David's dreams. His priorities began to organize themselves naturally around the future he envisioned. Although David's business results had generally been extraordinary, his work became even more satisfying and fulfilling. Even his partnership with his wife, Carolyn, strengthened. David began working fewer hours and getting more rest. His health began to improve, which had been one of Carolyn's major concerns for David since his heart surgery. "I didn't experience being any less intentional about things," says David, "I just became more focused, and with a lot less anxiety."

We do, in fact, believe that our timetext for, or relationship toward, time is extraordinarily predictive of our experience of health, accomplishment, happiness, fun, and love in our lives. In fact, it's possible that our mental approach to time has extraordinary impact not only on our own satisfaction, but on our ability to perform, to excel, and to realize our dreams. Historically, there can be no question that time as a constraint has contributed to increasing people's stress. We have found that time as an opening appreciably reduces our clients' stress.

That's fine, you reply, but what difference do perceptions make in the practical management of my life? It's quite obvious that, no matter what my point of view, time really is limited. I simply don't have enough time to do my work, play with the kids, catch up on reading, and just plain relax. There are trade-offs to be made, obligations to fulfill, and lower priorities are often set aside. Exactly! It's and/both, not either/or. One doesn't give up deadlines and scheduling actions. On the contrary, you still strive to meet deadlines, take actions, align your to-do list, and schedule choices with your dreams.

A Senior Perspective, Indeed

Thinking from time as an opening, people gain a senior perspective on the details that sometimes take over their lives. With this new view, or timetext, they can begin to align their practical use of time with their genuine priorities and concerns. "I don't have time" becomes "I have dreams, and I'm looking for new ways to fulfill them in the opening."

Traditional time management begins from a finite and given amount of time, which is then parceled out to meet various needs and obligations. Time as an opening begins from a future in which important intentions are realized and major goals are achieved. From that future, actions can be initiated to set in motion that which is required for that future to be fulfilled.

"We are experiencing a profound shift in time orientation. The time orientation during the long agricultural period was to the past. The type of orientation in the industrial period was today: 'Now. Get it out. Get it done. Bottom-line.' But the time orientation in the new global Information Era is the future. Things are rushing by us at an accelerated speed, getting more and more complex. We can't get hold of it. It's too complicated. It's moving too fast. So, we create a vision of what we want it (the future) to look like . . . Then that vision instructs us backwards in how to get there. The vision sorts out our decisions."
—John Naisbitt, co-author of *Megatrends 2000* and *Megatrends for Women*

Let's Start With Outcomes

Time as an opening begins with outcomes. Standing in the future, standing in the reality of outcomes, time becomes one of the key resources that assist us in realizing our dreams with all the other necessary resources. Time is no longer the constraining context. Time is a resource of the opening.

So, Amid All This Rushing, Where Do I Begin?

Suppose you resolve right now to begin a transformation of time in your own life. It makes sense to alter your perspective and be determined to make your schedule reflect what's really important in your life. What concrete steps can you take to set this shift in motion today? Well, you can begin by doing the following exercise.

"Even a thought, even a possibility, can shatter and transform us."
—Friedrich Nietzsche

EXERCISE

In what areas of your life have you experienced time as a constraint? Make a list. Once you've completed the list, select one item from the list and look at it from time as an opening. Make it a project for one week. Schedule a date one week later to review the project.

Top business leaders say that the biggest problem they encounter in effecting real change is the need to keep the vision present, visible, and alive for each person, at each moment, through each task of the day. Clearly, we won't work on what we don't see. When the vision evaporates, all that's left is the tedium, the busy-ness at hand.

So perhaps we begin by designing a physical environment, a structure or system that maintains our vision before us at all times and draws clear links between the daily activities and the final result. If we see the potential that time as an opening could offer—if we are willing to fundamentally shift our relationship with time—then we say it is possible for us to work out the battle between our visions and our to-do lists. It is possible to experience each moment as itself, not defined by the past or the future, but more like a clean canvas calling for our paintbrush.

When Germaine started training for her first marathon, she was stuck in time as a constraint because of all the training runs; there just wasn't enough time. Germaine decided to time transform how she approached her marathon training. Thunderbolt! Germaine now runs at 4:30 a.m. each morning with a group of running buddies. "It's changed my life now that I'm running between four and nine miles each morning during the week. I know what I'm accomplishing, and it is reflected in my mental and physical well-being." Germaine gets all her exercise (running followed by yoga or weights) before she gets to the office.

It is time we liberated ourselves from the restraints of our old, well-worn time-management thinking, or timetext. We stand at the threshold of a new era called time as an opening. Today, instead of knowing time as linear and immutable, we can know time as a vast, energetic network where people's intentionality, dreams, and outcomes intersect. Instead of knowing time as a constraint, we can discover time as an opening: a new timetext. With this new timetext, the canvas of our lives is enlarged and inviting. Let the artistry begin!

Wait a Minute!
How Do I Coach People Using This Tool?

"If the rower is 100% committed, giving 100% effort and not winning, then it is up to the coach to find a way to help him win."
—David Kucik, head crew coach, Purdue University

Easy! When our clients get on the rampage about not having enough time, we always go to the outcomes. We allow them to voice all the things that they have to do and ask, "Given the outcomes that need to be produced, what are you going to do?"

Time as an opening helps us to sort out our priorities rather than giving in to doing a lot of activity. Sometimes things may look different from the way that we imagine doing them. Germaine never once thought she would hit the pavement at 4:45 in the mornings. Things begin to change when you think from outcomes. The model below is great for coaching people through their chatterbox about time to focus on outcomes. Time as an opening is that simple—an opening within which to produce outcomes.

You design today thinking from a future you intend to have, rather than working toward the future, wading through the many tasks of what is merely urgent instead of what is important for realizing your dreams.

Figure 7.3

Summary

Time as an opening continues to be a revelation for us, providing more and more insights as we play in the opening. We hope that your experience from this chapter is also enlightening or at least has you inquiring into the nature of time. Our chatterbox, or our internal dialogue, impacts our perceptions—in this case, our perception of time. Perhaps you realize too that you wake up each morning with the same attitude toward time: 24 hours in a day, so much to do, and so little time. Time as an opening can pull you out of your head and allow you to view time differently. Time as an opening allows time to become just another resource like money, people, and information. Time as an opening can give you the freedom for choosing how you want to accomplish your outcomes rather than being shackled by the limitations of traditional time management and the old inherited paradigm.

Time Transformation starts with the willingness to approach life from the point of view that time is an opening and not a constraint. It is an inquiry into the possibility that who you are, what you do, and what you have are not constrained by time.

Are there things you've dreamt about but haven't found the time? Time as an opening will help you realize your dreams!

In spite of endless attempts to take control and change how we are about time, we often find ourselves on the same treadmill, doing, thinking, and approaching time the way we've always done it. Not only that, our approach to time hasn't changed in hundreds of years; it's still scarce, and we are constantly being constrained by it. Time transformation offers a new approach to time, one that has us think about our priorities, our goals, and the results that matter to us, and have those be our focal point.

We've put together an assessment inventory about time to help you coach your players with one of life's most precious assets. You'll find the inventory in Chapter 16.

The next chapter continues to delve into the possibility of time transformation.

CHAPTER 8

"You and I are essentially infinite choice-makers. In every moment of our existence, we are in that field of all possibilities where we have access to an infinity of choices."
—Deepak Chopra

THE MAGIC OF GENERATING TIME

Outcomes for this chapter:

- Discover methods of generating or capturing time from low-value activities to invest in high-value actions.
- Examine time traditions and their potential negative influence on your productivity.
- Invent a time-generator checklist to help you capture precious minutes to invest in realizing your dreams.

Technological innovations allow us to instantly have commands and controls at our fingertips. In a moment's notice, you can communicate to a large mass of people just by pressing the send button in your e-mail program. Things are moving by so rapidly—and we're able to access more all at once—that we're consumed with accomplishing and doing more. This is exciting, and yet how often do we wish we had the witchery powers of Samantha, accomplishing more in less time with the twitch of our nose?

The Notion of Saving Time

In our desire to get more accomplished, we search for ways to save time, to squeeze more into our already-busy schedules. Germaine enjoys running marathons. When she first started training, she experienced some frustration from adding her daily run to her schedule. In her quest to save time, she realized that she couldn't run any faster than her body would let her. Saving time was an illusion. You cannot save time. Yet we hear the notion that you can save time regularly. Save time here; save time there. Actually, there is no such thing as saving time. In fact, the notion that we can save time keeps us less powerful and a bit naive with regard to the phenomenon we call time.

You simply cannot save time like a thing or commodity. You cannot bank time. You cannot bank "now." If there were a time bank, to explore the analogy a little further, your account has a finite balance for which you cannot get an accurate statement. You have unstoppable, automatic withdrawals! You spend a day, every day, no matter what. There's no saving time. Each and every week has 168 hours in it, and you can never get it back. You use it or lose it!

> *"Yesterday is a canceled check; tomorrow is a promissory note; today is the only cash you have—so spend it wisely."*
> —Kay Lyons, author

Now, we have said that you cannot save time, but we didn't say that there weren't things that you can do to capture time and make the time invested more productive. In fact, in a certain sense, you can "generate" time.

Time Is Pretty Potent Stuff

As a practice, Jed and Germaine make a game of looking for ways to get more done or to fit more into a block of time. It's a great way to generate time. For example, we were driving to see a movie early one evening and noticed that we had about 15 minutes to spare. The little chatterbox in Germaine's head took this opportunity to remind her that she needed a speakerphone! "Aha!" Germaine said, "Let's go for it, Jed. Whad'ya say?"

"Whew, fifteen minutes, I don't know, Germaine. There are so many different types of phones and features to choose from," Jed said.

"Jed, it's a game, remember? We can get the phone and make the movie on time. Let's generate some time. Pull in here!" So we parked the car and ran into the closest store in the mall that sold telephones. We rapidly selected the speakerphone, paid the cashier, and dashed for the movie. We arrived at the movie early, with enough time to get popcorn and drinks, and the next morning Germaine had her regularly scheduled, one-hour coaching conference call. And that morning, she suffered no "telephone ear" from the handset!

Generating time is a great game and can pay enormous dividends. One of the big benefits is that playing this game instantly moves you away from being a time victim. We are all time victims to some degree. You know you're being a time victim whenever you say you can't have, do, or be something because of time.

Routine Actions: a Great Source of Time Generation

A number of years ago, when Jed was in the insurance business, his friend Ted made a lasting contribution to him. Ted noticed how incredibly slow Jed was at getting dressed in the morning to go to work.

They were staying at a hotel and had overslept. The wake-up call never came. To make matters even more exciting, their ride to the home office was with the agency vice president, Stephen. They thought, with some reason, that it might be bad form to make Steve wait. Anyway, Ted was dressed in no time but marveled at how slow Jed was. Ted said, "Jed, will you hurry up! Steve's waiting downstairs for us. Move it!" He said other equally motivating things, and they finally made it downstairs. In Steve's car on the way to the office, Ted was telling Steve the story and said, "Jed's only got one speed in the morning: SLOW."

Well, that made an impact on Jed. He examined his morning routine. He discovered that he held the belief that it took at least an hour for him to shave, shower, and get dressed. He inquired of other men how long they needed for this daily ritual. Jed discovered that, on average, he took twice as long as everyone he interviewed. Thunderbolt! If he could invest just 15 minutes less every morning in this activity, he reasoned, he would generate more than 90 hours a year to invest elsewhere (91.25 hours to be exact). That represents nearly *two workweeks* for most of us! And that's high-quality morning hours, to boot! (Jed works most effectively in the morning.) So he set out to change his routine.

Jed conceived of the idea to make routines, like getting dressed in the morning, athletic events. That's right, athletic events. He even bought a stopwatch for this purpose. He shaved off seconds and minutes every day until he got getting dressed down to 22 minutes flat! That amounts to 38 minutes that he generates every day. That's 231.16 high-value hours per year or the equivalent of almost six workweeks. Or he can invest the time in vacations, tennis, golf, etc. How much time can you generate from routine actions?

Time Traditions
Breathe New Life Into Old Activities

"The bad news is time flies. The good news is you're the pilot."
—Michael Altshuler

This breakthrough discovery led us to examine all sorts of routines. We have named this discovery: time traditions. Time traditions are the personal habits we have with regard to regular activities that consume blocks of time. These traditions can be personal as well as cultural. Corporate cultures can harbor many unproductive time traditions. There are traditional meeting lengths, traditional meeting frequencies, traditional meeting times, traditional conference call lengths, traditional meeting locations, and the list goes on and on. We even have traditional vacation times. Unexamined and unconscious time traditions rob thousands of people precious time that could be more wisely invested in their lives.

Remember, just 15 recaptured minutes in your day are about two workweeks in one year. What could you produce with two extra weeks this year?

Here is the Time Traditions exercise from our Eagle's View Time Transformation Course:

EXERCISE

1. On the following page, add to the list of time traditions with your own.
2. Change the example time figures next to the time traditions already listed to match your own experience.
3. After you have exhausted all of the time traditions you can think of, go back and challenge the numbers.
   a. Estimate how much time you could commit to shave off each time tradition.

---

    b. Multiply each of the shavings by the approximate number of times you participate in this activity in a year's time. For example, 20 minutes x 52 weeks = 1,040 minutes or 17.3 hours.

    c. Calculate the total time you could possibly generate in one year to invest elsewhere.

4. Pick yourself up off the floor and go to it!

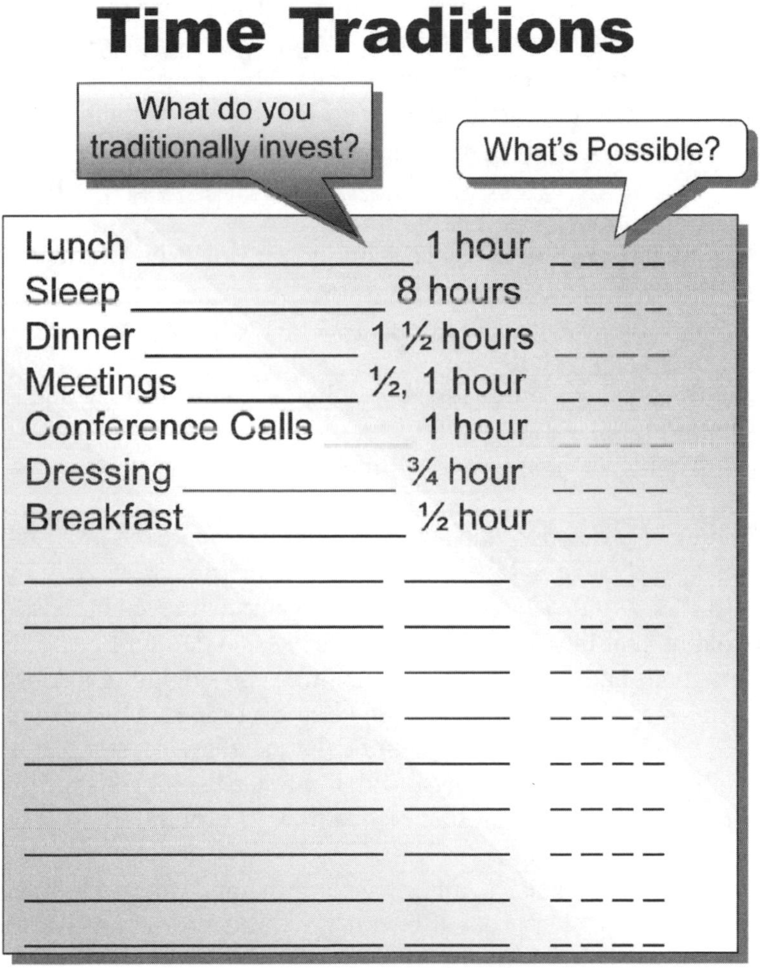

Time Traditions

What do you traditionally invest?

What's Possible?

Lunch _____	1 hour	_ _ _ _
Sleep _____	8 hours	_ _ _ _
Dinner _____	1 ½ hours	_ _ _ _
Meetings _____	½, 1 hour	_ _ _ _
Conference Calls	1 hour	_ _ _ _
Dressing _____	¾ hour	_ _ _ _
Breakfast _____	½ hour	_ _ _ _

Figure 8.1

Generating Time as a Practice

Another thing we've developed that has proven to be extremely useful is this Time Generator Checklist. We carry it permanently on a printed card for frequent review. It's a great little coaching tool.

TIME GENERATOR CHECKLIST

a. What do I do regularly that I can stop doing altogether or delegate?

b. What meetings can I eliminate or cut the time spent by 25 percent? 50 percent? 75 percent?

c. When people drop in on me, do I tell them how much time I have to speak with them and stick to it?

d. What trips (travel) can I eliminate or delegate? (43 percent of people find delegating difficult.)

e. What opportunities do I see in my schedule where I can get additional things done at the same event?

f. Who on my staff can I develop to do the things that I believe that only I can do now?

g. What routine processes should I checklist to save mental energy for myself and my staff?

h. Am I stuck in any time traditions?

We are not presenting this list as the last word on generating time. To the contrary, this list is by no means complete. In fact, we invite you to add to the list and to personalize it to meet your own special needs. People have told us that they have added things like, "What am I being too significant about and not getting into action? Who's doing my prioritizing today, me or my company? Where am I being a time victim, and what can I do about it?" One of our clients put the list on a large poster and hung it on an office wall to make a game of adding to the list for the staff. You can learn quite a lot from your staff about how to generate time. They see things you don't see.

We invite you to make a game of generating and capturing time. Have fun with it! Please don't have it be a heavy burden or chore. Experience proves that when activities are fun, people's results improve dramatically.

Summary

Although we're all equipped with the same amount of time, inside of the fixation of time, we are able to explore possibilities of generating time by the way we approach time. At each moment, we have power in the choices that we make. Time traditions are accepted by most people. We urge you to start questioning those traditions in whether they serve you in accomplishing your desires. You have the choice to generate time at any given moment.

The next chapter explores a variety of models to help you and your clients grow your businesses.

CHAPTER 9

"Truth ... will carry you through this world much better than policy, or tact, or expediency, or any other word that was ever devised to conceal or mystify a deviation from a straight line."
—Robert E. Lee

BUSINESS BY ACCIDENT OR BY DESIGN?

The Choice Is Yours

Part 1

Outcomes for this chapter (Parts 1 and 2):
* Illustrate how to translate analytical models into valuable processes for clients.
* Learn 5 Keys to Grow Your Business.
* Get an eagle's view of your business using the 5 Keys to Grow Your Business process.
* Discover which keys are strong in your business now.
* Identify which keys need sharpening.
* Design your next best actions to accelerate your business in any area.

During our careers as organizational consultants, we've used many consultative models and processes designed for large organizational change. As designers, we've found that many of these models are useful in coaching our clients to produce desirable results within their businesses, regardless of size.

In this chapter, we share with you the power of inquiry using tools to help you gain sufficient altitude to achieve an eagle's view of your business. Over the years, we have accomplished this by using several models, such as the 7-S Model (Style, Shared Values, Systems, Staff, Skills,

Strategy, Structure), by Richard Pascale, Anthony Athos, Tom Peters, and Bob Waterman for McKinsey & Company; and some of our own, such as the DreamMakers & DreamBrakers audit (see Addendum) and the Rapid Work Redesign process mapping method. The following consultative process is based on a model, Managing Complex Change, originally conceived in 1987 by Dr. Mary Lippitt, founder and president of Enterprise Management, Ltd. We've modified it into a coaching process tool and call it the 5 Keys to Grow Your Business. This dynamic process, also known as the 5 Keys, has assisted countless people in accelerating the growth of their businesses, large and small. In addition, it has helped clients enhance their particular departments' results by focusing on these five keys. This particular eagle's view, the 5 Keys, provides a window into one's business, enabling our clients to get their hands on the controls and rudders that shape their business results. We will describe the 5 Keys, the audit, and the companion action plan in detail. There is no magic in this model or any other model. As you will soon see, the magic is in the guided inquiry you facilitate for your clients to gain keen insights into their operation.

This chapter is highly interactive for you, the reader, if you want it to be. This can be an occasion for you to work on your business, not just in it-like most of us ordinarily do. This can be an extraordinary chapter for you in that, if you do the exercises we outline along the way, we are confident that you will experience several thunderbolts. And you will have an invaluable coaching tool through which to guide your players, if you choose.

May we coach you? This is important: If you choose to participate in the exercises outlined in this chapter, stick to one business, one organization, or one particular project in which you are involved. You will see why as you read on.

In this chapter, we'll ask you to think about, and from time to time examine, in depth, your business or organization and record your findings in the spaces provided. Or you may want to write them on a separate sheet of paper.

During the course of our many facilitations or explanations of this process, people have occasionally asked, "But what if these aren't the real five keys to grow your business? I mean, someone just made them up, right?" We reply that the value of these five distinctions or inquiries lies not in the truth of the model, but rather in the results of its use. We like the results. The power is in the inquiry into one's organization and its design, not the veracity of the model. The 5 Keys model is a likely story, if you will, that produces value for our players. First and foremost, that's what we are all about—bringing tools and techniques to our players that produce desirable results.

Here are some clients' results after getting an eagle's view of their businesses and implementing the changes they saw possible from the models and tools to which we introduced them:

- Estate planning firm in Boca Raton, Florida, reduced its process time with clients from an average of nine months to 6 weeks. The two principals became the #1 and #7 sales representatives for their life insurance company.
- Children's clothing store district increased sales in 11 stores, moving from #5 to #1 of 25 districts (200 stores) in one year.
- Hospital in Birmingham, Alabama, reduced the number of steps in its patient admissions procedure from 96 to 16.
- Regional food seasonings sales manager in Houston increased sales 5 percent and was promoted to national account sales manager.
- Ft. Lauderdale, Florida, financial administrative services firm discovered how to save $30,000 each month while improving service levels.

Distinguish Management, Leadership, Mentoring, and Coaching

The 5 Keys to Grow Your Business model will serve as a window into your business structure, organizational design, or project architecture. It will help illuminate some aspects of your business, or your players' operation, such that changes may want to be made.

To implement those changes, it is important to be clear about the role you'll play. Should you be a leader, manager, mentor, or coach? (You'll find these definitions in Chapter 1.) Please keep these distinctions in mind as you begin to discover any changes you might like to make in your own operation.

"Your definitions for management, leadership, and coaching in Coach Anyone turned my week of frustration into an easy-to-follow action plan to get the things done I needed done with each of my direct reports. I simply took my to-do list; designated each item with an M, L, or C; went to work, and enjoyed amazing results."
—Stephen Schwartz,
regional manager of a life and casualty company, Dallas, Texas

Design

We are going to examine the 5 Keys to Grow Your Business individually and all together. Individually they are designs, and together, they form a business operation.

Designs are both mental and physical. It is important to understand the effect of your business design on human energy and ultimately business results. Some designs are invisible, like culture, people's thinking, their motivations or their mindsets.

Make the Invisible Visible

Examining the 5 Keys helps make the invisible become visible. Once a design is in place, energy moves through that design by the path that offers the least resistance or obstacles. Said another way, energy moves where it is easiest to go. We're talking about a natural flow. In our Eagle's View course, we refer to this phenomenon as environment.

"You cannot outperform your environment."
—Clifford "Tex" Johnston

Most organizations of at least medium size have published policies and procedures to help ensure quality or maximize their efficiencies. But we often find that the practices of people in the organization can diverge a great deal from the prescribed procedures. Why? Because when a policy is too cumbersome or no one is looking, they find and take an easier road.

This is not to say that everything you do should be planned. A little chaos can provide an environment for high creativity.

"Contemplation often makes life miserable. We should act more, think less, and stop watching ourselves live."
—Nicolas Chamfort

And we have discovered a useful question to be asking ourselves from time to time: Is my business by design or by accident? Well, which is it? Has it evolved to its present shape through a series of unwitting mishaps over the years? In Robert Fritz' book *The Path of Least Resistance*, he points out that "If the riverbed remains unchanged, the water will continue to flow where it always has." So, if you want different business results from the ones you are getting, you've got to alter your business's design.

"Insanity: doing the same thing over and over again and expecting different results."
—Albert Einstein

People go through life taking the path of least resistance. The people of your organization take that path. Your customers and the players whom you coach will take that path.

An organization is a body of designs. It is a set of observable designs and less apparent *underlying* and often invisible designs. The designs of an organization, business, or project determine the path easiest to follow. Do your customers find it easy to do business with you, or do you put them through unnecessary steps to complete a sale or make a deal?

"Getting an eagle's view with your panorama card process mapping helped us discover how to reduce our patient admissions procedure from ninety-six steps to sixteen. And by the way, our team did it in two and one-half hours," Betty Ann Forest, chief administrator for a hospital in Birmingham, Alabama, told us. "What a huge difference this has made for our patients, not to mention their families," Betty reported.

If you can identify the designs of your operation, you can choose to do something about them. Otherwise you are at their mercy. The 5 Keys help you distinguish your organization's designs.

You Can't Fool Mother Nature

Design determines people's behavior. This is not to say that people are mechanistic. Each person is a rare and special individual. And each of us is subject to the powerful influence of design. You can't fool Mother Nature, and you cannot fool Mother Design, either. You cannot outperform your business design or your environment. Design is paramount—it overrides attempts to sustain desirable changes within it.

Here is the good news: You can shape, reshape, or change the designs of your business to improve your results. That said, you may be wondering where to start. We start by asking, What are the key design features of a successful, growing business or organization? What design features allow for business growth? What design features must be in place for growth to continue?

Here's an eagle's view of effective business design that allows for growth and continued growth. It was born during an inquiry we had several years ago with a handful of our management consulting colleagues. The inquiry was, "What are the key factors to examine when an organization is attempting to improve any of its results?" That initial conversation led one of our colleagues to introduce to us the Managing Complex Change model. This led us to design the process we now call the 5 Keys to Grow Your Business.

This eagle's view is composed of five design features or "keys": **Vision > Skills > Incentives > Resources > Action Plan**. It has served as a remarkably useful window into any type of business, organization, or large project.

And we have observed the inquiry to spawn other keys that our clients desire to examine, such as Systems. Although that could be included in Resources, the point is not to stick to the model in this procedure, but rather to allow the process to uncover important aspects of the client's organization that steer or limit business results. James Triplett, chief operating officer, for a manufacturing company put it, "I want to highlight systems as a key by itself. We have too many separate systems that can't communicate with each other. If we could fix that, we would dramatically increase our productivity." Whenever a vital key is uncovered in addition to the five, we encourage the client to include it in his inquiry, like James insisted. Perhaps you would like to add a new key yourself. Please, feel free.

The 5 Keys to Grow Your Business

Figure 9.1

To help our clients orient themselves and think about how each key relates to their particular situation, we have found the following set of synonyms highly beneficial.

Vision:
foresight, prophecy, idea, image, imagination, dream, mental/emotional picture, creative discernment or perception, aspiration, speculation, far-sightedness, insight from the future, visualization, purpose, future state, future condition, future environment

Skills:
talent, expertise, demonstrated abilities, competencies, proficiencies, aptitude, abilities through training, natural or acquired facilities, gifts, mastered methodologies

Incentives:
reward, inducement, enticement, payoff, motivation,
reason to act, encouragement, support, stimulus, compensation, impetus, spur, inspiration, reason for being

Resources:
operating capital, people, new ideas, know how,
line of credit, means, materials, inventory, reserves, wherewithal, assets, business structure, systems, expertise, knowledge, experience

Action Plan:
road map, preparation, diagram of events, strategy and tactics, milestones to achievement, design for accomplishment, systematic arrangement of activity, coordinated action, method of achievement, scheme, system, structured approach, deliberate process, articulated procedure, arrangement of actions, pathways for achievement

---

Figure 9.2

Now, what would a company or organization look like when one of the 5 Keys is missing, is lacking, or is insufficient in some way? What would be happening in a business where Vision is missing?

Figure 9.3

How would you describe the mood in a business where Vision is missing? Would you agree that the mood might be one of uncertainty or confusion? In our workshops and in-person with our players, their answers usually include some version of those. And what level of business results, or any type of desired organizational output, would you expect where Vision is missing? What effect might this have on customers?

Next, what would be happening in a business where necessary Skills are missing?

Figure 9.4

How would you describe the mood in a business where Skills are missing? Anxiety? Worry? What level of business results would you expect where Skills are missing? Not great, maybe? What effect might this have on customers? Might they be upset frequently?

What if meaningful **Incentives** were missing?

Figure 9.5

How would you describe the mood in a business where Incentives are missing? People just going through the motions until quitting time? Half-hearted effort? High turnover in a booming economy? What level of business results would you expect? Less than spectacular, you might imagine. A low plateau of output or even decline? Second-rate sales results? What effect might this have on customers? Fewer customers and mediocre treatment of those?

And if **Resources** were missing? What if the materials and the right people needed to get the job done were absent?

Figure 9.6

How would you describe the mood in a business where Resources are missing? Frustration? Worry? Resignation? Fear that your competitors will take your customers?

What level of business results would you expect? Low? Mediocre? A business headed out of business? What effect might this have on customers? Customers leaving? Few new customers? Low service levels, if any service at all?

And finally, if there were no **Action Plan**, what would you observe in any organization or project? What if there was no set of committed outcomes for which personnel had actionable steps to produce?

Figure 9.7

How would you describe the mood in a business where no clear Action Plan exists? People enamored with activity? No clear priorities? Confusion? False starts and false urgency? No urgency?

What level of business results or worthwhile organizational output would you expect without an Action Plan? Not the best, certainly.

What effect might the lack of a defined action plan for a set of intended outcomes have on customers? Erratic quality? Inconsistent care? Variable levels of service?

Now, here's a question that is usually met with soft, perceptive chuckles and sometimes loud guffaws: What if two of the 5 Keys were sorely missing? Beginning to get the picture?

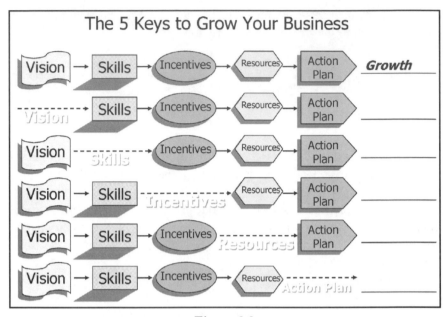

Figure 9.8

BUSINESS BY ACCIDENT OR BY DESIGN?
The Choice Is Yours
Part 2

Let's examine each key in some depth and notice how it relates to your personal business or situation.

Starting with **Vision**, you might want to first review its synonyms listed earlier in this chapter.

And here's an experiential demonstration for vision that many of our players have found impactful: Pick up a cone-shaped paper cup sometime-the kind you often find in a holder attached to some water coolers. It's the kind of little cup that comes to a point at the bottom without a base, so if you tried to set in on a table, it would fall over. Take the little cup, or imagine taking a cup, and with a pair of scissors, trim off the point at the bottom about a quarter of an inch or 6 centimeters. Now, hold the wide end up over one eye and close or cover your other eye. Look out into the room. Notice how much you are able to see and not see. Not much of a vision is it? Then, stand up and walk around with that sight picture or vision. Careful, now! Okay, stop, we don't want anyone to get hurt.

Now try this: Turn the cup around, and look through the small hole, being careful not to poke your eye. Notice the difference? You can see much more, can't you? Much easier to navigate around the room now, isn't it?

That's our dramatic metaphor for the difference between having a vision and not having one. Looking through the small hole in the cup, you can see the big picture. Add to that standing in the future, imagining the desired future, making it vivid and real in your mind—that's a vision. It's like looking into a crystal ball, only it's not a prediction of the future; it's instead an invented future.

> *"It's a poor sort of memory that only works backwards."*
> —Lewis Carroll, author, Alice in Wonderland

Is your company's vision clear? What do you want your business to look like in one year? Three years? Is it in writing? Do you have a mental and emotional imprint of it? Is your vision communicated to all stakeholders? Does each person in your organization own it?

Do you all think from it daily, and are everyone's actions consistent with building it? What about your customers? Know anything about their vision for you, like their vision for your customer service?

Now, on a sheet of paper, or on the 5 Keys Audit Worksheet you're about to see, describe what's present in your company, organization, or project with regard to vision and what's missing. What designs are present that allow your vision to be in place? What keeps it alive and well? What's missing, the presence of which would help have your vision be a living vision in your surroundings? Remember, you cannot outperform your environment, someone once said.

By the way, when we say *missing*, we don't mean that something is wrong. We hold the view that there is nothing wrong in an organization. Something like the way Haynes Smith, president of National Oilwell Varco Services, told us about how he operates as an executive: "There's no bad news; there's just news." There's nothing wrong—only what's present and what's missing.

So take a few minutes now, and write down notes about what's present and perhaps missing concerning your Vision in your business setting.

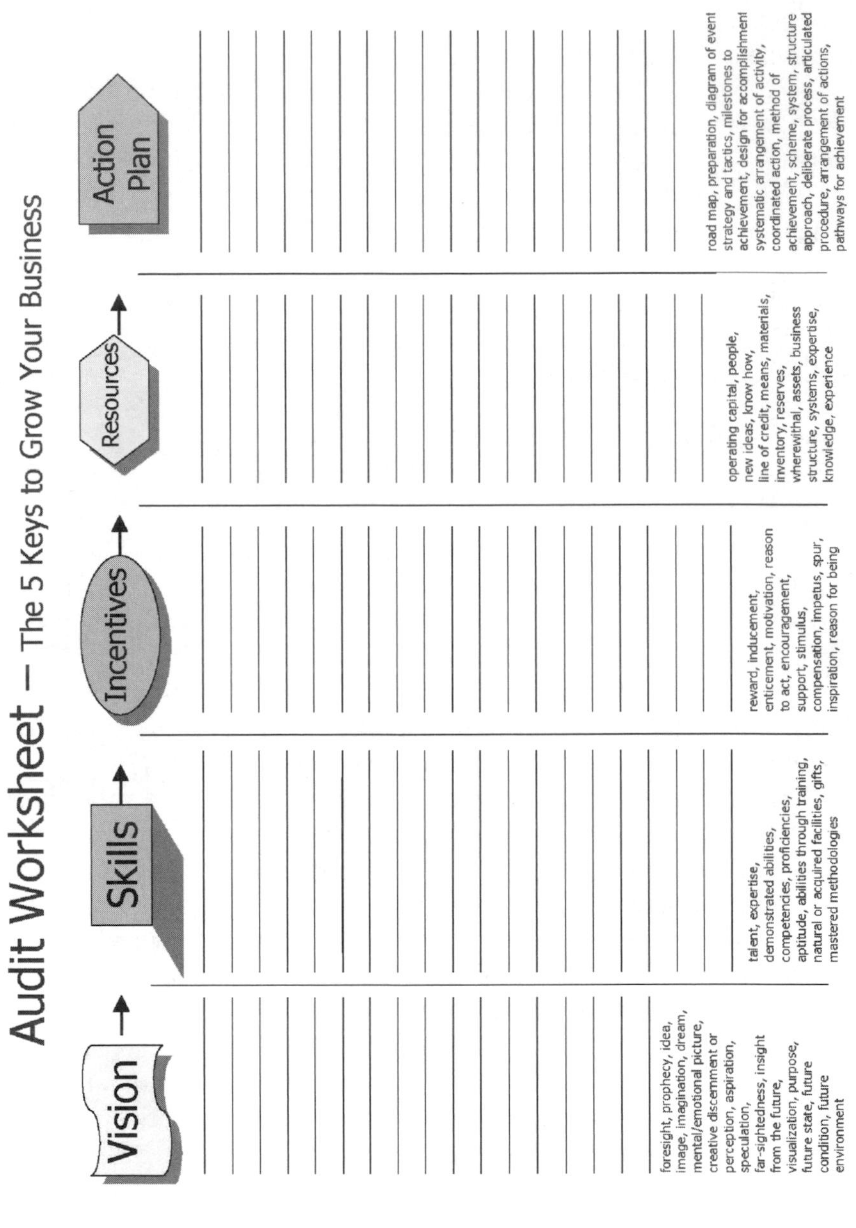

Audit Worksheet – The 5 Keys to Grow Your Business

Vision →	Skills →	Incentives →	Resources →	Action Plan

foresight, prophecy, idea, image, imagination, dream, mental/emotional picture, creative discernment or perception, aspiration, speculation, far-sightedness, insight from the future, visualization, purpose, future state, future condition, future environment

talent, expertise, demonstrated abilities, competencies, proficiencies, aptitude, abilities through training, natural or acquired facilities, gifts, mastered methodologies

reward, inducement, enticement, motivation, reason to act, encouragement, support, stimulus, compensation, impetus, spur, inspiration, reason for being

operating capital, people, new ideas, know how, line of credit, means, materials, inventory, reserves, wherewithal, assets, business structure, systems, expertise, knowledge, experience

road map, preparation, diagram of event strategy and tactics, milestones to achievement, design for accomplishment systematic arrangement of activity, coordinated action, method of achievement, scheme, system, structure approach, deliberate process, articulated procedure, arrangement of actions, pathways for achievement

Figure 9.9

Okay, now let's look at **Skills**. Skill is sometimes confused with knowledge by our clients. Do you know how to cross your arms? Of course you do. But try crossing them the opposite way. You understand, right? You have the concept of doing it or knowledge about how it might work. Right? But are you skilled at it? Go ahead, try it now. It takes most people two or three tries. How many times did it take for you to get it? That's a demonstration of the difference between skill and knowledge.

So, in this model, where do you put knowledge? Knowledge will most likely belong in the Resources column.

Review the synonyms for Skills now. What skills are necessary for success in your field? What management skills are essential? What management style is most successful? What sales skills are required in your business? Are they present? Do your employees have the necessary skills to produce your product or perform your service? Time-management skills, coaching skills, leadership skills, etc.?

What skills or help do your customers need? What kind of education do they need about your products or services? Jed's father, Ed, used to go door-to door educating people about the merits of natural gas and its safety. In Southern California in the late '40 s and early '50s, people were afraid of natural gas. If they ran their stoves and furnaces on natural gas, many people thought their houses might blow up! Although Ed was a civil engineer and not a salesman per se, many people like him had to actively, and in-person, educate potential customers. They had to persuade enough people in a neighborhood to subscribe to natural gas to make it financially feasible for the companies in the gas distribution business.

What necessary skills are present that enable your business to flourish? What skills are missing? Describe what's present or missing on your 5 Keys Audit Worksheet page or sheet of paper.

Now let's take **Incentives**. Review the synonyms for Incentives. What do we mean by incentives in a business context, for example? One way to begin looking at it is, if your business is a rousing success, what difference will that make and for whom?

Why are you in the business or field you are in? What is your motivation for the type of work you do?

If someone does a really great job, do you notice and do you tell her? Do you give your employees or collaborators feedforward? Perhaps you acknowledge them in subtle ways?

Do you reward outstanding individual performance or team performance? Do you have a recognition program? By the way, just because you have an incentive program in your company doesn't mean it acts as an incentive to everyone.

One of our clients had an incentive plan for their 200-person sales force. But no one understood it. The salespeople couldn't figure out how to win. So they gave up trying to figure it out and just complained about it, which was a disincentive.

What incentives are in place for your customers? What things motivate your customers to buy and continue buying from you? Describe what's present or missing in your scenario.

How about **Resources**? Review the synonyms for Resources, if you wish. Do you have the right people?

"We're either going to have to change people or change the people."
—Jack Welch, former CEO and Chairman, General Electric.

Do you have enough staff to get the work done? Too many staff? Do you have sufficient product inventory? Sufficient knowledge? Do you have sufficient operating capital? Do you need a line of credit? What shape is your customer database in? Do you belong to a powerful networking group?

What is your most valuable resource or asset? Maybe it's you. If that's the case, any work you do to improve your own effectiveness will have a huge impact on your business results.

Now describe what's present or missing on your 5 Keys Audit Worksheet or separate page.

Last, but surely not least, the **Action Plan**. Let's look at synonyms for action plan. Vision is about the big picture, like looking through camera lenses seeing the panoramic landscape. Vision is concerned with the future, perhaps three to five years out. The action plan, however, is like looking through a different set of lenses or magnifying the view—a much more narrow focus here and now. It's about day-to-day and week-to-week planned actions born out of a designed strategy to deliver that strategy for the current month or year.

Do you have the proper deployment of people and resources?

Will your plan fulfill your vision? Can you help your customers achieve their objectives through your action plan? Do you have a clear strategy and an actionable set of tactics to implement it? Are all the stakeholders aware of it and operate from it? Do they own the strategy and action plan?

By the way, some of our clients feel so strongly about strategy that they prefer to think of it as the sixth key and examine it separately from action plan. Like we said earlier, bring into play whatever gives you the best insight into your operation. We have no interest in making the model right. In fact, when clients question other keys, it's a validation of the inquiry process—evidence that they are authentically thinking, probing, and inquiring, and gaining insight into the workings of their organization.

Take a few moments now and examine your action plan for your business, organization, or project. Describe what's present or missing on your 5 Keys Audit Worksheet or separate page.

Next Best Actions

Now review your notes or your 5 Keys Audit Worksheet. Do you see things that you can do immediately to help your business grow? Write them down wherever you record goals or actions to be taken for yourself. And you might want to consider how best to realize those outcomes or implement those actions: would they best be implemented through management, leadership, mentoring, or coaching?

Out of Sight, Out of Control!
Practical Use of a Handy Tool

Germaine used this tool with one of her clients to help him design a growth strategy for his company. During one of their coaching telephone calls, Tim Radisson, owner of an environmental services company, expressed that he felt he had lost sight of his strategy and was behind plan. In fact, he mentioned to Germaine that he was not keeping up with the plan they designed together, and he was floundering. Germaine immediately went to the results that her client actually accomplished. She asked him to start by telling her the total revenues earned so far for the year. As Tim reported the numbers, Germaine added them up. Germaine also reviewed with him all the business in the pipeline. Once they had gone over all the numbers, Tim was surprised to discover that it was only midyear, and he realized that he had already reached 90 percent of his annual goal. Tim nearly shouted, "How about that!"

By the end of the conversation, Tim gave a sigh of relief, realizing that he actually was on plan and even beyond. It just didn't look and feel like he had imagined it would, because he had implemented new ways of doing business. He had begun implementing the use of contract retainers with some clients, and it had the effect for him of hiding booked revenue. Out of sight, out of mind.

At that point, they designed and implemented a new action plan to ensure the closure of the business in the pipeline by using new and creative means. One commitment Tim has is to stand out from his competitors by adding more value to his clients. A quick review of the 5 keys included continued marketing, hiring resources to work on the website, utilizing his present resources in the most effective way possible, and managing his inner voice to stay focused on facts, not interpretations based on how he felt. This whole conversation lasted maybe only ten minutes because Germaine and Tim were referring to the model as Germaine asked the appropriate questions to get to the facts. In addition, Tim recognized how he could work with his clients using the 5 keys to better serve them as well.

Summary

The 5 Keys to Grow Your Business assessment is an occasion for your clients to work on their business, not just in it. Most people are so busy working that they rarely step back to get an eagle's view of their operation. Some people never do and are doomed to a business by accident rather than a business by design. The 5 Keys model and any other model enabling an insightful eagle's view or look into an organization's inner workings can be a marvelous contribution to your players' businesses. We have observed that even slight design adjustments in any one of the 5 keys can have a profoundly positive impact on a whole system.

In our next chapter, we will examine how an organization might go about building a world-class coaching culture.

CHAPTER 10

"Research has shown that self-assurance, not self-awareness, is the strongest predictor of a person's ability to set high goals, persist in the face of obstacles, bounce back when reversals occur, and, ultimately, achieve those goals."
—Marcus Buckingham, co-author, *First Break all the Rules: What the World's Greatest Managers Do Differently*

BUILDING A WORLD-CLASS COACHING CULTURE

Outcomes for this chapter:
- Learn how to launch and implement a coaching culture in an organization.
- Discover the pitfalls associated with organizational cultural change and how to avoid them.
- Acquire a viable architecture for building a world-class coaching culture.
- Become acquainted with the law of gradual progress.

Throughout this book, we've shared with you tools and innovative ways to use them for individual players as well as for teams. Now we turn our focus to the organization. During the last two decades, we've helped introduce and implement coaching into organizations as a means to achieving organizational goals. Some of these consulting interventions have been widely successful in organizations, and some less so. In the process, we have learned a great deal. With that in mind, we present to you a possible architecture to launch and successfully implement a world-class coaching culture.

Building a world-class coaching culture inside an organization can be a daunting task. We've discovered that the key ingredient in accomplishing this feat is to begin at the top of the organization: the CEO, the business owner, the executive committee, the people in charge.

You may be thinking that you've had success within an organization without buy-in from the top. We agree, you can have some success at different levels; however, to build a world-class coaching culture across an entire organization, the buy-in from the top is paramount to its long-term sustainability. Getting buy-in at the top of the organization speeds up the process, provides necessary resources, and helps to pave the way through and around obstacles inside the organization.

Let's take a look at how this may unfold. We've crafted a design, or architecture, for implementation organizationally—to introduce and sustain a coaching culture. Let's go through the steps and phases.

Gaining Buy-in From the Top

This phase sets the foundation for creating and effectively launching a coaching culture.

When working with the organization's CEO, executive committee, or owner, there are questions that will have to be answered, of course. For example, what is the business case for coaching? Why should the organization invest time and resources to shift to a coaching culture? What will be the return on investment, or ROI? What outcomes are expected from successfully establishing a coaching culture? When we say *coaching*, what exactly do we mean—what does that look like? Should coaching become part of the company's guiding principles? How widespread can coaching become? Is coaching adaptable and flexible enough to be used at all levels within a company? Can coaching be used by the human resources department as well as sales, accounting, and manufacturing?

Your job, as executive coach and consultant, at this point in the game is to have the top decision makers understand that this is a strategic business initiative with specific, measurable outcomes-not just a fluff/feel-good program. Have them be clear on the reasons that a coaching culture will benefit their company's bottom line and longevity.

Great Processes Alone Don't Produce Great Results

We always point out to our clients early on that while they may have state-of-the-art processes and technologies, those alone cannot guarantee world-class results. In addition, competent people are essential to run the processes to have them be successful. Can a machine change how the machine will operate to adapt to all situations? Some situations, certainly; but not all. Only a human being can intervene to handle mechanical breakdowns of any magnitude. Coaching focuses on working with people, expanding how they think and work together to meet the company's immediate challenges and changes in technology and the economic environment.

> *"Processes don't work. People work processes."*
> —Porché/Niederer

People are a company's number one resource, and if given the right training and opportunity, they can turn an entire company around—and in short order!

Off With Their Heads!

Whenever we begin a client engagement, especially when we begin with some type of education session, one of the first questions that we're asked at the first break is always, "Has our management team participated in this training yet?" Even if top management kicks off the meeting and shares their commitment to this cultural change, they still ask. Why? Because the training messages being delivered are bumping headlong into the existing culture, which isn't yet organized for coaching. And the employees/participants aren't sure yet that if they implement the coaching practices we suggest that certain top managers won't lop off their heads!

Therefore, we take the time to not only sell the program to the top, but immerse them in the new language of coaching and its underlying principles. And we warn them that if they don't walk the talk and practice the tenets of the new culture, the coaching program will ultimately fail. We recommend continually coaching the decision makers at the top to coach each other and their direct reports throughout the progression of the implementation of the coaching culture.

"We must walk consciously only part way toward our goal and then leap in the dark to our success."
—Henry David Thoreau

A Coaching Culture Implementation Architecture

The following architecture is iterative in that the process repeats itself. This is how to get more people in the organization involved. When the first wave of teams realize their charters and complete the projects, new projects are formed as needed. These may be projects already known or new ones discovered from current projects in progress.

"If you want to build a ship, don't herd people together to collect wood and don't assign them tasks and work, but rather teach them to long for the endless immensity of the sea."
—Antoine De Saint-Exupery

1. Educate and coach the CEO/executive team/business owner.
    a. Create a charter or contract for expectations, establishing intended outcomes and time frames. Write a clear definition of what is meant by *coaching* as it applies to this particular organization. Bear in mind that the team or a core team should remain in place throughout the implementation of the results. (Sometimes this could go beyond the initial project by a year.) The coach will want to continue coaching the implementation or core team through completion.
    b. Devise a compelling case for action to be communicated during the launch phase. Answer the question most employees will have: "What's in it for me?"
    c. Assign an executive to be the sponsor or champion for internal coaches to be developed. This may be someone from the human

resources department or from workforce development or talent management. This person must have the respect and admiration of the other key players at the top. If not, continue to work with the executives until they choose a person whom they do respect and is right for the job.

d. Map out who the key influencers are in the organization and who will enroll them in the idea before the official launch. It's also not a bad idea to include as many of these centers of influence as possible in the design. Remember, people tend to be very much in favor of that which they invent. And it's almost never too soon to include these people.

e. Orchestrate an organization-wide launch. Roll out difference-making projects: business initiatives that cannot be accomplished without a team; work groups that are assigned an internal or external coach.

f. Schedule regular report-outs (presentations) to the executive team on the progress of these projects.

g. Educate and coach the executives on how to coach the teams during their presentations (See Chapter 14, Coaching Teams in Coach Anyone, Volume I.)

2. Designate a key person or core group of people to kick off the Internal Coaches Program.

a. If at all possible, we recommend designing this program as voluntary and self-selected. These people can be invited to participate in the program as a unique opportunity to forward their careers.

b. They may first have to go through all the necessary training to get familiar with what is expected of them to discover whether they're a fit for the job. The self-selection process is one where they choose to continue to participate by selecting themselves in, or discontinue by not selecting to move forward with this new challenge.

c. In either case, it is best if their choice is truly born of an invitation to participate, rather than a mandate, with no repercussions if they decide not to continue.

3. The Coaches Certification Program

a. We collaborate with our client and design a program to produce the outcomes that the organization is seeking. The framework for the training is a customized version of our CoachLab workshops. We teach the principles of coaching; coach participants in working with their internal or external clients; and work closely with the executives in accomplishing all the tenets of the coaching culture design.

b. The certification process is concurrent with getting real work accomplished. Participants start out by shadowing, or observing, us-partnering with us. Then we shadow and observe them in action-more coaching, more teaching. Point number 4 below is an example and explanation of what we mean by shadowing.

c. A completion/graduation program is designed to put the participants through the test. Yes, we'll gather a panel of executives, external experts, and other qualified personnel to sit on a panel and test the new graduates through this oral examination. We end with a nice celebration for their accomplishment.

4. Coaches go to work and produce results! Easier said than done.

Just because someone has been through training doesn't mean he's ready to take on a team to coach. We recommend that this be a gradual process (more on this later) where they shadow us coaching others; then we shadow them coaching.

During one of these shadowing sessions, John Weathersby, an engineer who was steaming ahead coaching his team, was being shadowed by Germaine. The team was discussing a phase in their project that was close to John's heart. He was the expert in this area and owned that particular process. Germaine noticed the excitement in his voice as he coached and participated with the team. In fact, he was so involved that the team requested he do some research for them and report the findings at the next team meeting. John proudly accepted the request. With a huge smile on his face, he sat next to Germaine, who was silently shadowing him.

Germaine looked at John and said, "Congratulations. You've just stepped out of your role as coach and became part of the team. How are you going to clean up this mess?"

John, realizing the misstep he made, replied, "Hmmm. I best take care of this right now."

John stood up and explained to the team that in his enthusiasm for the project, he had stepped out of his role as coach and into the role of team member. He explained to them that, as a coach, his job was to facilitate their team rather than become part of the team. Since he had vital information that the team needed, he suggested that a team member take on the request to get the information to the team by scheduling a time to speak with John in his role as engineer. The team immediately understood what happened, and a team member stepped in to be accountable for the action.

That was the day that John learned how easy it is to slip into your natural role at work and forget about the role of coaching. He learned more ways to help him stay in the role of coach instead of engineer, thereby avoid becoming a team member.

One small trick was to sit on his hands whenever John felt himself slipping out of his proper role. It helped him from becoming a pair of hands for the team, doing their work for them. This may sound silly to you, but it's sometimes the little things that can make a big difference. John didn't like sitting on his hands, so he learned to stay in the coach's role pretty quickly.

"Individual commitment to a group effort-that is what makes a team work, a company work, a society work, a civilization work."
—Vince Lombardi, American NFL Head Coach, winner of two Super Bowls with the Green Bay Packers

Well, I Think They're Going to Replace All the Supervisors With Those New Coaches

5. Communicate positive results to the organization. This is so important because after a program is underway, employees are curious about what is going on with it. In hard economic times, we wait to hear about layoffs or the extra work that we have to take on as a result. People will make up things, especially during a cultural change. When there is no clear communication and changes are taking place, people's imaginations take over.

To at least have a say in steering the gossip mill, we recommend that over-communicating is better than none or very little. You see, the more you communicate to the organization about what is going on, the less room you leave for gossip and rumors. What should you communicate? RESULTS! Let people know how the program is moving along, the little wins and results that are made possible because of the program. You can have teams report results as well as the difference it makes to have a coach work with them. There are many pathways through which to communicate with the organization. Here are just a few examples:

a. Newsletters
b. Company radio station broadcasts, when available
c. Company intranet sites, websites and blogs
d. Special e-mail reports of specific, measurable, positive results
e. Other company media, such as brochures sent through intercompany mail and posters set up at heavy traffic locations, perhaps near building elevators
f. CEO and executive committee members speaking at employee gatherings
g. Lunch and learns (brown-bag gatherings of interested employees who want to be updated)
h. Water-cooler conversations and bulletin boards

"Simple, clear purpose and principles give rise to complex, intelligent behavior. Complex rules and regulations give rise to simple, stupid behavior."
—Dee Hock, chairman emeritus, VISA

Hey, Hurry Up, Will Ya! I Got Things to Do, People to See.
A Word About Gradual Progress

When implementing change, we've noticed that many people start out expecting change to occur immediately. Just because you are being trained to coach doesn't mean that everyone will embrace the coaching with open arms. People are used to doing things in a particular way, the way they've always done them. When rolling out a cultural change, in this case, coaching, you have to earn the trust and confidence of the employees in the organization-and that takes time.

It's the Law!

This reminds us of gradual progress. While participating in a chi-running workshop with Danny Dryer, we learned about the natural law of gradual progress. The following is an excerpt from one of Danny's newsletters.

"Here's one of my favorite principles taken from t'ai chi that should be required learning in all our schools from kindergarten through college. It's more than a principle; it's a universal law that applies to all things and in every situation. In order for anything to progress and develop, there is a principle to be followed. It's a law that applies to development and it says that everything that grows, whether it's a plant, an animal, a business, or a relationship, must follow the law of *gradual progress*.

"What the law states is this: Everything in its developmental stages of formation must follow a simple pattern of growth by starting small and gradually increasing in size until it becomes its complete size from smaller to larger."
—Danny Dryer

Now, let's apply this law to change.

Critical Mass

According to the law of gradual progress, buy-in will begin with a small group of people until it grows into a critical mass. That too is our experience of successful organizational change.

At the moment your program is announced, if you divided the employees into thirds, one-third of the organization will be enrolled or happy for the changes; another one-third will be on the fence; and the remaining one-third will be against the proposed change. During this beginning stage the most valuable way to invest your time and money is to concentrate on the one-third who are on the fence. It's pretty obvious that the people who have already bought in or are enrolled in the change don't need to be enrolled further (but do not take them for granted—communicate coaching successes to keep them enrolled). They're already there, willing and ready to participate. You'll want to utilize their talents and influence within the stages of this change as much as possible.

Now, the one-third who are totally against the change may eventually come around but will need a lot of work to be enrolled. You can make a bigger impact faster with those who are sitting on the fence. Remember, for any change, you want to impact the critical mass and grow it as much as you can as quickly as you can.

"Business mirrors life-at the end of the day, both are always about relationships and people."
—Al Ritter, management consultant, author

Summary

Building a world-class coaching culture in any organization requires a viable architecture to launch, sustain, and deliver competent coaching. Beginning at the grass-roots level and working up through the organization to the top is a slow, arduous process and will almost never establish a new culture. Therefore, it is recommended to start at the top of the ladder of decision makers and enroll them in the business benefits of creating a coaching culture.

Although it is well-recognized that people are a company's most precious asset, developing people alone is usually not the compelling reason for a company to invest its resources. However, presented as a strategic business initiative with consequential improvements in key areas, creating a culture of coaches can be extremely attractive to management. Therefore, it is necessary to identify areas in which coaching can make a difference early to improve specific, measurable business results.

Coaching certification programs can be designed internally to build a cadre of competent coaches. These coaches can be made available for team projects and the coaching of high-potential managers and executives.

Embracing the law of gradual progress is essential to ensuring that the coaching cultural change program is not jettisoned too early for lack of immediate, spectacular results. Time is invested in enrolling the centers of influence in the organization to guarantee enthusiastic adoption by the company's departments and informal persuasive groups.

In our next chapter, we explore various delivery methods for coaching and the possible consequences of each.

CHAPTER 11

"Whenever you are asked if you can do a job, tell 'em, 'Certainly I can!'- and then get busy and find out how to do it."
—Theodore Roosevelt, 1858-1919, twenty-sixth U.S. President

COACHING DYNAMICS AND DELIVERY SCENARIOS

Outcomes for this chapter:
- Inquire into various forms of coaching, and study their implications.
- Be exposed to a variety of coaching delivery dynamics that shape your coaching achievements.
- Explore matching your player's specific intended outcomes with a particular coaching method.

In the previous chapter, we explored a possible architecture to design, launch, and implement a coaching culture in an organization. Here we examine the levels and attributes that distinguish the nature of the coaching delivery that might employed.

Types of Coaching

Sometimes we are asked our opinion about the value of informal coaching. "What do you think about ad hoc coaching that takes place in the hallway?" A fair question.

There is no doubt that water-cooler coaching can have a positive impact. On numerous occasions during our careers, we have benefited from this unstructured form of coaching ourselves. When asked what we think about it, we have to start by saying that it all depends on the results you want produced with an individual or team. And our estimation of its value is really one of and/both rather than either/or. We mean to say that a type of formal coaching is often necessary to impact and develop a player to the extent desired and that informal water-cooler coaching or mentoring can be a welcome addition along the way. The gold standard for coaching is not the approach with the most bells and whistles, but rather the one that is a match for the player's particular intended outcomes.

Coaching Levels and Elements

Our experience and research into the different varieties of coaching have cast light on nine main coaching elements. These variables comprise three levels of coaching and six possible elements that shape the modes of coaching. Uh-oh, here comes the rocket science. Relax, please. We've assembled it all into an easy-to-grasp, vivid display below in Figure 11.1. That's right, another eagle's view.

And please think of this as an inquiry rather than the definitive parade of every viable type of coaching. The purpose of the matrix is to prompt an inquiry: What coaching structure is best in light of the outcomes you intend to produce with your player? What are the probable consequences of the different types of coaching?

"I learn something new about the game almost every time
I step on the course."
—Ben Hogan, American professional golfer, ranked second-greatest
player of all time (behind Jack Nicklaus) in 2000
—*Golf Digest magazine*

Coaching Dynamics Matrix

In the background: **Commitment to Development**

	Technical	Collegial	Challenge	Individual	Team	Group
Formal	Integral to Training Program	Mentoring, or buddy system	Specific, measurable objectives	Coaching Outcomes Contract	Team Leader, Charter	Seminar
Informal	Casual, occasional, tips and techniques	Peers; up or down; counsel on any topic	Problem Solving; Guidance to winning	Peers; up or down; counsel on any topic	Visiting Expert	Guest Appearance, appropriate topic
Ad Hoc	Spur of the moment	Advice, opinion	Advice, opinion	Advice, opinion	Advice, opinion	Advice, opinion

In the foreground: **Specific, Measurable Results**

Figure 11.1

In the background of all coaching, no matter the type, is a context or commitment to developing the player. In the foreground are the desired results, in some cases, specific, measurable results. But keep in mind that there is always some manifestation of a result from any coaching conversation no matter how informal the coaching. Coaching results will, at the very least, be measured against someone's intentions and standards, if nothing else—or just how the person feels about the coaching moment.

Coaching Dynamics: Levels and Elements

Here is our list of nine coaching factors, three levels and six elements, with some examples and explanations for each:

1. **Formal**—Written contract with specific, intended outcomes; structured delivery; regularly scheduled coaching sessions.
2. **Informal**—No written contract or regularly scheduled coaching sessions. This could be normal practice. Delivery could be infrequent or frequent as part of day-to-day contact or employment.
3. **Ad Hoc**—Unplanned, casual (although the manner of the interaction may be intense); on occasion, as needed ("May I coach you?") or requested ("Would you have a minute to coach me on something?").
4. **Individual**—A person being coached by an individual, duo, or team of coaches.
5. **Team**—A formal team of people coached by a company sponsor, assigned coach, or scheduled visiting expert.
6. **Group**—A group of persons coached by an individual, duo, or team of coaches.
7. **Technical Application**—Help in applying specific knowledge toward becoming skilled.
8. **Collegial**—Persons included in delivering the coaching are peers, levels above and levels below, about various topics.
9. **Challenge**—Coaching for producing specific, measurable outcomes and results beyond business as usual.

What Flavor Coaching Would You Like Today? Strawberry or Chocolate Chip?

In the Coaching Dynamics Matrix, Figure 11.1, read vertically to examine the three levels or styles of the coaching delivery: formal, informal, and ad hoc. Read across for the other six elements that shape the coaching types. And in the boxes, you will find a salient or a noteworthy characteristic of that type of coaching that begins to describe the flavor of that coaching method. For example, when the coaching is **Collegial** and **Ad Hoc** (passing in the hallway or standing by the water cooler), the flavor of the coaching tends to be merely opinion and advice about anything on one's mind at the moment. However, when coaching is of the **Challenge** type and **Formal** (regular, planned coaching sessions), the tenor of the coaching is typically an honest and researched inquiry for the accomplishment of specific, measurable goals. As you read through the matrix, notice how many of the different types of coaching you engage in.

Diane Wintergarden, director of talent management for her accounting firm, visited Jed one day at his office and asked for some advice.

"Jed, I've got this guy who needs coaching. I'm not sure if he needs an informal mentor or something more formal, like the coaching you and Germaine usually do," Diane said pensively as she rolled a pencil between her thumb and forefinger. Jed pulled out the Coaching Dynamics Matrix display, and while beginning to explain what it was to her, Diane thrust a finger, landing on one of the boxes in the matrix. Tapping on the matrix, she looked up at Jed and declared, "That's it, right there! He should have an outcomes contract. Let's see, yep, formal and individual coaching, that's the ticket!" Then she studied the matrix again for a moment, looked up grinning and said, glancing back and forth at the model, "Oh, and thanks, Jed, for this little ... informal ... uh, challenge coaching session."

An Interesting State of Affairs
Methods for Coaching Delivery

The delivery methods for coaching are more numerous than you might imagine until you consider the many options. Take a moment and review the several aspects involved in the delivery of coaching below, and see if you agree.

Delivery Media:
- Face-to-Face
- Telephone
- Internet
- E-mail
- Regular mail or expedited shipment

Delivery May Involve Many Persons:
- 1 to 1
- 1 to many (team or group)
- 2 to many
- 2 to 1 (two coaches, one player)
- 2 to 2 (two coaches, two players)
- Other possible scenarios

Delivery Categories:
- Business
- Career
- Education/Learning
- Performance
- Personal/Life
- Skills

What Is the Right Medium for Delivery?

Selecting the appropriate medium or vehicle to use for delivering coaching in a given situation is important, whether you're coaching a team at a Fortune 500 company, having a one-on-one session with a client, coaching your direct report or the Cub Scout troop before their Pinewood Derby model car race. The right channel may also be a blend of media, such as the telephone plus e-mailed information for a particular coaching occasion, followed by an overnight shipment of a book you recommended that your player read.

And don't assume that face-to-face coaching is always the best. Sometimes the telephone is preferable because your client is an airplane ride away or you've discovered he listens better on the telephone. It may be more convenient to meet by phone. Sometimes you can get more work done with fewer interruptions. (For an in-depth discussion on this subject, see Chapter 15, Coaching by Telephone, *Coach Anyone About Anything*, Volume 1.)

And what's wanted and needed by your client may require more than just you to get the job done. "Germaine and I talk on the phone every week at the same time for forty-five minutes to an hour," says Larry Driver, an Austin, Texas, business owner and entrepreneur. "That helps me get what I need to achieve my objectives for the most part. Then for long-range planning or program design, we might meet for a whole day in Houston, face-to-face. And sometimes she has invited Jed to work with us on a particular aspect of my project," Larry recalls.

"If I were to wish for anything I should not wish for wealth and power, but for the passionate sense of what can be, for the eye, which ever young and ardent, sees the possible. Pleasure disappoints, possibility never. And what wine is so sparkling, what so fragrant, what so intoxicating as possibility?"
—Soren Kierkegaard, 19th-century Danish philosopher

Summary

Coaching is delivered every day in a variety of ways. Coaches who are informed about coaching in all of its forms and the implications of each have an advantage in serving their players. An inquiry into the relative value of methods of delivery can inform and inspire coaches to design their coaching practices to deliver the maximum value to their clients.

The mastery of coaching is a bold undertaking. The examination of key characteristics of the different types of coaching, matched with the player's intended outcomes, increases the coach's odds of hitting a bull's-eye with his coaching. The Coaching Dynamics Matrix provides a catalyst for creative thinking with regard to coaching approaches and structures. Coaches committed to applying state-of-the-art methods will appreciate the inquiry into the nine factors and are bound to invent other useful distinctions during their exploration.

In our next chapter, we will delve into a special brand of coaching known as sales coaching.

CHAPTER 12

"Finish each day and be done with it. You have done what you could. Some blunders and absurdities have crept in; forget them as soon as you can. Tomorrow is a new day. You shall begin it serenely and with too high a spirit to be encumbered with your old nonsense."
—Ralph Waldo Emerson

SALES COACHING AND GETTING AN EAGLE'S VIEW

Outcomes for this chapter:
- Gain two simple sales planning and tracking tools that can help your clients catapult their sales actions and results.
- Expand your ability to help your clients get an eagle's view of their sales operations to increase their sales results.
- Discover an easy and efficient way to locate files on your computer by designing a custom desktop background.

Many of our clients are involved in selling directly to customers, and all of our players' businesses ultimately depend upon sales to thrive and survive.

Here are a couple of simple but effective tools for you to share with your selling clients or use yourself to help build your own coaching practice. They both involve getting an eagle's view, a concept we use over and over, again and again, in our work to gain altitude and clarity in all kinds of situations and endeavors.

You Do the Math

In many cases, selling is a numbers game; sometimes it takes large numbers of sales actions to make a single sale. Make a certain number of sales contacts, convert them into appointments, and convert those appointments into sales—that's the formula. Plug in some numbers, do the math, and you will know how many actions and outcomes of what kinds it probably will require for you to generate the level of income you desire from selling.

This Is Rocket Science!

"Discipline is the bridge between goals and accomplishment."
—Jim Rohn, American entrepreneur, author, motivational speaker

No, it's not really rocket science, but it's scientific enough after you record some numbers through experience. At the beginning of a new sales year (Germaine was in real estate and Jed in life insurance), it always empowered us to know, based on our past year's ratios (calls to appointments, appointments to closes, closing interviews to sales), what we must do in the coming year to make the money we wanted or needed to make.

Simple, right? Yes, and logical too, but not so easy sometimes to have salespeople or yourself take the necessary actions. Why? Well, people ordinarily don't take action for one form or another of these five reasons: money, time, fear, trust, or urgency. In the sales arena, crude examples of each are **No Money** for a new laptop computer; **No Time** to make phone calls; **Fear** associated with being rejected by potential customers; **No Trust** in the sales process formula or sales manager/coach; and **No Urgency** to spur the person into action.

Duct Tape

Our friend Clifford "Tex" Johnston, an experienced sales manager and owner of a coaching practice, once asked Jed for coaching. "If you were a sales manager again, what is the one most important thing you would do to assist your sales professionals to gain new clients?" Tex asked.

Jed's answer: "Duct tape."

Incredulous, Tex laughed and asked, "What? Did you say duct tape?"

"Yes, duct tape. You know, that silvery cloth tape plumbers use?" Jed continued, "I would tape every salesperson's hand to the handset on her telephone and tell her to 'dial for dollars.'"

Well, Tex certainly didn't expect that answer from Jed, but he understood it. Having the magic formula is useless without the discipline to box yourself in and take the actions necessary to meet new prospects.

The following eagle's view of a sales process and formula has helped countless salespeople and coaches build their practices (Figure 12.1).

A Selling Scorecard

New salespeople often don't see the flow of things—how things fit together or how different sales actions provide leverage. You can create a similar graphic scorecard for yourself, vividly displaying the essential actions you want to take to enroll new clients to build your coaching practice. This can be a great assist for your clients who sell to get an eagle's view of their sales operation as well.

Our long-time friend and client Marvin Freeman, a headhunter based in Phoenix, keeps track of substantive phone conversations and has an objective of at least 50 each week. Why? Because the guy who trained him 16 years ago told Marvin that's what he needed to do to be successful—and it worked. He has learned that 50 substantive conversations serve as a foundation for his success. Achieving that goal each week gives him confidence that he is on the right track, whether he uncovers a new candidate for a client that particular week or not.

Take a moment to study the scorecard on page 138, and you will see that it is not only a place to record essential sales actions taken, but it is also a dramatic display of the sales process—and the formula when you add in objectives for each category. These objectives might be based on ratios from experience or estimated targets for a new salesperson. When we've used this scorecard/formula model with new salespeople or people considering a selling profession, their typical comment after they understand the flow is, "Oh, I see. So, that's how this sales game works."

If you are in sales yourself, or the methodology somehow applies to your work, try penciling in some of your objectives below on the blank Selling Scorecard.

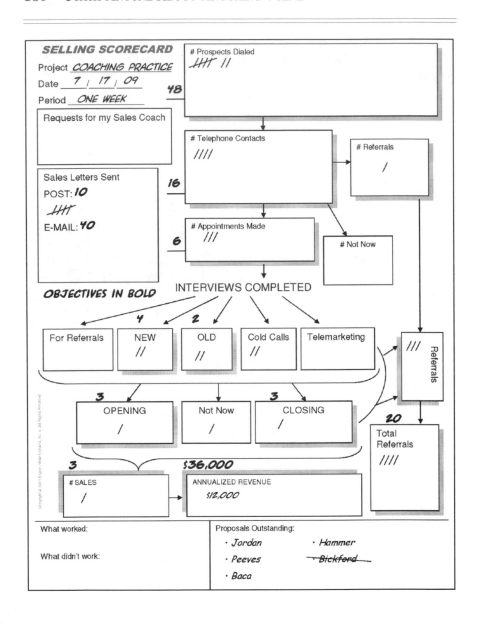

Figure 12.1

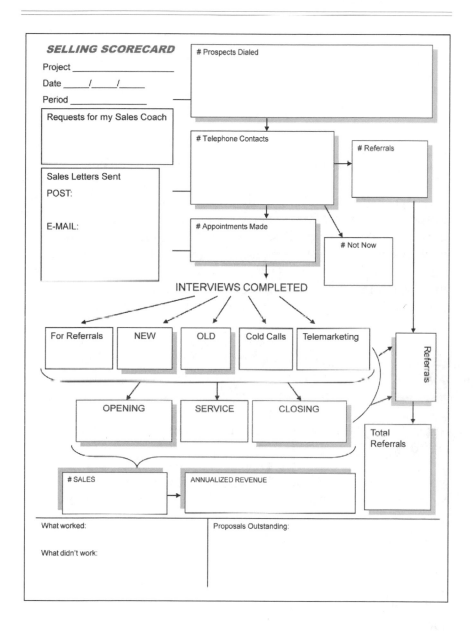

Figure 12.2

The Ultimate Week
Another Eagle's View

"The only thing even in this world is the number of hours in a day.
The difference in winning or losing is
what you do with those hours."
—Woody Hayes, Head football coach, Ohio State University
Two national championships, 13 Big Ten conference championships

If you ask salespeople with what would they like help the most, the answer you will get quite often is time management.

Sales Executive Council[1] studies reveal that salespeople don't really know where they invest their time. Why? Well, one reason is that they don't keep track, of course. But the primary reason is that they don't plan well enough in the first place. They don't write out a plan of where to invest their time to be able to look back and see if they did what they planned.

New salespeople often don't have a clue how to arrange their actions to get the maximum value from the time they invest. Top sales professionals invest the bulk of their time in customer-facing activities, while mediocre ones invest a preponderance of their time in non-customer-facing, the Sales Executive Council reports. While this may not be surprising, what is surprising is how just a little planning can improve salespeople's results markedly.

Here we present one of our favorite and most effective tools to help salespeople get a handle on their time and, more importantly, the outcomes they need to produce to have their sales operation run brilliantly (Figure 12.3).

Creating an Ultimate Week is the process of designing a model week so that you have the right people and the right things, in the right amounts, in the right places, and at the right times to produce the right results.

The Ultimate Week is your ideal week. It provides an eagle's view of how you would have your week play out if it were the perfect week. Ask yourself, "What do I need to do, and when is the best time to do it?"

---

[1]The Sales Executive Council, Arlington, VA, conducts case-based sales best practices, research, and quantitative research, globally in all industries.

Monday	Tuesday	Wednesday	Thursday	Friday	Saturday	Sunday
DALLAS	AUSTIN	HOUSTON	NEW ORLEANS	DALLAS		
5 :30 Run, Stretch, Crunches, Dress	6 : Dress 6:30 Study Product Line	6 :30 Run, Stretch, Crunches	6 : Dress 6:30 Study Product Line	6 :30 Run, Stretch, Crunches	6 :30 Run, Stretch, Lift Weights	
7:00 Breakfast Appointment	7:30 Telephone for Appointments	7:00 Breakfast Appointment	7:30 Telephone for Appointments	7:00 Breakfast Appointment	7:	7:30 Mass
Appointments	8:			8:00	8:30 Youth Soccer	
9:	9:00	9:00 Prospecting Calls		9:30 Prospecting Calls	9:	
	10:00 Appointment	10:00 Appointment	10:00 Appointment	10:00 Appointment	10:	10:00 Family Outing
11:30 Strategy Mtg. Coaching Session	11:30 Lunch Appointment	11:30 Lunch Appointment	11:30 Lunch Appointment	11:30 Lunch Appointment	11:	
	12:		12:00		12:	
1:30 Appointments	1:30 Appointments	1:30 Appointments	1:30 Appointments	1:30 Prospecting Research	1:	
	2:00	2:00	2:		2: Big Bros/Big Sisters	
	3:		3:		3:	
4:00 Write Proposals, Return calls	4:00 Prospecting, Send E-mails, Thank Yous, Return calls	4:00 Write Proposals, Return calls	4:00 Prospecting, Send E-mails, Thank yous, Return calls	4:00 Debrief Week, Coaching Session & Plan Next Week	4:	
5:00 Plan Tomorrow, Write Call Plans	5:00 Plan Tomorrow, Salesforce.com data entry	5:00 Plan Tomorrow, Write Call Plans	5:00 Plan Tomorrow, Salesforce.com data entry		5:	
6:00 Lift Weights	6:	6:00 Lift Weights	6:		6:	
	7:30 Light Study		7:30 Light Study	*SAMPLE*		7:30 Prepare for next week – think through
8:00	8:		8:		8:	
	9:		9:		9:	

Ultimate Week for: _____

Date: ____/____/____

Figure 12.3

The Ultimate Week is where you want to be located physically, what you want to be doing and when in a perfect world. The idea is for you to complete one weekly display, as in Figure 12.3, as your Ultimate Week.

So if you could have things during any week go exactly as you would want them to go, what would that look like? It would look like your Ultimate Week. Of course, things come up: unexpected interruptions and customer emergencies, for example.

Therefore, not every week will turn out precisely the way your Ultimate Week would. In fact, you will rarely have a week that turns out exactly like your Ultimate Week. But you still plan your week to give yourself the maximum opportunity to be the most effective in your work. Have you ever planned your day only to have your plan ruined by interruptions? Sure, who hasn't? But salespeople who give up on planning may as well give up on being wildly successful. All the research bears out that a major difference between the top 1 percent of sales professionals and everyone else is that the top 1 percent plan better.

You may want to begin crafting your own Ultimate Week on page 135.

When designing your Ultimate Week, you map out geography: what location do you plan to be in and when, what day and what time? You map out actions: the things that you must do to get your job done. When will you enter data on your sales report, for example? You schedule when you will complete your call plans. Maybe you write them at the end of the day for the next day, from 4:30 p.m. to 5 p.m., or maybe you do them a couple of days in advance and send them to your sales manager/coach, making yourself available for her coaching.

Having designed your Ultimate Week, with a hard copy in front of you, you telephone to make your appointments with customers. You schedule them into your calendar where and when you want to see them. A sample phone conversation might go, "Jennifer, I'm going to be in New Orleans this Thursday. May I see you at ten or would one-thirty be better?"

We distinguish *prime time* as the most optimal time to be doing the actions you must take to get your job done brilliantly. For example, if the very best time for you to call to make appointments with customers is between 7:30 a.m. and 10 a.m., you block out enough time in your Ultimate Week to make enough appointments to fill the next week in that prime-time timeframe. Let's say that you have calculated from experience that five hours per week of telephoning for face-to-face appointments with new customers is sufficient to make enough sales appointments to fill the following week. What's the best day to reach people—probably not Friday afternoon in the United States, right? So perhaps you decide to make calls for $2^{1/2}$ hours on Tuesdays and Thursdays from 7:30 a.m. to 10 a.m., and you block out those times in your Ultimate Week.

As mentioned earlier, you have your Ultimate Week in front of you while you are on the telephone making those appointments so that you don't schedule to see a customer face-to-face when you plan to be phoning for appointments.

But what if the customer can only meet with you face-to-face during your phoning slot? Well, you have to choose between phoning and seeing that customer. It's a judgment call, and you weigh the consequences. You

Monday	Tuesday	Wednesday	Thursday	Friday	Saturday	Sunday
	5:		5:		5:	
	6:		6:		6:	
	7:		7:		7:	
	8:		8:		8:	
	9:		9:		9:	
	10:		10:		10:	
	11:		11:		11:	
	12:		12:		12:	
	1:		1:		1:	
	2:		2:		2:	
	3:		3:		3:	
	4:		4:		4:	
	5:		5:		5.	
	6:		6:		6:	
	7:		7:		7:	
	8:		8:		8.	
	9:		9:		9:	

The Ultimate Week for:_____

Date_____/_____/_____

Figure 12.4

might choose to see the customer the following week instead if you judge that phoning for new appointments this week is time better invested than seeing your customer this week. During your scheduled phoning session, you might make five appointments. Maybe five new customer appointments are worth more than one face-to-face sales meeting with this customer. Or maybe you are absolutely certain that this particular customer would sign a five-year contract for $30 million for your products and services if you can just get in front of him. Duhhhh. In that case, you would schedule that customer in place of telephoning and reschedule your phoning session, wouldn't you?

It's a Big World out There
It's All in How You Look at It

As we mentioned earlier, one vital point of view to consider when designing your upcoming week from your Ultimate Week template is *geography*. Where do you plan to be? What city? What part of town? Schedule all your customers located in a single area for that day or part of the day. What is the best location to perform which actions to run your operation? What are the best surroundings or environment in which to conduct what part of your business? If you require peace and quiet to think and plan, arrange for that.

As a first year sales agent for Provident Mutual Life, once Jed resolved for himself that he was going to manage his business not only for the convenience of his customers but also himself, his results skyrocketed.

In the beginning, whenever a potential customer agreed to meet with Jed, he would go anywhere, anytime, just for the chance to make a sale. He found himself bouncing like a billiard ball all over the Seattle area and even the Great Northwest to see prospects. Then he read *The Critical Path to Sales Success*, by Frank Sullivan, CLU. Frank described in this seminal book his idea of a dream week. That was just the inspiration and information Jed needed to stop traveling from one extreme end of the city to another and back again and then back again, all in the same day!

Actions

Plan essential actions. Plan into your week the things that must happen to keep your sales operation running smoothly and to produce brilliant results. Schedule everything: telephoning for appointments, face-to-face sales calls, data entry into your CRM (Customer Relationship Management system), lunch, writing call plans, writing thank-you notes, handling e-mail, writing proposals, returning phone calls, coaching sessions, and studying new products. Schedule every critical action that should occur for your sales operation to run well, now and in the future. Take into account actions that must happen at different intervals: daily, weekly, monthly, or quarterly.

We have witnessed hundreds of salespeople have thunderbolts when they begin to map out their Ultimate Week. For one thing, they begin to realize, whether they knew it before or not, that if they don't schedule the things they must do, the likelihood of those things happening is somewhere between slim and none.

Prime Time

When is the best day and time to take which actions to be the most effective? When are you at your personal best? If you usually find yourself tired or sluggish in the late afternoon, you will want to avoid seeing customers face-to-face then.

What follows is a list of typical benefits that Ultimate Week users enjoy:

Reduced Stress, Improved Sales Results

- Less stress in managing outcomes through effective scheduling.
- Increases in productivity (often dramatic improvements).
- Attention to and completion of things that used to fall by the wayside.
- Ability to plan time more strategically with an eagle's view of the week.
- Help in setting realistic objectives for the week and avoiding unrealistic expectations.
- Reduced stress and travel time going to see customers through wise geographic scheduling.
- Sales manager/coaches are better able to coach their sales professional/players by seeing a vivid display of where they plan to invest their time and attention.
- Sales professionals discover what actions and outcomes must happen, when and how often, to have their sales operation flourish and meet or exceed their sales objectives.
- Help in distinguishing action versus activity. Action being things you do that materially contribute to realizing your sales objectives, and activity being those things that do not. You can choose to reduce or eliminate activities and increase productive actions.

Happy Holidays!

One of Germaine's clients, Jerry Colacino, is a professional recruiter in the engineering field in Texas. He likes to send her his schedule every week, in Ultimate Week fashion, with all his appointments and scheduled actions for that week. This gives Germaine, his coach, the opportunity to ask questions about his plans for the upcoming week. Although he has been a successful recruiter for 14 years, she sometimes sees things that he misses.

For example, one week Germaine asked, "Jerry, I notice here in your week that you are scheduling phone calls on Thursday afternoon with a target of reaching twelve people. Most people are off Friday because Saturday is July Fourth, Independence Day, do you …?"

He jumped in and said, "No, no, you're right, Germaine. A lot of my customers like to leave early the day before a holiday weekend begins. I need to make those calls on Wednesday, instead. Thanks for catching that." Now, Jerry is by no means stupid. Here was a veteran, successful sales professional who had doubled his placement results in the first six months of that year. Yet Germaine was able to glance at his plan for the week, ask a simple question, and make a substantial difference. The value of coaching is sometimes that we coaches simply see things our players don't see. Assuming that seasoned professionals are keenly aware of everything all the time is unwise. Any novice tennis player can coach his instructor's serve better than the instructor can coach himself. Why? The instructor cannot observe himself serve.

Put Out That Fire

Numerous times sales professionals and sales managers have said to us the following (in one form or another), just like William Emerson did: "You know, we can plan our week, but then we have a ton of interruptions and emergencies that we have to handle and fires to put out. It's just so hard not to be reactionary all the time in our business. And *we keep struggling to get back on track*. I agree that an Ultimate Week is a good idea, but it's just so hard to stick to a plan in this business." William was sales and operations vice president for a corrugated board manufacturing company.

Now, all the sales professionals that tell us this are telling us the truth. They aren't lying. They aren't lazy. They aren't just making excuses. We believe that they all want to produce extraordinary sales results. They are honestly describing as accurately as they can how their world occurs for them. And in every single one of those conversations, there is a coaching opportunity.

Germaine said, "William, do you remember your saying, 'we keep struggling to get back on track'? Well, without an Ultimate Week, you have no track to get back on. No wonder you're all struggling!"

This was a thunderbolt for William. Laughing out loud, he said, "Well, you sure have a point there—point, game, and set!"

"I gave up on planning at one point. Too many interruptions continually upset my plans. But I began to notice that when I was without a daily plan, I was a sitting duck for anybody's nonsense. It is always an ill wind that blows when a ship has no destination. So, I became a better planner."
—Ted Zouzounis, CLU, President, D/A Financial Group, Orinda, California

Raise Your Hand if You Use a Computer
Thank You. Here Is Your Very Own Eagle's View Desktop Organizer

Would you like to discover an eagle's view that you and your clients, friends, and colleagues will find immediately useful? Nearly every time anyone sees our PC's desktop for the first time, we get comments and/or questions, soon followed by a request to show him how he can build his own desktop background similar to the one he sees on our laptop.

We used to keep photos of pleasant scenes, family, or our dogs as background for our desktops on our computers. You too? Then, a couple of years ago, we invented the eagle's view custom desktop organizer. Here is a sample (Figure 12.5) of one we built while we had sequestered ourselves to write this book.

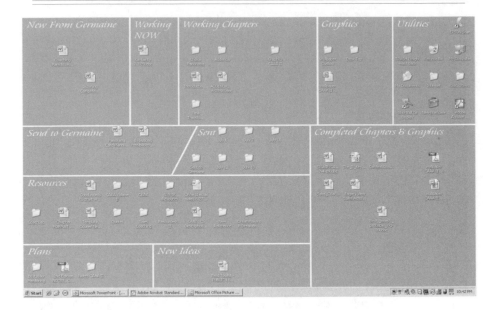

Figure 12.5

The desktop background above is the one Jed used on his laptop while we were writing this book. Germaine used a similar version. This desktop background helped him keep track of what we were writing to build the very book you are reading now.

You can build different backgrounds for special projects, like this book. And you can have a standard display for your day job. Here's one (Figure 12.6) Jed uses on a daily basis for his work.

Just imagine your own desktop populated with icons of your files and folders organized in a fashion that makes sense to you. What if your desktop helped you to swiftly apprehend the file or folder you need to find so that you can start work?

This is especially handy for managing the sales process and for coaching your clients through that process as well as other projects. The key projects that you're working on are easily accessible with the click of the mouse. You don't have to go through the arduous search for the documents that you need in a moment's notice.

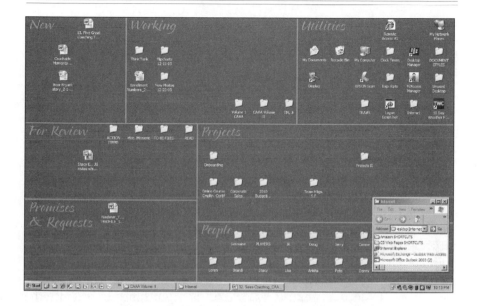

Figure 12.6

Cut the Suspense
Show Me How, Now ... Please?

Start a landscape PowerPoint file and name it something clever like *Desktop Background_2-11-10*. Build a background display that embraces the nature of your work so that when you fire up your computer, it helps you get to work fast.

After you get the PowerPoint to look the way you want it, save it as a PDF file. Then save that PDF as a JPEG. (If you save the PowerPoint directly to a JPEG, it will show up quite blurry—not at all crisp and sharp. If you wonder why that is, ask the nearest 10-year-old. Please do not call or e-mail us asking why. We do not know, nor do we care. Thank you in advance for your kind cooperation.)

Now right-click on the JPEG you created, and up will pop options, one of which will be Set Desktop Background. Click on that, wait three seconds, and then minimize the JPEG and you should see staring back at you your very own custom desktop organizer. Then, depending on your generation, you will exclaim, "Far out and groovy!" or "Awesome!" (BTW, either would be equally acceptable and appreciated by these authors.)

Summary

Recording sales actions can be a laborious and sometimes meaningless chore for salespeople. The eagle's view Selling Scorecard, on the other hand, can make the recording of one's sales actions motivating and even uplifting.

Succumbing to urgent demands, abandoning planning, and ultimately swimming in low-value activity is not a pretty picture. Instead, you can empower yourself and your players/clients to manage the unexpected interruptions and take high-value actions for greater sales and service for your customers. Building an Ultimate Week is the process of designing a model week so that you have the right people and the right things, in the right amounts, in the right places, and at the right times to produce the right results.

Inventing eagle's views of projects and one's routine work processes can enhance productivity and improve the quality of output.

In the next chapter we present five more tools for your coaching endeavors.

CHAPTER 13

"For the flower to bloom, you need the right soil as well as the right seed.
The same is true to cultivate good thinking."
—William Bernbach

FIVE GREAT TOOLS FOR YOUR COACHING TOOL KIT

Outcomes for this chapter:
*   Increase your value to your clients by having more tools to help them achieve their objectives.
*   Introduce five proven coaching tools that enable players to move forward:
    1. The three Ps: Prepare, Polish, Perfect
    2. Evaluating Possibilities model
    3. Three powerful questions: Best, Worst, Probable
    4. The Choice Panorama
    5. Roles and Responsibilities with R-A-C-I

We believe that, as coaches, the more equipped we are, the bigger the difference we can make with our clients. Knowledge is power, and the more facile we become with an array of tools and methodologies, the more value we can bring our clients. In this chapter we will introduce to you various tools and share with you how we use them. Please make them your own, and predictably, they will give you an edge in empowering your clients.

Ready, Set, Go!
The Three Ps to Success

Before you begin examining the following tools, we're introducing you to the three Ps: Prepare, Polish, and Perfect. Their purpose is to tune your listening as you read on. Here are the three Ps defined:

Prepare: Whether you're starting a new project or preparing a presentation for a new client, the Prepare stage is one in which you are planning, researching, getting ready, and starting the work. During this stage, focus is on getting all the information, tools, and knowledge needed to get the job done. Once you've done all the research and planning, you're now ready to move to the next stage.

Polish: The Polish stage is the actual practice and implementation of all the research and design work that was done in the Prepare stage. It's called the Polish stage because you have the opportunity to buff, shine, or clean up any imperfections. Questions for diagnosis in this stage:

What worked?

What didn't work?

What's missing?

What could be done differently?

Once these questions are answered, it's time to go back to the drawing board and polish or redesign your work. You're now ready for the next stage: Perfect.

Perfect: This stage is ongoing. As you continue to implement your redesigned process, you continue to perfect it and shape it to the audience, to the outcomes, and to the different situations. As you continue to perfect the process, your confidence, knowledge, and competence levels increase. You master your work. It becomes second nature to you. This is an iterative process because as you continue to perfect your work, you go through the Prepare and Polish stages within the Perfect stage.

"He who is too busy doing good finds no time to be good."
—Rabindranath Tagore, Indian poet, playwright, and essayist; Nobel Prize winner for literature, 1913

Coaches are all busy people, and if there is one thing about which we are certain, it is that if you don't schedule things you intend to do, odds are they won't happen. We suggest you schedule debriefing, or "perfecting," sessions with yourself or your colleagues after every coaching event. This will help ensure that you perform the important Perfect stage.

Putting the Three Ps to Work

We encourage you to keep the three Ps in mind and work through the stages as you are introduced to the following coaching tools. The Prepare stage is discovering and learning about the following tools and designing a way to use them within your work. The Polish stage is your practice of the implementation of your work and Perfecting the process or tool until it becomes yours-you own it totally.

The Evaluating Possibilities Grid

"Ordinary people believe only in the possible. Extraordinary people visualize not what is possible or probable, but rather what is impossible. And by visualizing the impossible, they begin to see it as possible."
—Cherie Carter-Scott

Have you ever facilitated a team of people in a conversation for possible actions and outcomes for a sizeable project? A team who feels free to put forth, uncensored, any and all ideas as to how to achieve a major objective? If you have, then you know that a handful of people can invent hundreds of possibilities in a short period of time.

As you use the Evaluating Possibilities grid, this is what you will accomplish:
- Discover a proven and uncomplicated device to efficiently display and evaluate the numerous possibilities that a team or an individual may invent to accomplish the outcomes of a major project.
- Learn how to facilitate the conversation for evaluating possibilities conceived by your players, whether they be a team or an individual.
- Expand your ability to assist your clients in thinking through possibilities and options to improve their business results.
- Be exposed to a process that acknowledges not only people's creativity but their business acumen as well.

I Am Covered Up With Possibilities!
Now What Do I Do?

"Ideas have a short shelf life, you must act on them before
the expiration date."
—John Maxwell

After the team or the individual has generated a plethora of possibilities and can't think of one more possibility to advance, then the question becomes, "How do we evaluate all these ideas?" Which ones are better than others? Which ideas should we eliminate? Which ideas cannot be implemented by our deadline?

We have used to great advantage an easy method of sorting the wheat from the chaff, or finding the richest possibilities to pursue among the myriad of choices. We call it the Evaluating Possibilities grid. (See Figure 13.1) This method is extremely helpful at the beginning of a project and is also worthwhile to perform at appropriate junctures along the way.

Let's Find the Good Stuff

After an inventory of possibilities has been created, it is time to evaluate each possibility. Usually there are so many possibilities that no one person or group can execute them all and, as freewheeling possibilities go, there are those that are not of sufficient value to even bother with. The trick is to find out which are which.

In using this evaluation technique, the primary step is to have the team or individual determine the two main criteria with which they will judge the possibilities. On our grid sample we are measuring just two things: relative value on the vertical axis and time on the horizontal axis. The point at which the two axes intersect represents the date when the project is due or by when it must be achieved or implemented. So if you have six months to work on the project, every idea you plot on the left side of the vertical axis is fair-and-in-play territory because you estimate that it can be accomplished within six months. For an idea to be of use to any project, the possibility must be able to bring value to the completion of the project within its time frame. Otherwise, it is plotted somewhere to the right of the vertical axis in the out-of-bounds terrain.

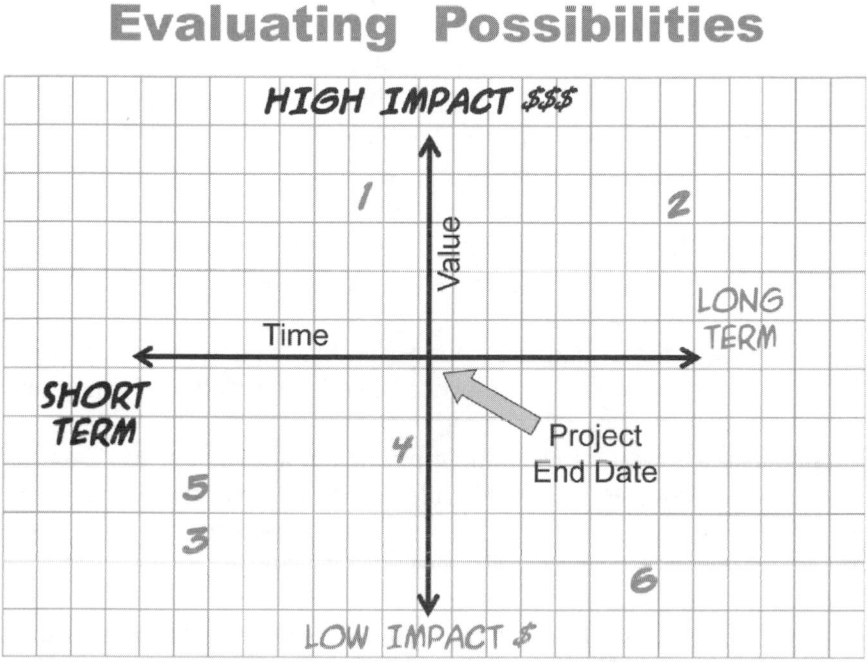

Evaluating Possibilities

Figure 13.1

Action: The Mother of Results

Here's a brief description of the process in action: Take one of the possibilities on your list and ask, "Can we produce this possibility inside our time frame?" That's the first question. But before you can plot that possibility's identification number on the grid, there's one more question to answer: "What relative value is this idea to us for this project's success?" That question brings us to the vertical axis of value.

The vertical value axis could represent any form of value you like. The top of the axis signifies high-impact value, and the bottom end denotes low-impact value to the undertaking. For our illustration on the sample grid, we chose to illustrate the category of impact with dollar signs ($$$) to symbolize the monetary impact or value. But it must represent just one variety of value, not more than one. It might stand for revenue dollars, profit, or cost savings. You must select just one of those, not all, for each

Evaluating Possibilities grid. You may, however, have more than one evaluation grid.

Sam Arnstein, team member of a high-performance project team at a zinc mining company in Canada, asked, "We've got more than one impact to consider with these possibilities, Germaine. We are estimating the immediate or short-term revenue value of these possibilities, but we also want to weigh their potential for long-term, sustainable revenue generation."

One of his teammates, Sandra Smoot, chimed in, "Hey, Sammy, why don't we have two grids—one for short-term revenue potential and one for long-term?"

Of course, Sandra had the solution, and Germaine nodded, smiling, and whispered to them both, "I love it when the client delivers their own coaching, don't you?"

In our illustration we are estimating the impact value $ and the time, short term to long term, that the idea or possibility will require to be launched and implemented. For simplicity and visibility in our example, we're only plotting six possibilities. And know that there are normally dozens of ideas to be plotted.

Possibility #1 is estimated to be of high value and can be accomplished during the life of the project or time span selected—and it is expected that the result of it will occur toward the end of the project. That's why it is close to the vertical axis representing the due date for completion of the project at the horizontal time axis. Possibility #2 is high value but won't happen during this project's time period. Perhaps that possibility is so potent that it launches an additional project immediately with a longer time frame. Or the idea might be put into an existence system so that it won't be forgotten for future endeavors.

Possibility #3 is low value but can be done quickly. So it is plotted far to the left of the deadline and low on the grid because of its relatively low impact value to the overall success of the venture. In this example, it is deemed low value because it doesn't generate a lot of money, yet it still may be worth doing if it is relatively easy to carry out and it smoothes the way a bit for your project. These kinds of ideas are commonly known as low-hanging fruit. The metaphor refers to things within easy grasp, like apples on the lower branches of the tree, and some positive contribution to the project. Looking at Possibility #5, you can see that it is in a comparable situation.

Look at Possibility #4. Why would you think it is positioned on the grid in the lower-left quadrant? If you thought something similar to low value and takes almost the entire life of the project to finish, then you would be accurate.

What about Possibility #6? Well, it's in the least enviable placement an idea could have, given the two criteria. It has low monetary muscle and takes too long a time to implement. Without further investigation you could predict that this idea is headed for the junk pile.

Where the Grass Is the Greenest

So, now what would you say is the most favorable quadrant to find yourself in if you were a possibility? It would be the upper-left quadrant, and the best position in that quarter of the grid would be the far upper left. Why? It has the highest estimated value and is judged to be quick to implement-most likely one of the easiest to implement as well.

By the way, during the team's discussions of where to place a possibility, we facilitate the deliberation until we have a consensus of where the team feels the possibility should lie on the grid. Keep in mind that these are estimations and assessments of the possibilities based solely upon the available information the members of the team have at this point. We are counting on participants' experience and existing expertise in the area to give us informed appraisals.

After the original plotting, upon further inspection and due diligence on the part of the team members, it may be discovered that a highly rated possibility should be sent to the scrap heap. And it may be revealed that a previously assessed low-value possibility climbs the grid way above the value midline because new favorable monetary benefits were discovered. Frankly, this is rarely the case in our experience, but it has been known to happen.

"In the beginner's mind there are many possibilities, but in the expert's mind there are few."
—Shunryu Suzuki, Japanese Zen priest

It was a beautiful, sunny spring day in the Catskill Mountains of New York State. We were at a resort and conference center, there to facilitate an offsite summit meeting for a pharmaceutical client. This was a large gathering of 100 persons, composed primarily of research scientists and top management.

The participants had arrived from all over the world to determine the future of the company. Their charge was to invent and launch break-through project teams to develop new drugs and improve systems to more quickly bring those medicines to patients. One might think that the par-ticipants would rather have been outside boating, golfing, or hiking rather than inside stuffy meeting rooms with their noses to the grindstone. Nevertheless, these people were committed to bringing breakthrough ideas to the table to help millions with their afflictions and to save lives. It was our privilege to be their coaches.

We divided the group into eight teams for various reasons, ranging from possible new drug and work redesign to bring the medical break-throughs to market faster. The executives had already written charters for the eight teams, detailing what was to be accomplished.

The teams were given instructions to generate possibilities to accom-plish the objectives mandated by their charters, without judging or evalu-ating them in the moment. There would be ample time for evaluating their merit later in the conference. The teams broke out into different rooms and went to work. They brainstormed possibilities and listed ideas on flipcharts for 90 minutes. There was a team leader for each team who facilitated these sessions. At the end of 90 minutes, we met with the team leaders.

The team leaders were delighted with their teams' output of ideas but worried about how to sort through them and come out of the process with some kind of sensible direction. We showed them how to weigh the pos-sibilities with the Evaluating Possibilities grid and coached them a bit in facilitating the consensus-rating process. But first we coached them to reorient everyone in the outcomes intended for the project, prescribed in their charters. Then we coached them to make sure their respective teams understood that their evaluations must all be in light of achieving those targets. The team leaders said they understood and all agreed to get the job done in the fashion we described. Back to work …

Trust Yourself

We were like air from then on; that is, we were everywhere. You never know how well even the most proven tool will work with a new group of individuals. You just cannot predict the future. There is always the risk of failure. But you can trust yourself to get the job done and know that you will help the team leaders use the tool to their full advantage and produce an acceptable work product.

"Excellence is the enemy of good enough."
—David Reid, Global Account Vice President, National Oilwell Varco

We went around listening in as the various teams deliberated upon the value of each idea. There were moments of inspiration, excitement, lethargy, and boredom. It was an emotional/mental roller coaster for everyone. But in the end they were all sorted out and pleased with the result. Looking back, all agreed it was a first-rate method for separating the ideas with promise from the possibilities that would lead nowhere special. Coming from predominantly scientific and highly critical minds, this was welcome support.

The teams came back the next morning and reported to the entire group what their plans were to produce the outcomes of their charters. As the teams shared their goals and insights into their achievement, you could feel the enthusiasm and commitment well up in people's hearts and minds. Questions from the group were the in the spirit of designing ways forward rather than shooting down the painstaking work of the teams. All in all, it was a stellar result for the conference.

"Man is so made that when anything fires his soul,
impossibilities vanish."
—Jean de La Fontaine, French poet, 1621-1695

Best, Worst, Probable

One of the things that we regularly encounter is one of our clients considering undertaking a new venture or project. Our publicity coach, Carmen Wisenbaker, gave us the following tool, which has been quite useful in building our own business as well as an eye-opening tool we now use with our clients.

The Best, Worst, and Probable tool is a simple but powerful tool that will help you to:

- Learn a proven method of assisting clients in assessing new possible undertakings.
- Improve your client's design of the way forward on new projects.
- Enhance your clients' confidence in producing successful outcomes.

So, you want to take on a new project or launch a new product or publish a new book. Ask yourself the following questions:

What's the best that could happen?

What's the worst that could happen?

What will probably happen?

Defining Terms

What's the best that could happen?

The purpose here is to discover what your vision is for the project. That is, what are the results you are after? What will those results make possible in the future? What are you building? Is it worth doing? Who will benefit and in what specific ways?

What's the worst that could happen?

If the project doesn't go well, what will be the cost? Financially? Psychologically? What bad things might occur? What will you be stuck with? What monsters might it create? (An example of a monster is a monthly newsletter that was a good idea at the time, isn't producing the results you expected, and is now a bad idea because you are stuck producing it every month because you promised you would.) What could you lose? Will it damage any other opportunities that you might have had?

What will probably happen?

Another way of asking this is, What is predictable? This can be estimated by examining the past results you have personally obtained from similar endeavors. What were those results? If you wanted them to be greater, what might have you done differently? What was missing, the presence of which would have improved the results? What were the circumstances then and now? Who was involved? What resources were employed? What was the market environment then? What is it now? Can you live with only the probable happening?

Or perhaps you got the idea from someone else and can examine his results. The trouble with this is that you are probably only interested in this new venture because he was successful in the first place. In any case, you must consider probabilities from some source to answer this question.

The Inquiry Process

- Imagine the future. Assume that the probable happened. What happened that the best didn't happen?
- If you want better than the probable to happen, what must happen to move the final outcome toward the best category? What actions will you take?
- Imagine the future once again. Assume you didn't take those actions. What happened that you didn't take those actions? What structures can you put into place to ensure that those actions will be taken?
- If only the probable happens, can you live with it?
- If the worst happens, can you live with that?

We have found that after a thorough and honest examination of these questions, the client is better prepared to win—which is what coaching is about, is it not? Projects that sounded good at first blush are sometimes dropped. Ventures that are undertaken are done so with greater clarity of the path ahead, better structures in place to ensure success, and more confidence in actions taken.

"The plan is nothing. Planning is everything."
—Dwight D. Eisenhower, supreme allied commander in Europe,
Second World War; 34th U.S. president

In addition, it is possible to use these three questions—Best? Worst? Possible?-to examine any possible action a person might take. This is especially appropriate when the risks associated with the action are high.

Lucy in the Sky

Lucy Gustafson, a successful chiropractor, got the idea to put on client appreciation days to acknowledge her existing clients and attract new patients. She had read about the idea in one of her industry's publications and had heard of other chiropractors doing it in other areas.

So Germaine asked Lucy the first question, "What's the best that could happen?"

"Well, my existing clients will feel appreciated, and I'll get some new patients," Lucy proposed.

"Good, how many new patients?" Germaine asked.

Lucy said, "If I could get five new regular patients, that would be great."

"Yes, but is that the best that could happen, Lucy?"

Lucy started to get the idea, and after more conversation she was certain that ten new patients was the best that could possibly happen. Germaine and Lucy went on to look at the number of possible existing clients who could attend and what was the best number of them attending. How many guests might they bring, and what percentage of those would need to become new patients for the best to happen?

As Germaine and Lucy continued the inquiry, Lucy began to see more and more things that she and her staff could do to ensure the event, if taken on, would succeed. She saw the things her staff would have to begin doing that very week. Lucy saw the preparation that must be done to serve that many people on a single Saturday. As they continued, she recorded the many details that were being revealed through the inquiry.

Lucy decided to take on the project. The outcome was tremendous for Lucy and her staff, not to mention their patients. Forty-eight clients felt appreciated that day, and eight of their guests went on to become regular patients.

In summary, the coach is frequently presented with the opportunity to serve his or her client in examining new approaches to enhancing their business or endeavor that may or may not be wise. The best, worst, probable tool can assist greatly in the examination of the practicability of the new idea. It can provide remarkable insight into the undertaking far beyond the cursory examination people commonly perform before they leap headlong into a new venture. This inquiry can uncover needed structures to put into place to ensure the success of the new project. In addition, the three questions-Best? Worst? Possible?-can help assess the value of any action.

Decisions, Decisions, Decisions!
The Choice Panorama—A Decision-Method Model

Business was growing rapidly, the phones were ringing constantly, clients were knocking at our doors; we needed a sharp, witty assistant with lots of potential to help us bring order to a chaotic situation. You're right if you're thinking this happened before 2008. As a matter of fact, we were sitting in the luxurious offices of one of our clients in Boca Raton, Florida.

A packed day of interviewing was scheduled to find the right person who would bring order and sunshine to the business. Before Patty Fisher actually started interviewing the candidates, we gathered around the conference table to align on the qualities and skills the person needed to fulfill the job position. Many times when we're interviewing candidates for jobs, we have a tendency to choose people whom we are drawn to personality-wise. Their personality may be so charming that they steal our hearts, and the skills needed dwindle to a nice thought—or better yet, they can learn as they go.

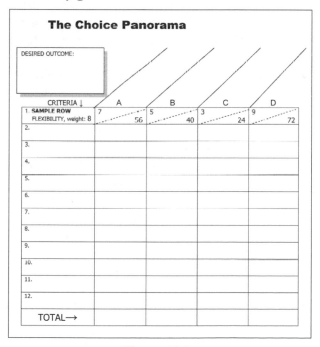

Figure 13.2

We used the Choice Panorama above to write down the skills needed to do the work and weighted them according to their importance. What happened? We met the "great personality," and she was lacking some of the skills needed. The Choice Panorama helped us to stay focused on the outcomes needed without getting enamored with someone who would wind up costing the company more money in the long run. Patty was able to hire someone with talent and a great personality. Interviewing so many people back-to-back, the Choice Panorama allowed Patty to stay the course with the criteria to achieve desired outcomes. She didn't have to hold the information in her head.

The Choice Panorama has very wide application.

- First, be clear about your desired outcome, and write it plainly in the box provided.
- Then list the criteria you want to use to make your decision down the left-hand column below the criteria.
- Weight each criterion on a scale of 1 to 10.
  List the possible choices across the top: A, B, C, and D. Add columns or pages if you have more than four possible choices.
- Rate each possible choice against each criterion on a scale of 0 to 10 in the upper left of the box to the right of that criterion for each possibility.
- Multiply the possibility's rating number by the weight of the criterion to get the score, and write it in the lower right of the box for that possibility for that criterion. For example, you may have a project to hire a new associate. You determine that one of your criteria is Flexibility, and you weigh its value an 8. You rate candidate A a 7 in Flexibility. You then multiply the weight, 8, times A's rating of 7, and you get 56. That's A's score for Flexibility.
- Rate each candidate for each criterion in this manner. Then total the scores at the bottom of each column.

Now you have a relatively objective look at a number of possibilities ranked against a number of criteria.

The higher the total score, the better the choice, at least against your criteria and judgment.

Of course, the model doesn't make the decision for you. But what it does do is give you a panorama of possible choices with the relative value of those choices against the criteria that you selected.

Roles and Responsibilities + R-A-C-I

The following consultative tool is one that we've used many times over the years to help our clients get very clear about putting the right people in the right job. For work teams already in place, this tool helps to ensure that the right talent has the right responsibilities to fulfill the job at hand.

Germaine used this approach with her client Rhonda Williams and her work team. Everyone attended the workshop prepared to report out their role and responsibilities. As people started reporting to the group their responsibilities, it became evident that some people took on too much work and others were clueless about their part in certain activities. This is where the RACI tool came in handy.

Under Rhonda's supervision, everyone became very clear about their role, the responsibilities of such role, and others who should be notified, updated, and consulted with during various stages of projects. The completed RACI tool (Figure 13.3) was then posted on the company's intranet for the team's ongoing use.

Role: Position, function, job; the part a person plays in the organization. Example: Marketing Materials Coordinator.

Responsibility: Specific work or task to be performed. This work might be performed on an ongoing basis or at intervals or only once. Example: Provide up-to-date marketing and sales materials to all stakeholders on a timely basis.

Outcome: A specific, measurable result or condition is present or has been achieved. Synonyms: Result, product, work product, ending, conclusion, effect. Example: Marketing materials communicate clearly the benefits and features of our offerings to potential clients and customers and assist our salespeople in making sales.

R-A-C-I

RACI is a tool used to distinguish the parts that people play in achieving a particular outcome or set of outcomes for a project or performing a particular task. The following definitions are expressly for the application of the RACI tool and may or may not apply to other conversations for the division of work or the description of work in the organization.

- **RESPONSIBLE:** The people who actually do the work. They are held to account by the accountable person (below).
- **ACCOUNTABLE:** The person who is called to account for the result being produced or not produced (where the buck stops). This is usually one person.

Note: Co-accountability is ordinarily ineffective and inefficient.

- **CONSULT:** People who are to be consulted for their expertise or opinion concerning certain decisions and changes.
- **INFORM:** People who must be informed when decisions or changes occur.

These are formal distinctions, not informal. For example, inform doesn't mean that you expect the person to read about it in the company newsletter. Inform means that it is someone's job to ensure that the person is informed by a certain time.

What follows is a sample R-A-C-I tool for displaying the people involved and the parts they play in achieving an outcome.

Marketing Materials Production, R.A.C.I.

Name:	RESPONSIBLE	ACCOUNTABLE	CONSULT	INFORM
SUSAN		X	X	X
JEFF	X			
MARTHA	X			
JACK			X	X
HARRY				X
GARTH				X
YVONNE			X	X

Figure 13.3

Summary

Our commitment is to give you as many tools as possible to use with your clients. Some of the tools may be new to you, and some may be familiar tools used a little differently. We invite you to start with the three Ps to plan, design, and implement the best solution to your client's needs.

Helping our clients plan effectively has become one of the highest-value actions we can take with them. In our next chapter we explore a methodology for planning that can pay big dividends for you and your players.

CHAPTER 14

"Without leaps of imagination or dreaming, we lose the excitement of possibilities. Dreaming, after all is a form of planning."
—Gloria Steinem

MAKE PLANNING FUN AND EFFECTIVE!

Outcomes for this chapter:
- Learn how to accelerate and improve project planning for groups.
- Examine the shortcomings of common group planning practices.
- Expand your ability to design anything quickly by getting an eagle's view, without sacrificing the quality of the plan.
- Discover that planning doesn't have to be linear, difficult, and boring.

It was a windy, rainy March day in New York City when we met with the new vice president for a large retail company. We had walked five city blocks from the Hyatt Hotel to Ann Acropolis' office and were a bit weary, not to mention wet. She greeted us in the lobby. "Thanks for coming," Ann smiled. "Let's get you two upstairs. Would you like some coffee?"

We finally sat down with her in a spacious, brightly lit conference room and listened carefully as Ann poured out her concerns, worries, and fears. Ann Acropolis, a very strong and talented woman, on this particular day was nearly in tears from being overwhelmed. She began our meeting with, "I am at my wit's end. I don't know where to start. Everything is a mess and needs work."

The new president, Robert Strasberg, had given Ann a big job, and it needed to be accomplished quickly. The competition was starting to make huge inroads and threaten their historically dominated market share. Their largest account was in jeopardy of being lost. Ann's task was to restructure their sales force and service departments by the end of the year. In addition, she was charged with, at a minimum, to maintain their sales levels to match the previous year's.

In the Jungle, the Mighty Jungle

All that needed to be achieved seemed to Ann to be so complex and problematical. "Help! What do I do?"

Germaine said, "Well, first, Ann, you must discover that there is a *finite* list of things for you to be concerned with. It's not infinite. The list ends. But it feels kind of infinite because you haven't seen the end yet. You haven't laid it all out and looked at it. You need an eagle's view."

Ann said, "That sounds great! I'd love to see an end to the list. Now, tell me, how do I get this eagle's view, as you call it?"

Germaine pulled from her briefcase a stack of 3 x 5 cards and divided them up about equally among the three of us. We each had about 30 cards. We had begun a unique process that would end with a happy and empowered client.

In fact, the process would ultimately enable her to lay out, in less than two hours, a complete plan to accomplish her objectives for the entire year. Ann would rise out of her frantic anxiety and become ecstatic. She would be delighted not only then, but nine months later when she and her team had exceeded their objectives and laid the foundation for her company's enviable future. The following is a step-by-step description of the process that we employed with Ann.

> *"It's kind of fun to do the impossible!"*
> —Walt Disney

We Always Start With Outcomes
The Five Objectives of Panorama Card Planning

1. Dramatically increase group members' participation in the planning process and virtually eliminate "waiting to be heard." (This method can be used in small or large groups.)
2. Shape an environment that fosters creativity.
3. Substantially and easily reduce the time invested in the planning process.
4. Improve the quality of the overall plan, and ensure its execution.
5. Provide a potent panorama and eagle's view of the project.

The Commonly Practiced Group Planning Method
Is Inefficient and Often Ineffective

Project planning performed by a group is generally done by having one group member stand at a flipchart (or whiteboard) and record items offered by the team's members. The completed flipchart pages are then usually taped to a wall. During this scenario, three major drawbacks are experienced:

1. While the person recording the items is writing one thought, the other group members have to wait for the recorder to finish writing before they can voice their idea. This tends to suppress, or at best reduce, people's participation and creativity. (By the way, in our experience, almost any attempt to reduce chaos suppresses creativity.) This method is extremely time-consuming and, in a major project, extremely tiring. (We would add boring, but everybody knows that good people never get bored. Right?)
2. People's ideas and thoughts are recorded in a linear fashion on the flipchart, and their order cannot be physically rearranged without rewriting the items or cutting and pasting.
3. One or two outspoken group members tend to dominate the process.

The Panorama Card Planning technique cures all three shortcomings described above.

The Steps of the Panorama Card Planning Technique

A. Provide each group member with at least 20 index cards and a pen or pencil.
B. Gather the group around a conference table covered with butcher paper or flipchart pages taped together. Three flipchart pages will usually suffice. Later in the process, the cards will be taped to the paper.
C. The facilitator asks the group to do the following:

1. Think of all the items and aspects of the project that must be considered to ensure its successful completion.
   Call out the items as you think of them and write each one at
2. the top of a card. Throw the card, face up, in a pile in the center of the table.
3. Do not censure or vote on any ideas brought forth at this time. That would suppress people's creativity. Regard all items as valid for the moment. Assure people that you will edit and refine them later.

People typically call out and write items similar to the following:

- Determine our budget, written in bold caps at the top of a card as WRITE BUDGET.
- Design new incentive plan, written as INCENTIVE PLAN. Conduct employee survey, written as EE SURVEY.
- Establish milestones and timeline, written as MILE-STONES/TIMELINE.
- Get R.W. to buy in, written as R.W. BUY-IN.
- Include the Marketing Department, written as INCLUDE MARKETING.

D. The facilitator encourages group members to keep thinking of project elements, and the facilitator may participate as well. When the group seems to have exhausted all possible items to be considered, the facilitator has everyone stand up and move around to one side of the table. (Arrange the cards so that they can all be read from that side of the table.)

E. Instruct people to move the cards into like categories and groupings, and move them to a likely time position on the paper, with time moving from left to right. (See Figure 14.1) Now invite editing and additions. At first, we have observed that teams will tend to try to crowd all the tasks to be completed into the first two weeks or first month of a six-month to a year's project. Once they begin to get an eagle's view, however, they see how unrealistic and unnecessary that is. Then they begin to move the tasks/cards around into a more reasonable and thoughtful timeline.

F. After the group has more or less agreed upon where the cards ought to be placed, tape the cards to the paper loosely with cellophane tape. Now the whole display is taken from the table and tacked to a wall where everyone can stand before it and get an eagle's view of the entire project. Now further fine-tuning can take place, such as eliminating cards, adding new cards, rewording them, and repositioning them. Now you have a potent panorama of the entire project's elements placed relative to time.

G. Lead a discussion to determine by what date each item or outcome must be completed and by whom. The dates and the people's names who are accountable are written on the cards. More fine-tuning may happen at this stage too.

H. Soon the group will be viewing a full panorama, or landscape, of the project, complete with timeline, outcomes, action items, by-when dates, and the names of the people who will perform the tasks to produce the stated results. The panorama reveals the key aspects and critical pathways for the undertaking.

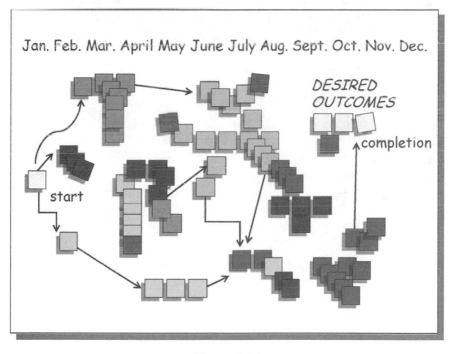

Figure 14.1

I. At some point, the process is declared complete. The panorama of the project can be typed in sections on a computer using PowerPoint and printed on standard-size paper. The pages of the sections can be joined together to recreate the panorama. In this way the panoramic plan can be easily distributed and exhibited in multiple locations.

J. Cards indicating ownership of certain project elements may also be taken by the owners after typing as described above. The information on those cards can go directly into people's personal project planners or Outlook to prompt them to take action.

Plan a Major Project of Your Own Using the Panorama Card Planning Technique

"Happy people plan actions, they don't plan results."
—Denis Waitley

Following the steps above, plan your own project. You can use this technique with a team, just one other person, or by yourself. On your own, you might want to plan a home landscaping project or addition to your home. Maybe you're getting married or planning your daughter's wedding. This is an ideal tool to lay out all the details that need to happen before the big day.

We employed this technique in planning to build our new home and then managed the various aspects of the actual construction from the cards we created during the process. Whatever project you choose, we're sure you'll do a fast, yet remarkably thorough job of planning using this technique.

Brandy Hickok, Training Manager for ACME Industrial, said, "I was blown away by how fast we were able to design our speaking skills workshop. In little more than an hour, three of us had a detailed plan laid out. And this is now one of our most popular and highly regarded courses offered to our employees."

One of Brandy's colleagues reports, "I saw Brandy's eagle's view on her wall. I was curious, and she enthusiastically explained to me how the process works. I'm an engineer, and this methodology is wonderfully helpful to me now in our project planning and even innovative designs."

Summary

Planning with a group of people can be a difficult and tiring process. The panorama card planning technique breathes life into planning anything and easily increases a team's participation and contribution in the procedure. Developing an eagle's view in this fashion results in a plan born of collaboration such that real ownership is shared by the entire group, with no one left out. Individuals benefit as well using this technique to free one's mind to think creatively and to craft actionable plans to make extraordinary things happen.

In our next chapter, we share with you inviting and fun ways of getting work done. Games at work can be just what the doctor ordered.

CHAPTER 15

"Games lubricate the body and the mind."
—Ben Franklin, American statesman, diplomat, scientist, inventor

GAMES WORTH PLAYING
How to Design Games That
Improve Player Results

Outcomes for this chapter:
- Learn the essential elements of every game.
- Discover the do's and don'ts of successful game creation.
- Examine 15 design principles for profitable games.
- Understand how to promote a game and build momentum.

Coaches who know how to help their clients invent compelling games can be an invaluable resource. How can we improve our results? This question is forever on the minds of thoughtful executives, business owners, managers, supervisors, employees, and enthusiastic volunteers. A useful tool for improving any organization's results can be the introduction of a well-designed game.

It is well-known by accelerated learning aficionados that games can relieve tension, sharpen focus, and enhance learning. Similarly, games can enhance business results through fun and concentrated effort.

Sometimes a problem that an organization is experiencing can be resolved with a game. Or an opportunity might be capitalized upon with a game. Safety can be improved. Sales can be increased. Costs can be reduced. All are possible with well-conceived games. The trick is in the design, including the proper launch, of the new game. Let's examine some of the basics and some of the finer points of designing successful games.

But How Long, Spock? How Long?

Games have varied lengths of duration. Some games last from one quarter to a full year and are generally referred to as *campaigns*, while other games are short-term and may last anywhere from one day to one week to six weeks or even eight weeks.

But short-term games must not be the order of the day nor business as usual. Should they become such, the game will lose its burst of energy and action impact. Imagine a store where everything is always on sale. When customers recognize this, they stop being moved to action by the sale opportunity. The scarcity and novelty of the sale are lost and will not increase customer participation.

Build It and They Will Come. Or Will They?

How do you design a successful game? First, successful games always include the essential game ingredients, or elements, that are present in any game. Below are fundamental game elements:

- Players
- The object of the game
- Rules of the game
- Special materials (official scorecard, for example)
- Officials or referees
- Rewards for winning/playing according to the rules
- Penalties for breaking the rules
- Time limits: beginning, middle, end
- The possibility of winning or losing

Next, you can build a really great game by accident or by design. Here are design principles or guidelines that you can follow to create a game worth playing:

1. First, be clear about why you want to have a game and what you are trying to accomplish. Don't try to accomplish too much in one game. It will dilute people's focus and may add unwanted complexity.
2. Obtain buy-in from the players by having some of them help you design the game. The main advantage to this is that these players will own it and probably encourage their colleagues in playing full out.

3. When games are too complex, people tend to give up trying to play. And they may not tell you they have given up. They just give up and go about their work as usual. Then the game makes no positive difference and might even get in people's way. The game could just wind up being a nuisance.

If It Ain't Broke, Don't Fix It

For example, one company changed how it measured the salespeople's results at the beginning of a new year. The new scoring system was supposed to better reflect how well salespeople were doing for the company and themselves. But the new scoring system was so complex, hardly anyone understood it. Really! It was that ill-designed.

Furthermore, this was a 100-year-old company steeped in tradition and pride. The company's salespeople understood the old system perfectly, and no one had a problem with it. But someone somewhere in management had a good idea, proposed a better way to measure results, and sold it to the decision makers.

The salespeople in every office across the country used to eagerly await the monthly Scoreboard newsletter to be published. They wanted to see the rankings of each salesperson in the entire company. But after a couple of months, people stopped looking at the monthly Scoreboard newsletter. Why? Because it didn't mean anything to people anymore. People just couldn't relate to the new point system. They couldn't see inside the numbers anymore to see what kinds of things people were selling. Scoring stopped being a motivator. After a short while, salespeople just did what they did and hoped for the best.

Needless to say, the new scoring system was a complete failure and destroyed a long-standing and once motivating game.

Fortunately, there were enough salespeople and sales managers in the company who voiced their dissatisfaction to the executives who could do something about it. The following year the company went back to the old system. The salespeople were thrilled, and the motivational value of the monthly Scoreboard was revived instantly.

Looking Good

4. The game must be fun and attractive to the players.
   It must be a game that people can win and a game in which every-one has a chance to win. A player needs to be able to imagine her-self winning. The game should not give any person or group unfair advantage to begin with. The objective or goal cannot be so high or difficult to achieve that players consider it to be unat-tainable. This is debilitating rather than motivating. If the objec-tive is viewed as unattainable or people cannot imagine winning, they won't play They may not tell you, but they won't play.
5. Have the game be attractive by giving it a great name.
   Name the game well. Give it a name that inspires people or points to something players want to be a part of. For example, most peo-ple want to be associated with excellence. One of the best games we ever saw played out was one simply titled "Commitment to Excellence."

And sometimes people just want to beat the competition. One success-ful game in a high-tech industry was named "Get XYZ Company!" It got people's juices flowing in the right direction, and they accomplished some extraordinary results. The name of the game actually makes a difference.

"The difference between the right word and the almost right word is like the difference between the lightning and a lightning bug."
—Mark Twain, American writer, humorist, satirist, lecturer

Now, This I Can See

6. Players' results along the way should be visible to everyone. Ongoing results could be displayed at a central work location or on a website, or both. The players' results should be accurate and updated daily to stoke the fire and momentum. Design the display to be neat and lively, reflecting the importance of the objective and excitement of the game.

One vivid display we witnessed was a thermometer right in the lobby of the division's floor. You had to walk around it to get to the receptionist. It showed the total score each day. That division of a Fortune 100 company literally doubled its revenue that year with the game they devised.

7. The game should be in harmony with the organization's values and ethics. The game must be consistent with overarching goals of the company, its mission, and its values. Avoid games that may demean the industry or profession. These will backfire and cause damage. This isn't usually a problem, but it's a good thing to examine and then check off your design list. And, of course, the game ought to be lawful and not tempt people to break any laws in order to win.

He Ain't Heavy, He's My Game Plan

8. Designers should take care that games not become an administrative burden for the players. The game rules, for example, should not be so complex as to frustrate people. And results reporting should not be a difficult chore, either. Distributing personal, user-friendly scorecards can be helpful in this regard and also help keep the game visible.
9. Don't change the rules in the middle of a game. Unless you want to upset people, then by all means, change the rules midstream.

When Jed first started in the insurance business, his agency manager, Dave, announced a sales contest. Jed was young and eager and played the game in earnest. Furthermore, Jed greatly admired his manager and wanted to demonstrate to him that he had hired a winner.

Then one day during the month-long game, his manager laughingly announced at a staff meeting that he had changed the rules. Dave had a great sense of humor and thought changing the rules was funny. He said, "It makes the game more fun." The other older sales agents chortled along with Dave, but Jed saw no humor in it. He was furious about the rules change and told his manager so, privately.

"Don't take life so seriously, Jed. Lighten up, a little," Dave counseled. So Jed promised to himself that he wouldn't take his manager's sales games seriously anymore. Not exactly the result Dave intended with his sales game.

Uh-oh, There's a Fly in the Ointment

But what if you find out *during* the game that the rules don't work?

What if you found out there was a flaw in the game that made it unworkable or unfair? What if you discovered that you had launched a potential game disaster?

First of all, be extra thoughtful when designing the game and its rules so that this doesn't happen. Of course, that's no help once it has happened. But it's good to make the point here that games launched thoughtlessly can do more harm than good. Decide now to be careful and reflective in the design of your games.

> *"It is better to look ahead and prepare*
> *than to look back and regret."*
> —Jackie Joyner-Kersee, winner of three gold, one silver, and two bronze Olympic medals in track and field

If it appears that the rules are unworkable, make certain that this is actually the case; make sure that the rules really don't work. Sometimes the rules are workable, but a couple of vocal players don't like them and tell you, "These rules don't work." Not liking the rules is a lot different from unworkable rules. Investigate the situation thoroughly before you change the rules.

And then if the rules are in fact unworkable, one option is to cancel the game and find a way to take care of the people who were winning so that they are not left being upset. If you don't make sure they are satisfied, they will be, at best, reluctant to participate in future games. (And if you are certain you want to use some kind of game, you may want to wait a few days or weeks before you roll out a new one. If you can, wait until the dust settles.)

Another option is to call a meeting or schedule a conference call to explain the flaw you found in the rules to the players. Announce your proposed change, and get the players' feedforward. Give everyone a chance to communicate. They might even help you with a more workable solution. And if everyone is fine with the change, go ahead with the game.

10. Promote the game along the way. Don't launch a game and hope it floats in the right direction by itself. Help it along. Promote it. One way to continue to have the game well thought of is by promoting people's successes during the game. Posters, reminder e-

mails, Web postings, and meetings can all be opportunities for promotion. And the leading player in the game could also play the role of cheerleader and help promote the game that way.

Here is a checklist of things to do along the way to accelerate results and build or maintain momentum:

— Build in smaller wins/milestones. These can build momentum and rekindle enthusiasm when communicated properly.

— Post results/updates daily: website, e-mail, etc.

— Have multiple winners: It is valuable for everybody to win something just for playing. But have a minimum result that signals real playing.

— Provide peer acknowledgement in the moment to reinforce success and inspire others.

— Share with others important lessons someone learns in the process of the game in order to capture them. Utilize e-mail, website, or call a brief meeting or conference call.

— Be interested in how people are doing. Make impromptu calls to find out. Be interested in what people need and provide it, if appropriate. But don't play favorites. Take care of everybody!

Rah, Rah, Rah!

11. Have cheerleading happening along the way. And being a cheerleader doesn't have to look a particular way. You don't have to shout, jump up and down, and wave your arms. No one has to change her personality to encourage people.

Here is one of the best examples of low-key cheerleading that we've ever heard. This was a brief phone call from our friend's supervisor. It went like this: "Janice, how are you doing?" She proceeded to tell him. He listened and didn't interrupt. When Janice had finished communicating, he said, "Janice, do you need anything?" Janice said she didn't and he said, "Thank you for your good work, Janice. Good-bye." Janice got off the phone completely inspired and went back to work with renewed commitment and enthusiasm. A two-minute phone call. No hype, no jazz; just sincere concern and acknowledgment produced authentic inspiration and lift for Janice.

> *"No coach has ever won a game by what he knows;*
> *it's what his players know that counts."*
> —Paul "Bear" Bryant, American college football coach,
> won six national titles

12. Think about what you want to promote in your organization as a corollary to the game's main objective.
Games can be the kind where the focus is on individual performance. Or games can be designed with teams competing against one another, fostering cooperation, synergy, and teamwork. What do you want to promote? Is it teamwork or individual responsibility and performance? Or do you want to promote both? Perhaps you want to promote people sticking their necks out and taking risks?

> *"I've missed more than 9,000 shots in my career. I've lost almost 300*
> *games. 26 times, I've been trusted to take the game-winning shot and*
> *missed. I've failed over and over and over again in my life.*
> *And that is why I succeed."*
> —Michael Jordan, American NBA basketball player, widely considered
> the best to have ever played the game.

13. Make the prizes or awards something that the majority of players will really want. Sometimes it's time off more than money that is desired. Close the office for two days when the goal is reached. Sometimes it's prizes that people would appreciate but might not buy for themselves. You may want to do a little research among your players before you decide. We've seen the prizes at the end of a game range from a bonus, a celebration meeting with dinner and awards, or a gift card to the winner's favorite restaurant. Depending on the scope of the game, the acknowledgment can range from one end of the spectrum to the other.

No Sweat, Coach

14. Avoid having the awards be too easy to win or having the awards too generous for too little results. Believe it or not, people really

do want to be challenged. And winning isn't winning if it didn't arouse competition and turn on people's jets. If winners experience it as a cakewalk, they won't feel like winners. People want to feel like winners.

"Talent wins games, but teamwork and intelligence win championships."
—Michael Jordan

15. Mark the end of the game with some kind of acknowledgment meeting or celebration. The celebration follows quickly behind the completion of the game. If you finish the game early, move up the celebration date and perhaps launch a new game.

Make it a big deal! Make the winners feel like winners. Bring all the players together somehow to acknowledge and celebrate the wins and underline what people learned in the process of playing the game.

"If anything goes bad, I did it. If anything goes semi-good, we did it. If anything goes really good, then you did it. That's all it takes to get people to win football games for you."
—Paul "Bear" Bryant

Do make sure the results for the game are clearly communicated to everyone in the organization. Otherwise, the next time you try to implement a game, you will be doing it over the top of people being incomplete about the last one.

A cost-reduction game was once launched and promoted in a company at its weekly staff meeting. Cash prizes would be awarded to people who submitted the best cost-saving ideas. But the game didn't have an announced end; no winners were ever announced, and it just sort of drifted away and disappeared. Months later a new kind of game was announced at the same weekly staff meeting. As the speaker outlined the game from the podium, several people seated in the audience began whispering to one another. Being sensitive to the group, she noticed this and asked, "What are you all talking about?"

"What ever happened to the cost-saving game?" one of them answered. Until the previous game was complete for people, there could be no fresh listening for a new game.

"Individual commitment to a group effort—that is what makes a team work, a company work, a society work, a civilization work."
—Vince Lombardi

A New Metric and a New Game

One of our clients, a copper smelter in New Mexico, had the worst safety record of any of this global company's sites anywhere. And it had been this way for 15 years. Cheryl Ducros, the new plant manager, asked us to help her assemble a safety team and coach them to quickly and dramatically improve safety.

First, we coached this new, eight-person team to write a charter with measurable results to be achieved within a specific time frame. Led by Manny Hidalgo, the plant's safety manager, the team chose zero accidents within the year. This was doable as it was now January and there had been no accidents yet. But taking their 500-employee plant from the worst safety record in the company to possibly the best would be an enormous task and require a cultural shift. Nevertheless, they were all absolutely committed to it.

"You know, the way we measure safety, loss-time accidents, is all after the fact," team member Patsy Ann Wilson, metallurgical engineer, said. "We need to get ahead of the game." And get ahead of the game they did. They created a new game: Near Misses.

Near misses was the metric the team invented to help prevent accidents. Every employee in the plant was invited to find, record, and submit any unsafe condition or "almost accident." The safety team made a game of it by setting their own target each month.

"We made it up," team member Buck Rivers said. "We didn't know how our people would respond, so the first month of the game we just picked the number, 25. Well, we hit 35! So the next month we set the bar at 50, and we hit 65. This was working—we could feel it and hear the water cooler conversations about it here and there in the plant."

The team arranged for an electronic sign to be placed in the most central and visible location of the plant. It had the number of near misses submitted for the current month, the target, and the company's up-to-the-minute stock price traveling across it brightly 24/7.

Employees began to feel that they could personally make a difference with safety, whereas they felt a bit helpless about it before. "I could manage me, you know, wear my safety gear, be careful, and maybe watch out for the guy next to me. But what difference was I gonna make with the other 498 of us?" Eduardo Rodriguez shared. "But by catching near misses, I saw that I could make a difference for everybody. And when I'd pass by the reader board and see how far off we were from our target, I would immediately start looking for a near miss to help us win the game."

The smelter won the Chairman's Safety Trophy that year by recording the best safety record in the company-from worst to first. The chairman visited the New Mexico smelter and rewarded the 500 employees and their families with an all-day picnic. As he walked around meeting the workers and their families, he heard the story of the game and 698 near misses that resulted in zero loss-time accidents for the year.

Summary

Well-designed games can be an effective vehicle for enhancing an organization's results quickly. Poorly designed games can backfire and harm the organization's results and even lower morale. So if you are going to employ a game, be very thoughtful in your design and avoid the pitfalls.

Good luck, and have a great game!

In our next chapter, learn how to be disorganized, guilt-free!

CHAPTER 16

"Until you value yourself, you won't value your time. Until you value your time, you will not do anything with it."
—M. Scott Peck

HOW TO BE DISORGANIZED, GUILT-FREE

Outcomes for this chapter:
- Discover the source of the nagging thoughts that can have you and your players feeling disorganized.
- Understand how to claim power in the face of chaos for yourself and your players.
- Learn new tools to coach your player into increased productivity.
- Complete the Eagle's View Inventory: A self-assessment to help you become more productive.

What's All the Rush About?
Take Time to Smell the Roses

Do you ever feel harried and rushed, nagged by the thought that no matter how much you've organized, how well you've prepared, something has still been left out? Do you have the sense that, in spite of your best efforts, you just can't get a grasp on all aspects of life-there's always something left to do? Do feelings of guilt, possible failure, or even impending doom drain you of all the energy you once had and leave you wondering what all this work is really for?

In our calmer moments, most of us recognize that we *have* accomplished a good deal, that in general our goals are being reached, that the chaos before us is just evidence of the many projects that are moving forward on different fronts at the same time. None of these thoughts brings much comfort for long. After all, everyone knows that a person who's *really* efficient, productive, and successful doesn't face massive chaos and disorganization. The people we really admire always complete their to-do lists, never leave loose ends dangling, and move confidently through a morass of competing priorities (work, community, and family life) with never a hint of distraction, frustration, or mental disarray. What, then, is keeping us from being the way we know we can be?

Did You Say Fantasy Island?

We have encountered thousands of people who have a very clear picture about how things should be. On an airplane, having just led our time-transformation course, Eagle's View, it dawned on us: All the conversations that people have with themselves when chaos seems to seize the upper hand are strange when you really look at them. We suddenly realized the problem: None of those conversations had any bearing on reality. They were, in fact, fantasies that we carried around with us virtually all the time—fantasies based on a picture of how life should be but never, ever is in the real, twenty-first century world. However, we saw a benefit in writing these down. Maybe some of these will sound familiar to you:

1. **Things should always go as planned.** Another way of saying this is that nothing should ever go wrong. If only things went the way they were supposed to go, my time-management system would work perfectly and everything would be just fine.
2. **When I accomplish x, it will solve all life's problems.** Someday, of course, I will manage to accomplish x, no doubt with heroic effort and brilliant organization. From that time on, I won't have problems anymore.
3. **I should never have too much to do.** I should always have just the right amount to do in the time I have available. If my to-dos take more time than I have available, whoever made up all those tasks was cruel, stupid, and unfair. Even if it was me.
4. **I should live a balanced life.** I should always have a perfect balance of work, play, and family life. I should never spend too much time in any one area. Life should always be balanced.

5. **I should always have what I want when I want it.** That's what being successful means, right?

6. **I should never feel pressured.** Oh, really?

7. **I should never make mistakes, and no one else should, either.** If I do make a mistake, I'm a bad person and probably incapable of achieving whatever I was trying to do. If someone else makes a mistake in something that affects me, he should disappear forever.

8. **I should never have to fix things.** The people who make things should make them to last forever.

9. **Life should have no interruptions.** I deserve a continual, unbroken cycle of productivity and bliss.

10. **Nothing should ever wear out.** This includes, especially, human beings. Youth, health, and vitality are our birthright forever.

11. **I should have plenty of time for everything I want to do, especially in this electronic-driven world.** See #3, above. If I weren't wasting time doing all those things I didn't want to do, I'd have time for the really important things in life.

Right about this time, we began to sound a bit like petulant 2-year-olds (or power-mad executives, we weren't quite sure which). But this was getting to be almost fun, so we continued:

12. **I should finish everything I start.** If there's a chance it won't get done in the time I have available, I probably shouldn't start it in the first place

13. **I should never fail at anything.** Failure is bad and to be avoided at all costs. If I fail at one thing, I'll probably fail at other things too, so it's best just to take on those projects that can't possibly go wrong. Projects I've already done a hundred times before are best.

14. **The things I have to do should always be enjoyable.** If I'm not having a good time, I'm probably not doing what I'm meant to be doing. Therefore, I won't succeed. So I should abandon anything that feels unpleasant and go to the beach.

15. **The things I have to do should never be difficult.** Related to the above: If it is too difficult, it wasn't meant for me and isn't worth the effort. *This* must be a task for someone who finds these things easy. Back to the beach!

16. **I shouldn't have to put in extra hours on anything.** Extra hours are not part of the deal. My job is to do only the things that fit into an eight-hour day.

At this point we thought we were getting a bit exhausted, and we thought we were finished … till we noticed the next conversation:

17. **I should never be tired.** Being tired is a sure sign of doing too much work that is too difficult or unpleasant. Fatigue, like failure, is a very bad thing.
18. **My in-basket should always be empty.** Even if I spent all my time accomplishing all those wonderful goals, I'd still have stuff piling up on my desk, and I'd still be behind. No fair.
19. **Everything should always be put away in its place, and nothing should ever be cluttered.** Isn't that the way your mother taught you? And isn't that the way your house always was as a child?
20. **I should always be totally organized.** The ultimate: It doesn't matter how much you accomplish and how well you do it, if you leave a trail of clutter and chaos, you didn't really succeed.

By this point, these conversations began to sound a bit silly, if not downright destructive. Yet we'd venture to say that at least a couple of these—or some variant of them-sound familiar to you as well. We like to call these the 20 Popular Unrealizable Fantasies about life and time. You might want to experiment with them and come up with variations or fantasies of your own.

These unspoken attitudes shape our entire relationship to ourselves and our productivity—preventing a real celebration of what is complete, and limiting our prospects for the future and how far we are likely to go. We like to refer to these statements, even the negative ones, as fantasies. Stated in this way, using *always* and *never*, they cannot be fulfilled. Life will simply not look the way you think it should all of the time. You're not going to be totally organized, things will be difficult and will wear out, people (including yourself) will make mistakes, and the most predictable thing about life is that it won't turn out just the way you've planned every time. Yet despite the impossible ideal they portray, each of us compares our actual life to the fantasies we've inherited or constructed and grow upset—usually with ourselves—when the two don't match. Somewhere, somehow, we've come up with the notion that life should be the way we think it should be. Someone, somewhere must have it really together, and those are the people we long to be.

Pour On The Guilt!
Arrrghh ... What Those Fantasies Can Do

"Sanity may be madness but the maddest of all is to see life as it is and not as it should be."
—Don Quixote

That first sense of being inadequate or at fault is where the guilt begins. After all, if your ideal says your in-basket or e-mail should always be empty, and it's now overflowing, you know you're doing something wrong. If you firmly believe you should never feel pressured, but you do-probably by people to whom you have a real sense of commitment—you're sure you don't measure up. In short, for most of us, every hour of the day could present a new confirmation of our own failings, and it reinforces our view that things aren't the way they should be; that fundamentally, life doesn't work.

Psychiatrists are familiar with a mental disorder in which the patient is compelled to keep everything in perfect order. These patients do not experience freedom, confidence, and a sense of being in charge of life-on the contrary, their lives are dominated by a fruitless quest to make, and keep, everything exactly the way it should be. While most of us don't go to such extremes, we can all relate to the sense of being run by our own compulsions to make life conform to the way it should be.

There is a certain freedom, however, in giving words to these once unspoken views and recognizing them as fantasies, nothing more. For decades we've been working with people on enhancing their own effectiveness, despite the chaos that often prevails. During that time, hundreds of people have told us that they experience a release, an unburdening, a sense of lightening up by simply acknowledging these ideals for what they are: unrealizable fantasies. Of course, we're not advocating that people should be disorganized or not care about managing their lives. What we do suggest is that for most people, the source of feeling disorganized, guilty, and upset comes not from what they are or are not doing, but from the unrealizable fantasies that continue to play in the background, invalidating all they do and inhibiting action toward future goals.

We're All for Organizing!

In fact, we strongly advocate organization; we find being organized is extraordinarily helpful in getting things done and relieving stress. But let's face it, none of us is wholly in charge of all aspects of our lives. Inevitably, we encounter circumstances, issues, and events that defy our best efforts at prediction and control. It is those situations that help us gain a new perspective on time and manage it in a way that inspires and motivates us, rather than presenting new obstacles to action.

We've discovered that the best organizing tool is one that works the way our minds work—creatively and chaotically—rather than organized around a particular system or structure for the way it should be. To build their own structures, we encourage people to draw an eagle's view of their life to see what does and doesn't work for them right now.

In fact, we've found that, for most people, keeping their focus on what works now, today, is more practical and more useful than designing systems around an ideal, or prospective, view of their lives. If your family life presents limitations on the way you work right now, why design structures for the life you hope you'll have when the kids are grown? If your greatest satisfaction is in learning and growth, why design your days to keep constantly moving, with no time to step back and reflect on what you've noticed or what you might have learned? When we shift our view from *what life should be to what's possible and available right now*, opportunities emerge that we couldn't see before-and at the same time, the guilt over not getting it right loses its grip.

We often find it useful to give ourselves permission to abandon a project that we are no longer working on, are not planning to work on, and are not realistically going to complete. Time—in some cases, years—is wasted in anxiety or worry over obligations to which we are no longer committed. This is in no way a justification for giving up on real commitments or simply walking away from challenging situations. However, we are all familiar with to-do lists that hold on to items that we have no intention of carrying out. Often, releasing ourselves from those fantasy commitments not only provides the relief that comes with telling the truth, but frees up energy and enthusiasm for commitments that we can and will fulfill.

It's Time to Celebrate

Another key to mastering our own chaos is the ability to acknowledge and appreciate what has been achieved. For the most part, we're so busy trying to do the right things that what is getting accomplished goes uncelebrated and even unobserved. By taking note of what has gotten done, even of the smallest milestones along the way—and by actually voicing these to someone other than ourselves—we are often able to complete the past, set it firmly behind us, and move forward with the new momentum that our real accomplishments provide. In doing so, we gain a fresh perspective about how we're doing en route to fulfilling our long-term goals; a new view not only of what's done, but of what isn't. By acknowledging our accomplishments and the things that we didn't accomplish, we're somehow freed up to move to the next thing without taking unnecessary baggage with us. We're left with continuing to do what works and improve upon what didn't work.

Try this on: Make a list of all that you've accomplished this past week. When the list is as complete as you can get it, find someone who is willing to listen. Read the list out loud to that person, and see how you feel.

We propose that you, too, can be even more productive when you allow yourself to be disorganized, guilt-free.

The Eagle's View Inventory
Assessing Your Use of Time

"Dig the well before you are thirsty."
—Chinese Proverb

The Eagle's View Inventory is an insightful tool to use to get a handle on the controls of how you spend your time. If you're a coach, this is one of those tools to help you and your player get to critical areas of coaching to improve productivity as well as efficiencies.

How to Complete the Eagle's View Inventory

1. Set aside a block of time, 20 to 30 minutes, to complete the inventory. You will be judging your experience of yourself or your sense of yourself; i.e., how you view yourself in each of 25 questions.

2. Rate yourself on a scale of 0 to 10 for each of the 25 questions. If you rate yourself less than 10, note why in the gap (see the sample on the next page). We suggest that you use whole-numbered ratings.

3. After you have completed all 25 questions, total your score and divide by 2.5. This will give you a numerical score relative to a percentage score on a 100 percent scale. For example, a perfect score of 250 (a score of 10 for each of 25 questions) divided by 2.5 would be 100.

4. Review each question in your inventory, and note what you intend to improve. You might want to make plans to accomplish these improvements and record them or share them with your coach.

5. Plot your score for each question on the Progress Graph that follows the inventory questions, and note the date and total score for this inventory.

6. We recommend that you retake this inventory in two weeks to measure your improvement.

Note: You apply your own personal standards when completing this inventory; therefore, your scores are not objectively comparable with others' scores.

SAMPLE

5. DELEGATION:

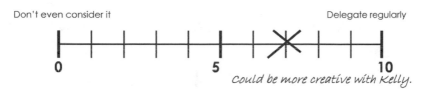

6. DAILY PLANNING & REFLECTION:

7. ABILITY TO GENERATE
   EXTRA TIME:

8. UTILIZATION OF OUTSIDE RESOURCES:

Figure 16.1

Eagle's View® Inventory

NAME_____ DATE ____ / ____ / ____

1. YOUR EXPERIENCE FOR BEING ORGANIZED FOR EFFECTIVE ACTION:

Not organized at all   Well organized

0   5   10

2. YOUR EXPRIENCE OF GUILT ABOUT NOT BEING ORGANIZED OR NOT GETTING DONE WHAT YOU SHOULD GET DONE:

Enormous guilt   No guilt whatsoever

0   5   10

3. YOUR EXPERIENCE OF GENERATING YOUR LIFE VERSUS REACTING TO LIFE:

Reacting totally   High frequency of generating

0   5   10

4. VELOCITY OF TRANSLATING INTENTIONS INTO ACCOMPLISHMENT:

Rarely happens   Happens when I say so

0   5   10

Figure 16.2

5. DELEGATION:

Don't even consider it   Delegate regularly

0   5   10

6. DAILY PLANNING & REFLECTION:

Rarely do it (or   I daily plan & reflect
do it to excess)

0   5   10

7. ABILITY TO GENERATE EXTRA TIME:

Weak   Highly Creative

0   5   10

8. UTILIZATION OF OUTSIDE RESOURCES:

Outside resources   Resources beyond myself
ignored   used creatively

0   5   10

9. WORK ENVIRONMENT:

Unsupportive   Extremely supportive

0   5   10

10. HOME ENVIRONMENT:

Unsupportive   Extremely supportive

0   5   10

11. PROJECT PLANNING:

Poor Planning (if any)   Highly workable plans

0   5   10

12. PROJECT MANAGEMENT:

Don't follow plans   Do what I plan

0   5   10

13. PLANNING FROM THE WHOLE OF YOUR LIFE

Planning restricted to   I plan daily from the
isolated area(s) of life   whole of my life

0   5   10

14. YOUR EXPERIENCE OF PUTTING THINGS OFF
THAT YOU KNOW YOU SHOULDN'T:

Too frequent an occurrence   Rarely happens

0   5   10

15. BEING "IN TOUCH" (IN COMMUNICATION) WITH PEOPLE:

Out of communication

In communication

0   5   10

16. AMOUNT OF PERSONAL TIME YOU HAVE:

Insufficient

Sufficient

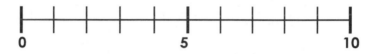

0   5   10

17. ACKNOWLEDGING (THANKING, APPRECIATING) OTHERS:

Rarely do it

Regularly

0   5   10

18. MAKING REQUESTS OF OTHERS:

Rarely do this

Regularly

0   5   10

19. KEEPING YOUR WORD
(DOING WHAT YOU SAY YOU'LL DO BY WHEN YOU SAY YOU'LL DO IT):

Low integrity

High integrity

0   5   10

20. YOUR EXPERIENCE OF FUN IN ACCOMPLISHMENT:

No fun   Lots of fun

0   5   10

21. COMPLETING THE THINGS YOU START:

Way too many   Projects rarely stall or
incompletions   incomplete for long

0   5   10

22. SIGNIFICANT, DIFFERENCE-MAKING PROJECTS OR TASKS:

Just can't seem to   Jump right in and
get started   keep on going

0   5   10

23. YOUR EXPERIENCE OF SUFFICIENT ENERGY TO MEET COMMITMENTS:

Tired and listless   Eager, alive and
                                                       ready to go

0   5   10

24. CELEBRATING COMPLETIONS AND ACCOMPLISHMENT:

What's that?   Celebrate often

0   5   10

25. INSPIRED ABOUT YOUR FUTURE:

Going thru the motions   Inspired future,
(or pessimistic)   optimistic

0   5   10

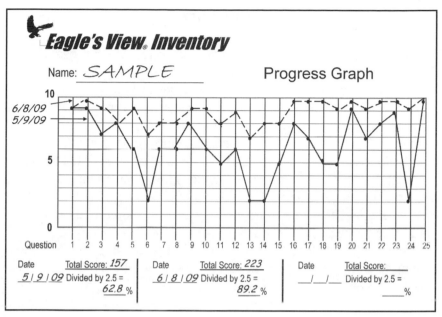

Figure 16.3

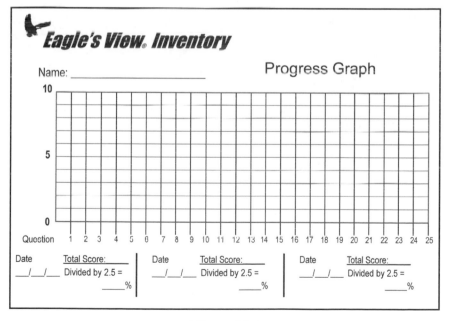

Figure 16.4

Summary

When the unrealizable fantasies are uncovered, we can begin to see how we paint our destiny of being guilty about being disorganized. Of course, when we use terms such as never, always, and should never, it puts us in a powerless position of being unable to accomplish whatever it is that we've made an impossibility. When we confront how we speak and recognize the labels that we've attached to our thinking, only then are we able to do something about them. The unrealizable fantasies help us to see the obstacles that we've unconsciously designed, relieve some of the guilt associated with those obstacles, and allow us to move forward.

The Eagle's View Inventory helps you to focus on areas that could improve efficiencies and productivity.

Next, we will explore ways of communicating the value of coaching to our players and prospective clients. For persons who have not yet been coached successfully in a business or organizational context, the value of the coach is not readily clear. It is part of our job as coaches to present to these people our incomparable value so that they may take advantage of it.

CHAPTER 17

"Don't go to the fishpond without a net."
—Japanese Proverb

THE VALUE OF THE COACH

Outcomes for this chapter:
- Gain a tool to help you describe the many possible benefits of being coached.
- Learn how to more easily enroll new clients.
- Discover the Paradoxical Commandments of Leadership.

There is no doubt that countless coaches have been of extraordinary value to their clients. Coaching is a growing industry, no longer in its infancy. However, at this point in time, the number of people in the world who have a complete grasp of the value that coaches may bring to their clients are in the minority. Toward the education of those who are unaware of its construct and worth, we have found the following list to be an important tool.

The Value of the Coach

A Strategic-Thinking Partner
- Helps you to visualize creative future scenarios
- Assists you to think beyond the constraints of what you already know and design new ways forward
- Aids in transforming dreams into commitments, enthusiasm, and results
- Facilitates the creation of plans grounded in reality
- Helps you set realizable goals and objectives, and provides feed-forward in their attainment
- Enables you to get an eagle's view of your endeavors and focus

on high-value actions versus low-value activities, thus eliminating wasted energy

You Are Not Alone
- Provides fresh perspectives and objective observations
- Helps you evaluate new opportunities and handle challenges to transform apparent obstacles into creative ways forward
- Regular dialogue and attention to working on your business, not just in your business
- Supplies experienced brainstorming for significant decisions
- A partner without the downside of a partnership
- A nonjudgmental sounding board
- A partner as committed to your success as you are

A Resource
- Experience and a resource to new ideas, insights, proven approaches, solutions, and help
- Supplies attention and momentum to projects that would otherwise never begin
- Someone with whom to collaborate, invent, and discover
- A source of new networks and alliances to expand your reach

In the initial, or enrollment, stage, The Value of the Coach serves as a useful device to help the potential client envision how we might be of assistance to her. For example, when meeting with a prospective player in our office or over coffee, we pull out this little gem, The Value of the Coach, usually early on in the conversation.

It serves as the basis for our value proposition, an important ingredient in enrolling any new customer. We have found that the checklist helps our potential clients think of specific ways in which we might help them. As they read it, they invariably begin to share about their own situation, ask questions, and comment favorably about some of the items listed.

What Do You Take in Your Coffee?
What Would You Like in Your Coaching?

Helena Russell, an owner-manager of two ladies fashions boutiques, and Germaine met at Starbucks to discuss the possibility of coaching for

Helena. As Helena began to read The Value of the Coach, she began to speak animatedly. "Oh, this one here, 'assists you in thinking beyond constraints,' I could really use some help with that. I like the term 'strategic-thinking partner' too. And this one … number, hmmmm, you should number these, you know … this one, 'fresh perspectives and objective observations.' Germaine, I can't get my people to bring me new ideas. They think I should have all the answers already." Helena continued to enroll herself in the possible benefits of coaching as Germaine made notes.

A Fair Question

In our coaching training programs, even with experienced coaches, we find all too often that coaches cannot clearly articulate their value proposition. We are not referring to a quick, 20-second elevator speech here (which is almost always missing as well). By value proposition we mean the many benefits that you can offer your clients to help them meet their particular objectives. What value can you bring to the client in her world? What can you provide that she cannot or will not provide for herself?

It always amazes us when we hear coaches complain about not being able to enroll new clients. Yet most of them have no clue where to start when we ask them to describe the value they could be to a new client.

During one of our coach training sessions, we asked Annabelle, an experienced coach with seven clients, "Why should I hire you to be my coach?" A fair question, don't you think?

Germaine: So, why should I hire you to be my coach?

Annabelle: Well, uh … maybe you have some goals that you aren't achieving, and, uh, I could help you with that.

Germaine: How?

Annabelle: Well, uh, I don't know, what aren't you doing about them?

Germaine: Excuse me?

Annabelle: Well, what's not happening? You know.

Germaine: No, I don't know. What are you talking about?

Annabelle: Okay. What are your life goals? Uh, what are your secret dreams?

Germaine: Hold on, I think you are getting a little too personal a little too fast.

Now ask a software salesperson what she can do for you. In our experience, she can tell you. At least she can give you a smorgasbord of possibilities pretty quickly. Ask a life insurance sales professional what he can do for you and your family. He can tell you. He can probably rattle off benefit after benefit after benefit. But ask the average coach what she can do for you, and she isn't always so sure.

Granted, to know exactly how you can help a particular person, you need to ask some questions. But we aren't talking about that. We're talking about a value proposition—a statement or list of possible benefits you could offer your client; a compelling catalogue of possible advantages that a player could have by contracting a coach. Don't you find that sometimes you have to earn the right to ask the questions you need to ask to tell someone how you might specifically be of benefit to him?

As coaches, we can forget that the average person isn't clear about the benefits of coaching. Whether we are in the process of enrolling new clients or simply explaining the value of coaching to the uninformed, we ought to be prepared to give our best. The Value of the Coach checklist has proven to be a useful tool to help us be successful in this effort.

May We Coach You?

If you are a coach, we invite you to create your value proposition and be certain about the benefits you can bring before you offer coaching to anyone. It can save you a lot of bobbing and weaving, but more importantly, it can help you to contract a new client for whom you could really make a difference.

> *"You cannot catch a trout by standing on the river bank, shouting at it and telling it what a great fisherman you are. You need a hook with bright colored feathers on it and you have to cast it into the water."*
> —Michael A. Tate, author, *Design a Life That Works*

Coaching Paradoxes

Coaching is a world of paradoxes: The less you talk, the more players learn from you; the more you listen to your player, the more he listens to you; the more you tell a player how things work, the less she learns how things work. The list is probably endless.

In 1992, Germaine and Jed were presented with a beautiful document by Jim Snow, one of the participants of a coaching workshop we had been facilitating. He was one of a group of 20 plant supervisors in the Johns Manville fiberglass plant in Winder, Georgia. John, the plant manager, had asked us to teach his supervisors how to effectively lead and coach their crews to produce extraordinary results.

During a break, "Big Jim" told us that he was a Boy Scout Scoutmaster and that a lot of what we had been talking about reminded him of a document he was given at a Boy Scout conference. Jim proudly gave us a copy of that document, which we have treasured ever since. Jim said he tucked it into his Scoutmaster manual and that he referred to it often.

What follows is a re-creation of the document Jim shared with us. It is our privilege to share it with you here. We have passed it on broadly and widely for years to the people we have trained to be coaches. We suspect that you will agree that these paradoxical commandments are just as applicable to coaching as they are to leadership.

Paradoxical Commandments
by Dr. Kent M. Keith, author

People are illogical, unreasonable, and self-centered.
Love them anyway.

If you do good, people will accuse you of selfish ulterior motives.
Do good anyway.

If you are successful, you will win false friends and true enemies.
Succeed anyway.

The good you do today will be forgotten tomorrow.
Do good anyway.

Honesty and frankness make you vulnerable.
Be honest and frank anyway.

The biggest men and women with the biggest ideas can be shot down
by the smallest men and women with the smallest minds.
Think big anyway.

People favor underdogs but follow only top dogs.
Fight for a few underdogs anyway.

What you spend years building may be destroyed overnight.
Build anyway.

People really need help but may attack you if you do help them.
Help people anyway.

Give the world the best you have and you'll get kicked in the teeth.
Give the world the best you have anyway.

© Copyright Kent M. Keith 1968, renewed 2001

"Our deepest fear is not that we are inadequate. Our deepest fear is that we are powerful beyond measure. It is our light, not our darkness that most frightens us Who am I to be brilliant, gorgeous, talented, fabulous? Actually, who are you not to be? You are a child of God. Your playing small does not serve the world. There is nothing enlightened about shrinking so that other people won't feel insecure around you. We are all meant to shine, as children do. We were born to make manifest the glory of God that is within us. It's not just in some of us; it's in everyone. And as we let our own light shine, we unconsciously give other people permission to do the same. As we are liberated from our own fear, our presence automatically liberates others."
—Marianne Williamson

GUTSY COACHING MOMENTS

Outcomes for this chapter:

- Discover the coachable moment and its potential impact.
- Showcase the incomparable value of storytelling as a coaching tool.
- Share a compilation of gutsy coaching moments contributed by some of our readers.

Coaches hail from a wide variety of backgrounds. And anyone who coaches for a living knows how far back in our experiences we sometimes reach to bring forward new perspectives for our clients. Your mothers, fathers, sisters, and brothers may have been some of your best coaches. Ours certainly were. And over the years we've been blessed with many other superb coaches: sports coaches, teammates, friends, bosses, peers, clients, authors, our heroes, role models, and the list goes on. Some of the best coaches didn't always call themselves coaches.

One of our discoveries that made an unmistakable difference in our coaching practice is that there are *coachable moments*: occasions when we all can contribute to someone. These are moments when we have the opportunity to coach, whether or not we are a professional coach. Sometimes we pass them up, or maybe we don't even recognize them. These coachable moments might occur in the kitchen, by the water cooler, or in your SUV while driving to the hockey game.

An Unexpected Coachable Moment

It was June—a hot summer day by Seattle standards—80 degrees Fahrenheit. Jed had recently graduated from high school and was working construction to help pay for college. This was his first day on the job. Today Jed would learn something about who his father was from an unexpected source. He would learn lessons in leadership, management, mentoring, and coaching.

Jed was part of a Mid-Mountain Inc. seven-man crew laying natural gas pipelines for Washington Natural Gas. He was a laborer, digging ditches and running the jackhammer. His father, Edward Niederer Jr., was senior vice president of Cascade Natural Gas Corporation. Ed would occasionally contract Mid-Mountain to help build Cascade's distribution systems outside the Seattle district.

Sitting in the shade of the welding truck, Jed was having lunch with Jake, the crew's welder.

Who's Your Daddy?

As they finished their lunches, Jake said, "Your last name ... I recognize it. Your father wouldn't be Ed Niederer?"

"Yeah, that's right," Jed replied, rolling up his brown paper lunch sack.

"I know your father," Jake said, as he wiped his face with a paper towel. "Our crew was short-handed the day I met your dad," Jake went on. "He had come by to check out the job, I guess. We were trying to line up a couple of pieces of sixteen-inch pipe so that we could weld them together. It was mighty slippery in that ditch—mud from all the rain—and it was still coming down, and the ditch was filling up with water," Jake said as he looked down the road strewn with similar pipe.

"Your dad saw that we could use a hand. Without a word he just took off his jacket, rolled up his sleeves, and jumped down into all that mud and water with us. Then he put his shoulder on a pipe so that we could weld it to the other one."

Then Jake looked Jed in the eye and said evenly, "I'd never seen an executive do anything like that before." Then he glanced down and kicked the dust with his boot. Jed just stared at Jake, trying to think of an intelligent response. "You didn't know that about your dad, did you?" Jake said laughing a little. "Well, enough of this jabberin'. Come on, we got some pipe to lay."

Jake's story had an impact on Jed. He learned many things that day, not the least of which was that to lead well, you shouldn't be above putting your own shoulder to the grindstone, right alongside the people who work for you. Jake's story also taught him that one's reputation could be built on a single incident, one single moment. He found that people retelling stories built reputations and taught valuable lessons. A person's name or standing in the community could be formed by memorable moments, not years. Every action counted, and people were watching your every move—even the moves of an 18-year-old kid.

Fast-Forward

Now, fast-forward 22 years later. Jed was now a management consultant and coach. On a flight to Seattle from Houston, he was telling his new bride the Jake story while they were on their way to visit Jed's family. Germaine said enthusiastically, "What a great story, Jed! What did your father say when you told him about it?" Well, Jed had to confess that he hadn't ever told Ed about it.

Germaine said, "You're kidding. What is this—a guy thing? You don't share stuff? Don't you think he would appreciate knowing?" So Jed promised Germaine he would tell him during this visit.

A Moment of Appreciation

Late one evening in his parents' den, Jed was alone with his dad, amidst golf trophies, bowling trophies, and business achievement plaques that his father and mother had garnered over the years. It was the perfect opportunity to tell his father Jake's story, and he did. But Ed didn't seem nearly as pleased as Jed had imagined he would be. Glancing away from the TV late-night news, Ed responded with an almost smile and a low, pensive, "hmmmm." Looking at the TV screen, Ed said, "How about those Sonics! Boy, your mother sure loves watching them play."

So much for trying to show my dad some appreciation, Jed thought. Well, at least I kept my promise to Germaine.

The Coachable Moment
An Opportunity to Contribute

The next morning, Jed's father drove him to the airport to fly home. Germaine had gone ahead of him to see one of her clients.

As they rode toward downtown Seattle on Interstate 5, Jed's dad said, "You know that story you told me last night?" "Well, that story reminded me of a story about my father, your grandfather." Jed's grandfather had been a superintendent in the natural gas business in Philadelphia, Pennsylvania. He had met his "Grandy" only once before he died when Jed was seven.

Ed continued, "When I was a little boy, eight I think, your grandfather took me with him one Saturday to look at a pipeline job. I loved going out to visit work sites with my dad. It was a hot, humid summer afternoon. Everyone was moving pretty slowly, everyone except one ditch digger, Mr. Flannigan. Mr. Flannigan came bounding up to your granddad and me when we got out of our car. He was very animated and excited about something. It turned out that he was complaining about a co-worker.

Mr. Flannigan blurted, 'That Italian guy over there isn't pulling his weight. He's moving too slow, Mr. Niederer. He's just lazy!'

Your grandfather glanced over into the ditch where the other fellow was shoveling. He watched him dig for a long moment. Then he called to the man, 'Would you come over here for a minute, Mr. Bonasera?' The man laid down his shovel, popped out of the ditch like he had springs on his feet, and ran over to where my dad and I were standing. He and his family had recently moved to America from Palermo, Sicily."

Dig This

"'Yes sir, Mr. Niederer?' Mr. Bonsera asked. My father said, 'Mr. Bonsera, how would you like to try to make a little extra money?' 'Oh yes sir, Mr. Niederer, yes sir. I would like to do this very much,' Bonsera said, grinning. He spoke with a heavy Italian accent. 'How about you, Mr. Flannigan?' Mr. Flannigan replied quizzically, 'Well, yes, of course I would, Mr. Niederer. But how?'

"'Good. Let's have a little contest then,' said your granddad. 'I'll pay twenty-five cents to the man who can dig the farthest distance in the next two hours.'

"Then your granddad led the two men out to the ditch line. Back then, everything was dug by hand with a shovel, leapfrog style, one ditch digger out in front of the other. Eventually the trailing digger would catch up to the lead digger and punch through the back of the lead man's ditch.

"So your granddad positioned the two laborers far enough apart so that the trailer wouldn't catch the leader in two hours. 'Okay, go to it, gentlemen, and I'll be back around four o'clock.' They began to dig, and we walked to the car to go inspect other jobs."

Money Isn't Everything

"When we came back, Mr. Bonasera was still digging ... and smiling. He had dug half again as far as Flannigan, who was now sitting under a shade tree, exhausted. Your grandfather walked toward the man under the tree. We surprised Mr. Flannigan and he rose to his feet quickly. Your grandfather, looking at the two ditches said, 'Looks like Mr. Bonasera is a pretty good hand after all, eh, Mr. Flannigan?' The man nodded wearily, staring at Bonsera who continued to dig.

"'You know, that Italian fellow doesn't speak very good English does he?' Mr. Flannigan looked at your granddad and then at the ground and nodded slightly. 'And you've been thinking he's a little stupid because he doesn't speak quite right.' Now Mr. Flannigan looked up from the ground at my father with sort of a how-did-you-know look. Then your granddad said, 'But Bonsera's smart enough to know how to dig faster than you, isn't he?' 'Yes, sir,' Mr. Flannigan agreed, speaking soft and low.

"'If I were you, Mr. Flannigan, I'd ask Mr. Bonsera if he wouldn't mind showing you how to dig the way he digs. The man knows how to pace himself. And in return, Mr. Flannigan, you might teach him how to speak English. What do you say to that?' The man looked at your granddad and thought for a bit, again staring at the man who continued to dig. Then he said, 'Yeah, I could do that, yes. I sure could do that, couldn't I, Mr. Niederer?'

"'Oh, Mr. Bonsera,' my dad called. 'Would you please come up here for a moment?' motioning with his hand. Bonsera leaped from the ditch and ran up to my father and Flannigan. 'Well, gentlemen, it was a fair contest, and you won, Mr. Bonsera. Congratulations.' My dad gave Mr. Bonasera twenty-five cents and shook his hand. Then Flannigan shook Bonasera's hand, and they all smiled."

The Contribution

"Your granddad and I went to our car. Just before we drove off, he asked me, 'Well, son, what did you learn today?' He would always ask me that after every outing. I remember saying, 'You can learn something from anybody.' And your grandfather said to me, 'Very good, son. Very good.'"

Jed's father passed away some years ago. Jed thinks of him often. Sometimes he thinks of the winter's day his dad drove him to the airport, the day his dad gave him his grandfather.

* * * * * * * *

Gutsy What?
Gutsy Coaching Moments

"Do the thing you fear, and the death of fear is certain."
—Ralph Waldo Emerson

The following pages are gutsy coaching moments that we want to share with you. They're shared by people in all walks of life, including one by Jed and Germaine. As you read on, you will realize how many of us are natural coaches, using many of the tools shared in Volume 1 and throughout this book. As you continue to read, we invite you to think about coachable moments that have made a difference in your life or someone you know.

Changing Lives One Life at a Time
—By Iris Hatfield[1]

"We make a living by what we get, we make a life by what we give."
—Sir Winston Churchill

One day, Bob, a national sales manager for a large printing supply company, called me with gloom and doom in his voice. Bob has been a client of mine for over ten years. As a professional handwriting analyst, I helped Bob select and hire top-notch sales people.

Bob's company had recently been purchased by another company, and he and his family were going to have to relocate again soon. He had become dissatisfied with his job and the changes in management. He wanted some direction and help with career and quality-of-life changes. Bob wanted a better lifestyle with less stress and less travel, but he was unsure about exactly what that would look like and how to make it happen. Since I knew him quite well through his handwriting, and saw his potential, I knew he was more than capable of making the changes he wanted to make to improve his life. (I use handwriting analysis to help me understand my clients and as a coaching tool to bring out the best in them.)

One of the first tools I use with my coaching clients to move them toward their objectives is the Powerful Five questions found in *Coach Anyone About Anything, Volume 1*. The five questions are:

- What must happen?
- Why do you think so?

---

[1] Iris Hatfield is president of HuVista International Inc., www.huvista.com

- How might that be accomplished? How else? How else?
- Who will/should/could be the one(s) to do it?
- By when must this be accomplished?

Bob's voice became light with a hint of enthusiasm as I began asking these questions. The questions were instrumental in helping Bob clarify and realize what he really wanted and what would be necessary to achieve his objectives. Over the next several months, the coaching process assisted and empowered him to make some gutsy moves. To live the lifestyle he wanted with his family, he would need to resign from his secure position with this company, find another position in another part of the country—never an easy task. But he was willing to take the risk because, through the questions, he saw it was necessary to attain his worthwhile goals. A few months later I received the following letter from Bob:

"Iris, I wanted to update you on my new home and career, but mostly I wanted to let you know how much I appreciate your coaching and guidance this past year.

"It was difficult making the jump from a 15-year investment with the same company, but then it wasn't the same company after several mergers. The exercises you suggested and coaching sessions helped me identify what I wanted, get energized, and find a sense of home and a career I can really sink my teeth into. We have moved back to our hometown, and my wife and I are very grateful for how things have fallen into place. Once again, thank you for all your help identifying my real desires and the encouragement to pursue them."

Coaching changes lives one life at a time. It is a wonderful profession!

Grab the Bull by the Horns
By Chris Bernal[2]

"Leadership is lifting a person's vision to higher sights, the raising of a person's performance to a higher standard, the building of a personality beyond its normal limitations."
—Peter F. Drucker

I had been working with Bill, VP of operations for a pharmaceutical manufacturing company, for four years. One day I received a call from Bill to discuss a challenge that he was experiencing with one of his plant managers, James. Bill informed me that James was failing at his job and that all attempts to help James were failing. As he provided additional information, I listened and asked questions to explore the nature of their relationship, the state of business results, and the culture of the plant.

By all accounts, Bill had a good grasp of the situation. There was little trust between them; plant results were poor; they were experiencing high turnover, low morale, poor product quality, poor compliance with regulatory requirements, and high waste; and to make matters worse, the FDA had begun taking significant regulatory action against the plant and the company for a variety of compliance concerns. Employees were disgruntled because they did not experience that management listened to them. In addition, there was a lack of confidence and trust in the management team, and they felt the managers were weak. On top of all that, employees feared for the stability of the plant.

[2]Chris Bernal is CEO of Effective Systems Consulting.
www.effectivesystemsltd.com

As we continued to dialogue, it became clear to me that Bill was not responding to the performance problem with James. We discussed two scenarios. Make a decision that James was not the right person for the job and replace him, or reach out and offer a process through which James could develop under a set of clear expectations and guidance to turn things around. I encouraged Bill to get off the fence and make a decision. He had his personal experience as a reference. Bill did and asked me to be available to coach James. I emphasized to Bill that the first step was for him to have a heart-to-heart talk with James, explaining the seriousness of the situation and offering him the possibility of a coaching process. If James was interested, he should take the initiative and call me.

When James called, I was reminded of how a bull enters the arena: strong, fearful, and ready to horn someone or something. He was upset, mad, rebellious, antagonistic, sarcastic. I listened and asked him why he had called me. He forcefully communicated, "Bill suggested that I get a coach, and he would provide support and participation in this process. He also mentioned that he started that same process with you several years ago and is still working with you."

Needless to say, this first conversation with James was quite difficult. His posture was assertive and demanding. I felt like I was on the defensive, and it took a lot for me not to respond in kind. He had a myriad of questions, including, "What is this process like? Does it provide for Bill to change?" I felt very challenged not to provide him the answers. I had to be patient and allow him to express himself and arrive at his own conclusions.

I remember thinking, Boy, what am I going to say next? Then I said it, "The real purpose you are here speaking with me today is not the obvious one (the relationship with your boss); it will only become clear at some point down the road. The process can't be fully understood until one is in it, and at some point, it requires a leap of faith." I went on to say, "I have listened to you with all my attention, and all I can say is that I can offer you a process that can help you to see the situation in a different light. I can offer you complete confidentiality as you are my only customer in the process; I am not here to report back to Bill in any way."

I was exhausted after this call. I remember thinking that I had just experienced one of those special coaching moments that one cannot prepare for, but must trust the process, the dialogue, and believe in the art of asking questions. We spoke for 1 1/2 hours; I asked him to think about it and call me in a few days if he was interested.

Several days later, when he called me back, James was in a different frame of mind. He was much more open and beginning to entertain the idea of coaching. The process was beginning to work! To make a long story short, he chose the coaching for himself. At the beginning, the coaching emphasized James' relationship with Bill. Through good, honest, and authentic dialogue, they were able to establish a trusting relationship. This led to amazing personal transformations that laid the foundation for plant changes, which ultimately became the real reason James was seeking the coaching!

A recent culture audit with emphasis on turnover revealed that employees now enjoy working in this plant and, by extension, have a favorable opinion of the company. Employees are being involved in important decisions and are engaged in the success of the plant; needless to say, morale has improved substantially.

Fast-forward to six months after initiating the coaching process with James; there is documented evidence of a seismic shift in the overall performance of plant operations. Employee safety-related events have gone down 60 percent, overall nonconforming investigations are declining, human error quality deviations are declining, scrap has gone down 80 percent, overtime is down and product supply volume is up, turnover has gone down 60 percent, and his plant recently received a clean inspection by the FDA.

The company is seeing clear improvements directly tied to the work James is doing to improve his approach through the Executive Coaching and Development program. His engagement in the program is undeniably the cause of this improvement. Largely because of the work Bill and James have done, there is a new culture of development taking root throughout the organization. Employees outside of manufacturing operations have now entered the coaching and development program; focus teams and employee involvement are on the rise. James has taken a leadership role in promoting this work, running several book clubs, mentoring others in the program, expanding his organizational development circle of influence, and becoming a champion of the process.

The future of the plant is bright, and many great things are happening every day!

I Don't Understand Why That Happened
by Neal Barnes[3]

"What separates those who achieve from those who don't is in direct proportion to one's ability to ask for help."
—Donald Keough, chairman of the board of
Allen & Company Incorporated

I work for a company that's growing fast. In fact, it's growing so fast that it's doubling in size every year, from £4.8 million to £10.5 million during the past year. It's now at a size where employees can't know everyone, and something needs to be done about it. There must be a way for us to capitalize on our people resources and talent.

As a result, my team is keen to implement a human resources database to capture current skills and future skill requirements and development needs. Part of this includes ensuring that senior HR colleagues have quality data in the system for their area of responsibility.

As part of an audit of the database, team member Alex followed up on the gaps with the HR team, and in her eagerness to get to the outcome, she upset one of the HR managers, Helen.

I was copied on a series of e-mails that flew culminating in Helen, the upset HR manager, calling me to share her feelings and concerns.

After hearing Helen's story, I asked Alex for her side of the story. Alex is also surprised and upset by Helen's reaction and can't understand why she has flown off the handle.

---

[3]Neal Barnes, group talent manager at Tullow Oil plc, London, England

I thought back to a time with my coach, Jed, when we worked together on a global change project. The words "Always have the courage to put yourself in their shoes before acting" had always stayed with me.

Alex and I went off for a coffee to discuss the situation:

Neal:	OK, so what happened?
	Alex carefully recounted the story again, still not understanding what had happened.
Neal:	Why do you think Helen reacted the way she did?
Alex:	I don't know.
Neal:	Imagine you're Helen.
Alex:	OK …
Neal:	What does it look like, what does it feel like, and how busy are you?
Alex:	I've got some pretty demanding managers who need an excellent service.
Neal:	What else?
Alex:	It's busy with lots to do, but I still wouldn't have reacted the way she did.
Neal:	I understand how you feel. Again, imagining you're Helen, what are you working on?
Alex:	I'm currently managing a new HR adviser, recruiting, organizing, training, and discussing business targets for the year and how I'm going to support them.
Neal:	Just so that I understand how busy you are … you're managing a new adviser, recruiting, organizing development for the team, and reviewing business targets and the impact on your work load. Sounds busy."
Alex:	It is!
Neal:	OK, so how do you feel when someone reminds you about a commitment you had agreed to at the HR team meeting a couple of weeks ago?
Alex:	Aaahhhh, I think I get it. But we still need to deliver, don't we?
Neal:	Yes, that's true, we do. Thinking about delivery, how else might you get the result you need?

Alex:	I'm not sure.
Neal:	OK, let's write down the different ways we could approach it.
Alex:	Well, we could offer support.
Neal:	Good, what else?
Alex:	See her face-to-face and offer to input the data or arrange for a temp to do it.
Neal:	What else?
Alex:	Say sorry for coming across so pushy.

I could see that Alex finally saw it from Helen's side. She visibly relaxed, having moved her thinking from the past problem to future solution.

Neal:	Great, so what's next?
Alex:	I better go over and see Helen, find out what I can do to ensure we have a quality database for the future. Oh, and say sorry!

A few days later I bumped into Helen, and she told me about the change in Alex and how things have really improved between them. Seeing things from another's point of view isn't always easy or comfortable, but the rewards can be significant in transforming people's working relationships from a bumpy road to a smooth highway.

Deadline? What Deadline?
By Vicki Aucoin[4]

"Being a leader changes everything. Before you are a leader, success is all about you. It's about your performance, your contributions. It's about getting called upon and having the right answers. When you become a leader, success is all about growing others. Your success as a leader comes not from what you do but from the reflected glory of the people you lead."
—Jack Welch, former CEO, General Electric

One of the exciting things about my job is that I manage a variety of projects that are time sensitive. It's critical that they be completed on time because there are so many components to each project that, if delayed, could cost us a lot of money.

One of my direct reports, John, was always working diligently on his projects but was continuously missing deadlines. I coached John a few times on his role and responsibilities because I noticed that he was always under the gun and appeared harried. Many times I questioned him about the task that he was involved in at a given moment. John would adhere to the coaching for a while and then return to his previous behavior.

It dawned on me that I should try a different approach if I wanted different results. I remembered an exercise from the book *Coach Anyone About Anything* that talked about activity versus action. I picked up the book and revisited that methodology for my next coaching session with John.

Upon reading about activity versus action, I knew this approach would make the difference that was needed for John to effectively work on his projects, maybe bring them in on time too. My next meeting with John was quite different. During our conversation, as John was updating me with the projects, I waited for the opportunity to ask him, "May I coach you?" He replied, "Of course, you may." I continued, asking John to envision the desired intended outcomes and then what possible actions he could take to complete the many projects he had started. This process allowed John to begin to visualize his thoughts with actions. Yes, John actually started to differentiate actions from activities and began meeting deadlines.

---

[4]Vicki Aucoin is integration manager, operations planning and development, Chevron Business and Real Estate Services, a Division of Chevron U.S.A. Inc.

John's voice and body language shifted as he began to see the end of the tunnel regarding his projects. This process worked so well that we made it a regular part of our conversations. John started eliminating low-value activities with high-value actions! The process helped John to stay focused and understand the obstacles that were hindering the completion of projects. The intended results clearly shaped the actions required to complete each job.

I was very happy that I invested time reviewing the activities versus action model and shared it with John.

The Significance Buster
by Doug Upchurch[5]

*"All courses of action are risky, so prudence is not in avoiding danger
(it's impossible), but calculating risk and acting decisively. Make mistakes
of ambition and not mistakes of sloth. Develop the strength to do bold
things, not the strength to suffer."*
—Niccolo Machiavelli

As a coach, I've had a number of gutsy coaching moments, but one
stands out above them all. It began when an entrepreneur that I look up
to and consider a great mentor asked me to coach him as he was finishing a new product that he was about to bring to market. The development
of the product had already taken a couple of years, and yet suddenly it
had stalled. This is where I came in.

As I began to talk with my client, it felt like he was stuck in the mud.
Every time he tried to move forward, he either got distracted or his energy dropped and he couldn't move forward. It wasn't clear to me why, but
it was clear that he had lost his passion for the project. I knew I had to get
him reconnected to the why of his project. I had to ask him what it was
that caused him to want to begin this journey several years ago.

It's important to note that this is someone whom I have a great deal of
respect for, and in order to take the next step, I knew I had to take him out
of the project and back to the beginning. I also knew that it might mean
that I would have to tell him that he needed to scrap the whole thing and

---

[5]Doug is president of Practical Soul, www.practicalsoul.com

start over. Needless to say, I wasn't sure where it would end up, but I knew I had to take him there.

So I started by asking him why he wanted to start this business and, in particular, this project. At first, he was a bit taken aback, but we kept talking and I kept asking questions. We got to the heart of what he was committed to. When he spoke about his commitment, he was passionate and the energy returned to his voice. I could see the seeds of this passion in his project, but it had been buried underneath layers of stuff that was really only there because he thought it was what was expected of a project like this. He had lost contact with the heart of his project by making it so significant.

Because the project was so important to him, significance took the form of being cautious, overly careful, and concerned, which turned his passion into a mundane project. I challenged him to think about what parts of the project were in alignment with his commitment. I suggested that he should be willing to throw out anything that wasn't aligned. It was this suggestion that required the most guts from me. He was the expert in my mind. I realized that I had to challenge him to give up everything he spent the last two years on in order to get back to the heart of his work.

After this, he went away to do some work on his own, and shortly afterward we spoke again. The passion and energy in his voice was back, and he was truly a different man. I was blown away. He said that by my encouraging him to let go of what he had and reconnect to his commitment, he was able to sift out the solid ideas aligned with his passion from those that were unnecessary. The result is that as of this writing, the project has radically transformed and is now on its way to completion and will be released to market within the year.

It's amazing what happens when we stop making things so significant!

Nailing Home a Point With a Velvet Hammer
by Susan Bagyura[6]

"Pretend that every single person you meet has a sign around his or her neck that says, 'Make me feel important.' Not only will you succeed in sales, you will succeed in life."
—Mary Kay Ash, founder of Mary Kay Cosmetics

Finally, Dan and I had signed our outcomes contract. It really took some patience and gentle prodding to reach that point. So gentle that, after his third failure to write up his desired outcomes, I suggested in an e-mail that it may not be the right time for him to do this and that I would be available in the future when he was ready. Within an hour, I had the contract back with some impressive thinking and goals along with an apologetic e-mail for the delay.

The following week, after very careful preparation, I sat and waited for the phone to ring. After waiting for 45 minutes, I sent off an e-mail to see if I could get his attention. I continued waiting and still no call or response to my e-mail.

While I was waiting for the phone to ring, there was plenty of time to think. I was wondering how I would handle this situation. For me, it was important to make it clear that we both be prepared and on time for our coaching sessions. At the same time, I had concerns about being so strong

---

[6]Susan Bagyura is a leadership coach, speaker, and author of The Visionary Leader. www.thevisionaryleader.com

that I would be confused with a parent or some other authority figure in Dan's life. The approach would certainly determine whether we could keep this on a professional business basis and still have a good foundation for actually having our coaching session. However, if this was not addressed, it would most likely be a recurring situation.

After waiting over an hour, the phone rang. It was Dan. He said, "I'm sorry for calling so late. I was tied up in a meeting that lasted longer than I had anticipated." I have 25 years of business experience that included meetings, deadlines, and promises. To simply accept this excuse would negate a lot of that experience, and Dan would lose out on an opportunity to learn and improve.

I said, "Dan, may I coach you?" Dan agreed. I continued, "It is really important to meet commitments whether it is a promised phone call or something else. We made a commitment to be on time and prepared for our calls in the outcomes agreement. I know that things can come up, but then it is important to inform the other person in time or, if necessary, excuse yourself from a meeting and call or e-mail the other person.

"Just the other day, I had a similar situation. I had made a commitment to call my coach at a certain time, and then an unexpected but critical meeting came up. I wrote her an e-mail saying that I would not be able to call her at the appointed time, and then, just to be certain, I called her at the regular time to say that I could not talk but could reschedule. All of this only took a couple of minutes but saved both of us a lot of time."

Dan said, "I understand what you are saying and agree that it is important. Can we leave this as a learning experience and go on from here?"

Of course, I agreed and then told him, "Dan, it is a privilege and an honor to be coaching you; your success is extremely important to me, and I will do what I can to help you achieve your goals." Over the telephone I could "hear" the smile on his face as he thanked me.

This transitional statement was key because it allowed Dan to feel good about himself and it provided a great start to the rest of the conversation. I learned a long time ago that being authentic and taking care of people can take you far. In this particular case, take someone from an uncomfortable but necessary conversation into a positive mood to continue a dialog.

That was the only time I had that conversation with Dan. He realized how taking care of his customers made a huge difference to them and his bottom line.

If You Care, Be Carefrontational
By Machen MacDonald, CPCC, CCSC[7]

"Resolve to be tender with the young, compassionate with the aged, sympathetic with the strong, and tolerant with the weak and the wrong. For some time in your life you will be all of these."
—Lloyd Shearer

As a coach, you will agree, I am sure, a primary reason clients hire us is to help them achieve goals they feel they would not otherwise accomplish on their own without a coach. Perhaps it may simply be to speed up the process, knowing they can do it, and they just feel they need support in staying focused and accountable.

For a coach to really be able to hold a space of success and fulfillment for his client, he must truly care about his client and be more committed to the client's winning the end game than the process along the way. With that being said, the process-as awkward and messy as it sometimes can be-is oftentimes the catalyst to personal and professional growth the client is really after. Be willing to get messy, awkward, and out of control, and encourage your client to do the same on his path to achieving his successes.

I like to refer to this discombobulating juncture in the coaching process as being carefrontational. Allow me to provide you an example of leveraging carefrontation in a gutsy coaching moment.

---

[7]#1 best-selling author Machen P. MacDonald, CPCC, CCSC, is a certified life and business coach with the ProBrilliance Leadership Institute in Grass Valley, CA. www.probrilliance.com

I'll refer to a situation that really brought this to life for me as it was close to home. My son was 13 years old at the time and a competitive gymnast. He was doing quite well, winning plenty of bronze and silver medals in various competitions. However, a gold medal appeared to be elusive. If anybody deserved a gold medal based on determination, hard work, and talent, it was this kid. Be that as it may, his current self-concept was not quite that of champion status.

Toward the end of the season at a California state qualifying meet, he performed exceptionally well, landing a second place overall. He achieved his best scores in all events, providing again silver and bronze medals but no gold. The ride home was heavy in emotion. When we got home it took all he had not to break down.

Up to that point we had been working on his visualizing winning a gold medal, and he was starting to become, shall we say, impatient. As his dad, who happens to also be a coach, I conveyed to him he just needed to keep with it, and what he wanted or something better would come. I jumped on my coaching box and attempted to pump him up, reiterating that he must really feel the accomplishment in his gut as he was visualizing his winning the gold. We refer to this as *visceralizing the gold.* Well, at this point in the evening he was fed up with gymnastics, visualizing, and coaching as he replied in a rather spirited way, "Dad, just quit coaching me! Coaching and visualizing don't work!"

Those words, from my son in that tone, were like a knife to the heart. Amazingly they were also a catalyst to my becoming a more powerful and impactful coach. For, in that moment, I found myself doing a gut check. I really checked in with myself as a dad and a professional coach. This was a crucial moment for me in my coaching career. My decision to make was this: Do I back off or do I step up and challenge my son to learn how to develop a skill and habit that will serve him for the rest of his life, well beyond his gymnastics career? Hopefully, the answer was obvious. I believed I needed to provoke his brilliance. In that moment, I could clearly see his championship potential, whereas he was mired in a temporary hallucination of being only second best.

As he was committed to his story of never being able to win a gold medal, the waterworks commenced. In that moment, I decided to risk my son becoming really upset with me, and I became carefontational and really called him on his focusing on what he didn't want. I coached him to redirect the current emotion of frustration and disappointment and imagine being on top of the podium receiving the gold medal. At first he pushed back, but his commitment for his limitations was not as strong as my determination for him to experience his championship potential, and he eventually redirected his focus to a more empowering image of winning gold at his next meet. By this time it was time for bed. Sweet dreams.

At his very next event, again he was on track to have his best meet yet as each event's score was better than those at his previous meets. His gymnastics coach does not allow the kids to see their scores throughout the competition. He feels that this way the kids don't get discouraged or overconfident during the competition and can be more present. They learn of their results at the awards ceremony at the end of the meet. However, my wife and I could see our son was on his way to his first gold medal.

At the conclusion of the competition, as they announced the results for the pommel horse, the announcer proceeded to reveal the name of the gymnast who secured the bronze and then the silver. For the gold medal they announced the pommel horse champion as … Drake MacDonald! His joy burst through as he stepped up to receive his medal. He went on to win two more event golds and was the overall champion of the meet.

After the ceremonies, my beaming son told me, "Dad, coaching works!"

That season, Drake went on to become the California state champion. That's what he visualized, and I permitted myself to be carefrontational along the way.

Learning to be carefrontational with all of my clients has catapulted them to achieving great successes sooner rather than later. It can be tough to step up and tell clients the way you see it and them, especially when they don't see it themselves. It may feel emotionally messy and awkward. If we had a choice to be smooth and cool, most of us would opt for that. That's not what our clients pay us for as coaches. Believe me. They want us to be carefrontational.

I Need You, but Do Not Want You
By Angelo Edwards[8]

"Success is not final; and failure is not final."
—Don Shula, NFL Football coach, record for most career wins (347)

Eugene was referred to me by one of his business colleagues. He had a small five-employee fabrication company making decent revenue. On August 25, 2005, his business changed dramatically, when Hurricane Katrina hit the New Orleans area. Seemingly overnight his services were in demand by federal government agencies and large private-sector construction firms to work on the recovery efforts in New Orleans. To service the requirements of certain contracts, he had to increase the number of employees to 25 and to seek financing to cover the mobilization cost for some projects.

Through this unexpected increase in work, Eugene realized he needed help in running his business. When he called me, we spoke for about 15 minutes for me to get a quick overview of his business and the situation he was confronted with. We set up an appointment and I visited him to discuss the coaching process. I conducted a needs assessment of the current position the business was in, I delivered a report to him, and we decided on the areas that coaching would be beneficial to him. Our coaching sessions were set, assignments were given to him, and we agreed on the anticipated outcomes from the Coaching Outcomes Contract.

From my Coachlab/Eagle's View training in becoming a coach, one of

[8]Certified Business Coach, Micro-Enterprise Institute, Inc., New Orleans, LA
www.microei.org

the vital questions to ask a player upfront is, "Do I have permission to coach you?" This was a question I posed to Eugene, and his response was yes. Almost immediately as the coaching sessions began, I sensed hesitation and frustration from my player. He became restless during face-to-face sessions, assignments were not being completed, and some sessions were abruptly canceled without prior notice, which was against the rules we outlined in the Coaching Agreement.

Numerous attempts at trying to find out why our coaching sessions were not yielding the desired results for both parties was now creating a sense of self-doubt in my abilities to coach. Moreover, what should I do about it since I felt I was not getting feedback that would give me some insight as to continuing with the Coaching Assignment?

During one coaching session in early 2006, things came to a head, and Eugene finally opened up to me and expressed his feelings regarding the coaching. "Mr. Edwards," he said, "I know you're capable of coaching and I know I need your services, but I feel you don't know enough about the fabrication business to be an asset to my business." It was during that discussion that I gained clarity as to what the problem was. Although Eugene needed a coach, he really was not listening to me; in his mind he was thinking that he should be the coach because he knew more about fabrication than I did. After that session, I knew exactly what to do. I reread Chapter 5 of *Coach Anyone About Anything*, and with renewed vigor I called my player and requested that we have an unscheduled session so that we could revisit the Coaching Outcomes Contract. From that session, I was able to listen more intently, and my player listened also. He agreed to commit to the sessions with the goal of producing outcomes beyond his expectations.

The outcome of the player's new commitment to coaching resulted in his gross revenue increasing by 40 percent in a five-month period; the net profit increased by 35 percent. He now had established business goal benchmarks and systems in place to reach the business goals. His employees were now well-informed about how their job directly correlated to the success of the business. The business is now seeking new markets and customers.

Fly Me to the Moon!
By Dick Huiras[9]

"Athletes, singers and an array of others have been using coaches for years. It is only recently that the business community has begun to see the wisdom of hiring executive coaches."
—Harvard Business Review

Having spent many hours as a pilot, I well understand the effect weight has on the performance of an aircraft. With extra weight, more thrust is needed to get the plane off the ground. With added drag, more lift is required to keep the plane airborne. But until reading Chapter 13, "The DreamMakers & DreamBrakers," in *Coach Anyone About Anything*, Volume 1, I had not related these principles to daily life. Ever since reading it, I have used this very simple, yet powerful tool frequently in my coaching practice. In fact, The DM & DB (DreamMakers & DreamBrakers) has become one of my favorite processes to help my clients make significant changes in their lives for the better.

Kathy Pendragon, a physician working in Texas at the Children's Hospital, was referred to me by a friend and client. Kathy called me and we scheduled an appointment, but before she left the telephone she said, "Dick, I hope this works. Nothing else has." Just from Kathy's parting comment, my sense was that the DreamMakers & DreamBrakers audit could be the perfect first coaching conversation to have with her.

Kathy came to my office the next day. I listened for a long while as she

---

[9]President of ICS-Connect, www.ics-connect.com

described in detail her trials and tribulations at the hospital. She was sorely missing a sense of accomplishment. I asked her if she would take a few minutes to complete the DM & DB audit with me. I drew the four quadrants on a flipchart: weight, lift, drag, and thrust. She began to tell me about the things that she experienced as weight and as drag (burdensome and annoying events or situations), and I listed them in the appropriate quadrants.

Eventually we got to the Lift and Thrust sections, those moments or activities that are uplifting and energizing. "What gives you thrust and lift in your work, Kathy?" I inquired. Kathy didn't speak for a long moment and just stared at the flipchart with the two empty quadrants. Then gradually she began to think of and share with me some of the joys and satisfactions of her profession. In a little while Kathy was in tears recalling why she went into medicine in the first place and the difference she wanted to make in children's lives. By the end of the process, no more than 45 minutes, she was beaming and walked out of my office with a short list of adjustments she would make to increase her lift and thrust and some requests she would make of the hospital administration to reduce the weight and drag.

"It's amazing, Dick. I actually feel lighter, like I could almost fly or something," Kathy said laughing.

The simple DreamMakers & DreamBrakers exercise gave Kathy the altitude she needed to examine her whole situation, not just the things that weren't working in her life. Because she had to look at all four forces, she was able to see the big picture and rediscovered her passion and commitment to children's well-being, while pinpointing issues she could take positive steps to resolve.

May the forces be with you!

It's All Fun and Games
By Cristin Farr[10]

"That's what learning is, after all; not whether we lose the game, but how we lose and how we've changed because of it and what we take away from it that we never had before, to apply to other games. Losing, in a curious way, is winning."
—Richard Bach, author, *Jonathan Livingston Seagull*

As part of my field base for my B.S. in Academic Studies degree, I was required to take a block of courses centered on children's literacy. This was a senior-level course block that was famous for making or breaking future teachers. It was an intense four months of teaching, tutoring, learning, and most of all, *stress!*

During all of this chaos and growth, I was able to work one-on-one with Henry, a second-grader. Henry was a struggling reader and a minority student in a poverty-stricken area. At this point in his schooling, Henry should have been reading at (at least) a level 16. However, he was only reading at a level 10, which put him far behind his classmates. This frustrated Henry and many times caused him to completely shut down during instructional time, especially when he was required to read.

After meeting Henry and having the opportunity to observe his behaviors in a class, I was asked by my professors to tutor him twice a week. To be quite honest, the thought of tutoring such a challenging child frightened me quite a bit! I mean, here was a student who, in addition to his refusal to work, also had major behavioral problems.

---

[10]Cristin is a senior at Sam Houston University

Henry seldom sat in his assigned desk; instead, he preferred to walk around and bother the other students. He could often be heard from other classrooms, yelling at his classmates when things were not going his way. So, in a desperate effort to find clues to effectively reach Henry (and to avoid any type of outburst during our tutoring time), I went to his teacher to find out as much as I could about him.

Based on the information she provided, I selected appropriate books and reading environments that would be in line with Henry's interests. I stressed to Henry that our tutoring was a special privilege that not all students would get to enjoy.

I learned very quickly that Henry really enjoyed competitive games. So I turned our tutoring into a game by working on second-grade vocabulary and having reading competitions between us. Not only did Henry respond positively to the idea of a game, he really began to try harder to "beat" me.

I was able to watch as our game time began to change Henry. His behavioral problems began to minimize, and he slowly started recognizing the second-grade vocabulary words that he was required to know. He also began to really enjoy our tutoring sessions! Henry would come to our sessions with a smile on his face, determined to win the game for the day. By the end of our tutoring sessions (just 3 1/2 weeks), Henry's confidence had significantly increased, and he actually advanced to a reading level of 12. Additionally, Henry could recognize almost 80 percent of his second-grade vocabulary terminology.

This was one of the greatest feelings in the world for me. I helped a child increase his confidence while reaching for new heights-just by changing learning into fun and games.

The Art of Consensus
Hey, That's My Idea!
By Larry Lamb[11]

"Setting an example is not the main means of influencing another;
it is the only means."
—Albert Einstein

Leadership and management require helping others to succeed. Many times the person you are coaching may stray off course, and you must find a way to get her back on track. This is always risky and sometimes even dangerous because most people don't like to be told what to do. Many do not even support a good, solid manager/direct report relationship.

I find that it's much better to lead people down the proper path rather than direct them or give an order of how to obtain the desired result. It has been my experience that everyone performs better if they can meet their objectives using their ideas and experience.

I think it is important to set goals and track performance between the coach and the person being coached. That is, the goals are a co-creation, not an imposed quota. The following are proven techniques and ideas that support coaching and managing a successful relationship with your direct reports.

- Promote an open-door policy.
- Be up-front and honest in your dealings.
- Create a *no-surprises environment*.
- Be sincere with praise and stern when issues arise. (And be equally sincere or honest when issues arise. You don't have to change

---

[11]Produce sales entrepreneur, Houston, TX

your personality depending on the outcome of another's effort. I recommend that you be sincere, honest, and simple.)
- Plant the seed: If the person you are coaching does not come to the desired conclusion on his own, begin making statements that promote the desired result.
- It may take longer to achieve the goal, although if it's the other's idea, everyone wins.
- Use the questions "What do you think?" "How would you …?" and "What would you do to …?"
- Say "we" rather than "I" as much as possible.
- Be patient.
- Care about others.
- Do not take credit for others' work.
- Other characteristics or concepts: Rule of reason-understand the strategy, follow the process, make goal setting a joint responsibility.

Example: Anthony Franco was national sales manager for a large manufacturing company. The company used a dealer network that was managed by zone managers. For several years the company had been consistently achieving its sales goals. This particular year, the company was changing its strategy. Inventing new products became part of its new strategy and new objectives. Profit expectations rose among the top executives due to this new leading-edge strategy.

When announced, the dealer network did not wholeheartedly accept the new objectives. Implementing change is never easy, and implementing a new business strategy may be one of the most difficult changes you will ever see. It was very clear to everyone that change needed to take place in some major markets. Revenue was declining and profit margins weren't what they used to be. Many of the zone managers reporting to Anthony had become good friends over the years with their dealers and were struggling to help them succeed.

This could have been a disaster. With the challenge ahead, Anthony knew he had to direct his zone managers to become more aggressive in key markets to achieve the sales objective and profit budget. How? Friends don't like to press friends ordinarily, and the zone managers were friends with their dealers, if not close friends.

So Anthony started asking questions of his zone managers. The zone managers began asking for feedforward on the new goals and commission structure. The following coaching questions were invented by Anthony and his zone managers to ask of the dealers:

— Is there anything standing in your way to achieve your budget?

— Sales success is a partnership; what could the company do to support you in your market?

— Do you agree with the new sales objectives? Why? If not, in what ways would you want your sales objectives to be adjusted?

After 60 days, the writing was on the wall. It was clear in which markets change was necessary. The zone managers submitted their recommendations, and in four out of eight markets, changes were made.

The result? All markets in the entire country reached their sales objectives for the year.

The zone managers achieved their desired results, and the national sales manager was pleased, of course. Anthony's team achieved the sales and profit objectives using *their own ideas*.

The result got accomplished because strategic coaching steps were followed.

Charlene Bernal

I know, I know

"Changing human behavior without understanding motivation is like trying to start a stalled car by kicking it."
—Ernest Dichter

One of our clients shared the following coaching moment with us.

Charlene was the manager of the number one store in a chain of boutiques. She'd trained twenty people or more in her three-year retail-management career. The owners of the chain sent people through her store to be exposed to this retail master. Charlene was good, really good.

Today Charlene wasn't feeling like she was good. Today Charlene was feeling like she was rather ineffective. The owners had sent Ruth, a salesperson, to work with Charlene before promoting Ruth to store manager of another location. Ruth was experienced. Perhaps she was too experienced. It seemed that every time Charlene tried to tell her something, Ruth would say, "I know, I know."

Charlene went home that night pretty down and frustrated with the way Ruth's training was progressing. Charlene relaxed with her roommate and began telling her about Miss Know-it-all at work. After a few laughs and a couple of glasses of wine, Charlene strategized her new approach.

The next day at the store, Charlene watched as Ruth straightened a pile of sweaters. "Charlene," she said to herself, "if you're going to contribute anything to this woman, it better be soon 'cause she's out of here next week. Well, here goes." Charlene sighed and walked toward Ruth.

"Excuse me, Ruth, may I talk to you for a moment?"

"Sure," Ruth said. They walked casually toward the back door of the store together.

"Ruth, may I coach you?" Charlene asked.

"Uh, what?" Ruth replied.

"May I coach you?" Charlene repeated.

"Okay, I guess so," Ruth answered.

"Great! Let me explain what I mean by coaching."

Ruth interrupted, "Oh, I know what you mean."

Charlene countered, "Would you be willing to consider the possibility that you don't know?"

Again, Ruth asked, "What?"

Charlene said, "Ruth, what I mean is that I think I have something to tell you that might be of benefit to you, but you'll never know unless you listen as though you might hear something new." Ruth just looked at Charlene. She continued, "Someday, Ruth, you're going to have to train someone who thinks she knows everything."

Ruth interrupted, "Oh, yes, I know that."

Charlene whispered, "Someone like you, Ruth." Ruth's eyebrows rose a full inch as she cocked her head to one side, listening to Charlene. "Oh, I realize you don't mean to come off like a know-it-all, Ruth. But you do anyway. And it makes it so hard to contribute to you even though I know you have a burning desire to learn and grow."

"That's true, I do want to learn and grow. I didn't realize I came off like a know-it-all. I apologize," Ruth said sincerely.

"Thank you," Charlene said. "Thank you for being so coachable just now."

"Now, what was the coaching you want to give me?" Ruth asked smiling. "Just kidding, Charlene. I got the coaching."

"Whew, I thought I was going to have to go to Plan B."

"What is Plan B?" Ruth queried.

"Don't you know?" Charlene said slowly. They burst into laughter and laughed for many moments more.

Sticky Situation
Taffy Candy Sticky
By Troy Henson[12]

*"If there is any one secret to success, it lies in the ability to
get the other person's point of view and see things from
their angle as well as your own."*
—Henry Ford

I was hired by the owners of an auto parts distribution company to make a difference with their GM, Randy. The problem was his communication style. He was constantly saying the absolute wrong thing at the absolute wrong time, putting the company in potentially dangerous legal situations. My directive was to transform Randy's approach. If that goal couldn't be achieved, he would be terminated. Prior to agreeing to the terms of the contract, I scheduled a meeting with Randy to see if I would be a good fit as his coach and, of course, to determine if he was coachable.

When I met Randy, I was delighted to observe that he was very open, welcoming, and looking forward to the opportunity to work with me. He fully acknowledged his communication challenges and was eager to change his bad habits. Unfortunately, that's not where the story ended. As is the case in many such situations, there was a bit of a he-said, she-said component. According to Randy, the owners were sabotaging the future success of the company through negligent decision making regarding

---

[12]Troy Henson; owner of Be Coaching & Consulting LLC in Phoenix, Arizona; coachtroy@becoaching.com

company finances. He agreed to start coaching with me if I would help him "fix" the owners' spending problems. Always a glutton for punishment—and knowing this was going to be a sticky situation—I accepted the contract on a 90-day trial basis.

The major challenge in this deal was that Randy would only agree to being coached if we were able to spend our time working on his issue with the owners, Brett and Tim. The white elephant in the room, though, was that Randy didn't realize the ultimatum the owners had outlined for his future employment. While Randy saw this as a bit of a two-way issue, Brett and Tim were more interested in turning around Randy's communication style. They didn't want to let him know there was a potential of losing his job for fear that would cause him to make a pre-emptive strike and quit.

To make matters worse, two weeks into our coaching work, Randy made his biggest mistake to date. While the owners were out of town on a business trip, Randy issued the annual bonus checks to the staff without Brett and Tim's approval. You can imagine the shock when they realized what had happened, especially since they had established a new bonus structure and the company was not financially prepared to lay out the bonus cash. The consequences were dire. How do you take back a bonus that has already been given, especially when they were already dealing with a demoralized staff with little faith in the current leadership?

I was flooded with e-mails and phone calls, some from Randy, who realized he'd messed up big time. The others were from Brett and Tim, who were colossally angry and worried about the potential repercussions of Randy's actions. I was called to a private meeting with the owners about whether or not it was worth the time and resources to try to help Randy. After much discussion, the decision was made to move forward with the coaching contract while they began exploring options for another GM to take his place.

Four weeks later, Randy had made great strides concerning how he was dealing with his perception about how the company finances were being handled. However, I was once again called to a meeting with the owners. "Troy, you've been great. We've really noticed a shift in the way Randy has been communicating. However, we've decided that he's still not quite at the level we need him to be. We're working on finding his replacement. We need you to stay on working with him for another four weeks while we get things squared away with his replacement. Of course, we need you to keep this conversation between us as we need to keep things running smoothly for the next few weeks. Thanks again; you've been great. It's definitely not your fault. We just realize we have the wrong person in the job."

My sticky situation had just gotten immensely stickier. I now had to spend four weeks coaching a dead man walking. I couldn't even tell him what was about to happen. I decided I had better take this challenge full on and do whatever I could to cause a miracle to happen. I couldn't tell Randy about the owners' plan, but I also couldn't let him be taken out like a sitting duck. Right away, I initiated a breakthrough-thinking brainstorm with Randy about creating a radical plan that would position him as an irreplaceable asset. He was all for it, and without me even touching the topic, he suggested it would be a good idea for him to spend some time working on a fallback option in case these plans didn't work out and he needed to find another job. "That's a good idea," I agreed, calmly.

Two days before the end of my extended contract, I was called to a meeting with the owners. "I'm not sure what you did, Coach Troy, but in the past month we've noticed an unbelievable shift in the way Randy has been leading, communicating, and thinking in terms of the future of this company. His vision is dead-on, his new strategies are right on track, and the entire staff is operating at a level of productivity we've never seen before. We've decided to keep him on. Whatever you're doing, it's working. Please keep doing it. Thanks."

I couldn't have been more relieved as well as excited for Randy's success. This turned out to be a bigger challenge than I ever anticipated. The true key to the success in this situation was Randy's willingness to take the coaching and do the work to make the changes. He took on each challenge and gave it a true fighting chance, even if he didn't know how it was going to work out. And I was once again reminded that, through a commitment to success, anything is possible.

Who's Afraid of the Big Bad Wolf?
The Wonder of Open Communication
By Shideh Bina[13]

"Fear makes the wolf bigger than he is."
—German proverb

I was hired by a C-level client to develop her new senior leadership team and establish alignment. I had previously done a very effective executive coaching engagement that had supported her promotion to C-job.

For this assignment she briefed me that there were some internal dynamics on the team that needed to be corrected or the team would not be able to effectively lead the necessary turnaround. Future success for the business would require a whole new business model, new cost structure, and new working norms. Yet the team could not even have the most basic business conversation or generate much collaborative behavior.

Prior to the offsite, I interviewed each member of her team so that I could familiarize myself with their perspective, gain greater insight into the issues, as well as establish a relationship. While no one said anything directly in the interviews, it was obvious to me that, for some reason or another, there was an undercurrent of fear, particularly of Judy.

As we began the two-day offsite, Judy would meet with me on each break to give me feedback so that we could make any course adjustments. Although I had worked with her very successfully and very intimately for over a year, for some reason I found myself feeling more anxious after each huddle, and I couldn't pinpoint why. I knew she trusted me completely, and

[13]Shideh Bina, founding partner, Insigniam Performance,
www.insigniam.com

yet somehow I was also becoming afraid of her. While the offsite was fairly effective as it progressed, I knew I had not yet delivered the outcome she was looking for.

In the middle of the second day, Judy made some comments as part of discussion, and I noticed my stomach tightening. At the same moment I looked around and could observe body language that indicated others were also anxious. I knew at that moment we were face-to-face with whatever the underlying dynamic was. I took a deep breath and I said, "Judy, I have worked with you closely for some time, and I know in reality no one has anything to fear from your management or leadership, yet I think something just happened that stimulated anxiety for some of the people here. I include myself, and I have nothing to fear from you." I could see people nodding and shoulders relaxing. "Can we use this moment to dissect this issue?" What transpired after that was a very open discussion, where we revealed that certain mannerisms, language usage, and tones of voice that Judy regularly employed to make her point were perceived as aggressive signs of displeasure. For Judy, she was merely amplifying a point.

Once we were able to have a direct conversation about people's fears and how Judy was amplifying those fears, she then had the room to honestly express her expectations. With these conversations, the leadership team really coalesced and moved on to make a dramatic impact in turning around the business. When I came back six months later, they were a different group, and she was much more relaxed and able to be herself as a leader.

Let It Snow!
By Stacey Winter[14]

"Training is usually an event. Coaching is an ongoing process."
—Porche/Niederer

Isn't it great when you go by the book even when you don't know you did?

In my role, I am afforded the opportunity to work with managers from a variety of backgrounds and cultures. During my interactions, I provide a sort of open-coaching forum wherein we strategically discuss how to help develop their employees while considering the needs of the employee as an individual and the demands of the business. These facilitated discussions bring managers into a room where I challenge them to think about their employees in the same way they often think about their products and financial obligations to the organization.

One such meeting was particularly memorable because of the action items associated with a specific employee. An employee was discussed during our session, and one of the action items noted by the manager was "be coached by Stacey Winter." While, yes, I was in the meeting and privy to the discussion surrounding the employee, I had no idea what specific outcomes the manager desired (or why he chose me).

The meeting was scheduled, and Sarah came to my office. I invited her in and did my usual light conversation to help her feel welcome, and she

---

[14]Stacey Winter is the director of employee development at National Oilwell Varco.

looked frightened. I stopped midsentence and said, "Sarah, why are you here?"

"Because Mike said I had to come see you," she said.

"Did he tell you why?" I asked.

"No. He said you guys were talking about me, and now I have to talk to you."

I assured her that I was not here to fire her. I explained what her boss meant by talking about her and then said, "Knowing what you know now, is there an opportunity for us to continue our discussion? If so, what do you want to talk about?"

She began to tell me about her career history. While she was speaking, her tone and body language said she was uninterested. We discussed the coaching contract, I gave her some homework, and we scheduled a secondary meeting.

During our second meeting, all of her questions carried a negative connotation. She would ask questions of me that were leading more toward a "what can you do for me" than a "what can we learn together" discussion.

I asked her to participate in a personality-styles survey to allow her to get to know herself and possibly understand why those around her were, in her words, "so annoying." My intentions were to take the results and discuss versatility in the styles. After she took the instrument, she listened to me explain the different styles and the ways we communicate effectively within them. She interrupted me to say, "You know, this doesn't really relate to me. How are you going to help me get a new job?"

I explained to her that it was not my responsibility to find her a new job, but to provide her with the tools and resources necessary to be more marketable in the one she has. She left soon thereafter. This left me thinking that maybe I wasn't the right person to coach her. That thought in mind, I approached one of my colleagues and explained what happened and my thoughts. I was advised to give her another meeting and to then determine the next steps.

In our third (and yes, final) meeting, Sarah and I talked about her anticipated outcomes and her willingness as a player in our relationship. She explained that she was so busy looking for me to be "really intelligent about something I don't already know" that she didn't really feel she was getting anything out the meetings. I agreed and volunteered to find her a new coach for the outcomes she anticipated.

In feeling like a failure as a coach, I turned to several resources. In *Coach Anyone*, Jed and Germaine speak about the snow-job effect. It made me realize that I was not only coaching someone who didn't want the coaching (hey, she was forced), but she was so busy looking for me to be intelligent, having all the answers, that she didn't listen to her own desires and actual needs for the relationship.

I also realized that I was on automatic. This one snuck up on me. Usually, when I am coaching someone, we are clear about the outcomes to be produced, and I take the necessary steps in working with my players. However, in this particular situation, because I was privy to the original conversation with the manager, I didn't stop to have everyone align on the outcomes. I assumed we were on the same page. A key learning for me is to ensure that the alignment meeting is always in place. So now, when anyone comes to me for coaching, we start with the basics:

What outcomes are you committed to producing? Are those outcomes aligned with your manager's outcomes for the coaching? And, yes, before engaging in the coaching, we get the OK from the manager, especially when the manager sends players to me.

In addition to the alignment meeting, I learned three things from this experience that I transfer to all my requests for coaching:

1) It's okay to not be a good fit.
2) I need to do a better job of coaching my managers on how to introduce the concept of coaching.
3) Coachability is key.

It's amazing to me that it doesn't matter how long one has been coaching, it is never too late to learn something new!

Coaching Someone With a Big Personality
By Jeff Powell[15]

"Life begins at the end of your comfort zone."
—Neale Donald Walsh

Many years ago, as a young consultant, I was working with a steel manufacturing company in the Midwest. This was a big project, and we were changing some key processes. I was working with a group that was a mix of union and nonunion, and we were working on effective communication.

These folks were a feisty bunch, full of thoughts, and were willing to express themselves not always politically correctly. I prefer a group who engages, rather than one whose thoughts you have to draw out, as it allows for great conversations.

The mill had gone through a lot, and the employees knew they had to make these improvements. So although they were boisterous, they were also serious about the work. With a group like that, there were many characters, a veritable USA miniseries worth of characters. Some were loud and some were quiet, but they were all smart and fast with the quips and jabs. As a consultant I had my work cut out and had to dance pretty fast.

In one session we were discussing requests and promises, and I was explaining how a clear request, very specific, can really provide only three

---

[15]Jeff Powell is managing director of Critical Business Solutions, www.criticalbusinesssolutions.com.

answers: Yes, I accept; No, I do not accept; or I counteroffer. They were explaining that saying no was not really an option, and I explained that if you can't say no, then yes did not mean much.

At this point one of the foremen, Steve, stood up. Steve was a literal giant of a man, about 6'5" and 290 pounds, and was clearly a don't-mess-with-me kind of guy. Steve was, without doubt, a strong voice in the group, and his opinion meant a lot. He did not start a lot of conversations, but he ended many of them.

I remember vividly his towering over me and looking down at me. He said, "Are you telling me that these guys can now say no to me? No one says no to me! We would have chaos here." Steve was not using his indoor voice at the time.

I am clear that I have a choice at this point. Not much of a choice, as all 35 members of the group were eager to see how this was going to play out. Watching Steve devour the young consultant was potentially very entertaining. Either I had to work this out with Steve, or I would lose all credibility with the group.

I thought for a moment and then said, "Steve, does everyone do everything you ask them to do, exactly when you want them to do it?"

Steve replied "Of course."

I probed a little. "Steve, does this happen all the time—without exception?"

"Well, sometimes a few of the guys are late with some work."

I said, "Would you prefer to know that it was going to be late, or do you prefer surprises?"

Steve said, "I hate surprises." His whole mood changed, and he laughed at the reality of what life really is like with no accountability in time, just threats, as he was not getting what he wanted, either.

"That's all I am saying, Steve. Coordination happens when we can be authentic and say I cannot do that by 3 p.m.; I can do it at 3:30 p.m. That takes the mystery out of when it will get done. I am not advocating we all say no; I am saying we should say no when we need to say no. If we have no choice, we have no power in our speaking, no matter how powerful we are."

This opened up a deeper and profound relationship with that team, who then took on some amazing projects. I look back on this group now as a wonderful experience, which could clearly have gone either way.

Coaching a Daughter/Artist
Does Father Know Best?
by John Gordon[16]

"It is very difficult to live among people you love and hold back from offering them advice."
—Anne Tyler, Pulitzer Prize-winning U.S novelist.

Coach Anyone About Anything is the title, so why shouldn't I coach my daughter Michelle when she started her career as an abstract artist a few years ago? Of course, I knew that there would be some challenges for both of us in putting aside our parent-daughter relationship so that we could establish a business coaching relationship. I like to call Germaine and Jed's book the "Coaching Bible."

Michelle began painting as a small child and never stopped, although she purposely elected not to attend art school because at that time she wanted to enjoy her painting as a hobby and not work it as a career. So she was working in a nine-to-five community activist job when some artists from Chicago "discovered" her and said her abstract oil paintings were terrific. They urged her to quit her day job to become a professional artist. So Michelle and I talked about this, and I gave her encouragement.

Michelle had never studied or enjoyed business and had no business plan or a concept of one. Nevertheless, she decided to take the leap and "… build your wings on the way down," as the Kovi Yamata quote from the Coaching Bible said. So it was natural for her to ask me how to build the wings since I was her father and business coach. And I am a business attorney. This was a gutsy coaching moment for me. Do I accept the

---

[16]John is the owner of several businesses and a family law practice—which is the third-oldest (1881) Kansas City-based law firm—and is a personal coach.

request to be her coach and perhaps put a strain on our relationship? I said, "Yes. I'll be happy to be your coach. And remember: I'm a resource, not an answer."

My coaching philosophy is that you have the power and the greatness. I just help you turn on the switch. I was able to coach Michelle through some business matters, and her career was advancing. Our good personal relationship got even better as we had this common cause. We had an understanding that our coaching relationship was business and that while I would challenge her, she should always be free to decline any challenge or suggestion by me. Then the test came when I lined up a beautiful venue in my city of Kansas City, Missouri, for Michelle to have an exhibit and a reception. I would invite friends and clients. I contacted a public relations company and our local paper, and I could foresee a huge success and great recognition for Michelle. She agreed it would be a great opportunity, and it was exciting for me as the proud father.

So we got the dates confirmed months ahead of time. Then, just a few weeks before the opening night, Michelle called and said, "Dad, I'm sorry; I can't do the show now in Kansas City. I need to show the artwork here in Chicago at another venue and I need to be here." That was a gutsy moment for Michelle. Of course, a lot of thoughts went through my head, most of them parental. I believed my venue in Kansas City would be much more successful than hers in Chicago, but I didn't say that. I remembered that the Coaching Bible encourages us as coaches to sometimes wait at least four seconds before responding. So I started counting. Then I remembered that the fifth point from "10 Ways to Get the Most From Your Coach" says that the player should "not be afraid to be contentious with your coach." Michelle was expressing herself. Then another quote from the Coaching Bible suddenly appeared: "Remember, coaching is about the other person."

So I shifted my focus to Michelle. I became so proud of her courage, which is an essential element to anyone's success. I then realized that I had successfully coached her in a very important way, and I felt joyful. Michelle is doing very well; our relationship is great. She inspires me as a coach, just like the coaching contract says. So, does Father know best?" Yes! But only when he asks for permission and listens well. I am grateful to Germaine and Jed for giving me the courage and the tools to coach my daughter and to deepen our relationship. You may view Michelle Gordon's art website at www.michellegordon.com.

The Wake-Up Call
By Paul Wang, PhD[17]

"Learning is the discovery that something is possible."
—Fritz Perls

I was visiting Houston, Texas to attend the oil and gas industry's popular OTC (Offshore Technology Conference). I was accompanied by some of my colleagues from the faculty team for an internal sales and management course sponsored by a large oil and gas manufacturing company. We all wanted to deepen and widen our knowledge of this industry so that we could better design our curriculum and delivery to our 40 sales management students.

I was invited to attend a large daytime gathering of the company's employees and customers as part of the week-long festivities of OTC. While there I was greeted by Jayme Sperring, a former student, and now friend and colleague. Jayme said, "Paul, you must ask David Reid to show you around OTC. He can give you a very special perspective on the exhibits and how everything fits together."

The next day, I found David at his company's exhibit and asked him if he wouldn't mind spending some time with me. "Jayme says that you can give me a unique perspective of what I see here." David humbly accepted my request and invested a good hour of his time with me. Indeed, Jayme was correct—I was fascinated by David's insights into the vast number of equipment displays and new technologies presented.

---

[17]Dr. Wang is Professor of Marketing Communications, Northwestern University, Evanston, IL

David offered to drive me from the OTC site to another of the week's many special gatherings. This time it would be with the alumni from our sales management course, current participants and faculty. As David drove us out of the crowded parking lot in his SUV, he asked me, "What was your experience of the OTC?" Without having to think, I responded emphatically, "Oh, I learned a lot!" David did not reply right away as he continued to negotiate the heavy traffic around Reliant Center, this year's home for the OTC.

After two or three minutes of silence David finally said, "When I was a young man, after growing up in Aberdeen, Scotland, I was rather precocious. Thought I was smarter than most people. Then one day, when I was about twenty-one, I guess, I spent time in California, where a wise and influential teacher in my life asked me the same question I asked you a moment ago. I admired this man very much, Pastor Daniel Brown. He was not only a minister but had a PhD in Higher Education and a Master's Degree in English Literature, and I had been able to spend eight months listening to his practical life-lesson teaching. I would hang on his every word during his eloquent lectures or sermons. As my time there came to a close, walking down the church steps to bid him good-bye, he asked, 'How was your experience with us, David?' I replied, 'This has been amazing Daniel, I have learned so much!' He smiled knowingly and said, 'Really David, I am not sure that you learned much at all. I think you may have just heard it for the first time. I think learning takes a longer time, and without discovery there is no learning.'

David continued, "I learned how to learn that day. Since then, I only consider that I have learned something when I have discovered something or have had an insight into the subject."

Suddenly I was jolted by the thought, "My God! David has just told me that I did not learn anything! Me, a university professor! Learning is my business! How dare he tell me that I did not learn anything! I had inspected equipment, I had asked questions, I had made notes, collected brochures and had already read some of them. I thought I learned a lot! Yet, this man suggests that I have learned nothing. I could not stop thinking about this possibility as we continued to travel to the new event. In fact, during the event, although I greeted students and enjoyed lively conversations, David's challenge continued to haunt me.

After the event, I went to my hotel room and spread all of the brochures and articles I had collected over the king-size bed and thought, "Okay, I have learned nothing. I have only seen it for the first time. For there to be learning, I must discover. All right then, what can I discover? Let me start learning. I had a purpose. What insight can I have now, looking at all this literature and marvelous photos of oil rigs and component parts?

I studied this makeshift collage for several minutes. And then it hit me. All of these many and varied pieces must fit together perfectly and simultaneously for the whole complex process to work! If they do not, the job cannot get done. All these different people from different companies must keep their promises to each other—work together in harmony for it all to come off safely. Safely! Then I thought of the Deepwater Horizon offshore drillship tragedy that the world was still reeling from. Now, insights began to explode one by one in my head like fireworks. I was discovering at last! I was learning. I got it! Yes, I had read before. Yes, I had researched before. But that didn't mean I learned anything. I got it.

Through my friend, my coach, David, I had experienced a gutsy coaching moment as a player—and I had profited immensely from his gentle *wake-up call*. He changed my life with his story—a special gift. I will never be the same. My lectures, my writing will forever be touched by my new view of what is required to actually learn and not "just see for the first time." I will pass this impact on to my students.

But even before that, Jayme was my coach to refer me to David. I shudder to think that I would have missed this magnificent opening for learning had I not accepted Jayme's coaching and sought David's unique perspective! Jayme knew that I had spent most of the day before at OTC and was ably guided by an experienced industry participant. Yet, he dared suggest that I go back, that I make the effort to ask David for his time. I discovered that coaching is a chain reaction of coachable moments, and in some cases "gutsy coaching moments"—those moments when one dares to challenge another's thinking, conclusions, or views in light of what the player seeks as his outcome. They are precious moments when one attempts to contribute to another at the risk of insulting a friend or losing a client. These are coachable moments when one makes a choice between seizing the opportunity to contribute to another or passing it up, watching it fade into oblivion. We will never have this moment again.

I learned that coaching is a discovery process. The coach may expose his player to a number of things—a whole bunch of stuff. It is ultimately up to the player to make sense out of it, to use it to achieve his desired outcomes. Coaching is not a string of pearls all carefully connected to one another. It is more like a billiard table—a lot can happen fast. One takes a shot and a whole myriad of things may take place ... like an explosion of possibility or an unintended scratch shot.

I bear witness to the profound difference that these magical coaching moments can make in our lives.

"Always have a 'Super Bowl' goal.
Maintain your positivity.
Don't ever let anybody steal your dream."

—Jeffrey Ross Ward, top U.S. outdoor advertising salesman, sold the largest-ever electronic sign in Houston, Texas. (From birth, Jeff Ward had to manage severe spina bifida. Neither Jeff nor his family and friends ever considered him handicapped.)

ADDENDA

1. The Coaching RoadMap
2. The Coaching Scope
3. Activity Versus Action
4. Coaching Outcomes Contract, Worksheet
5. Ten Ways to Get the Most From Your Coach
6. DreamMakers & DreamBrakers Exercise

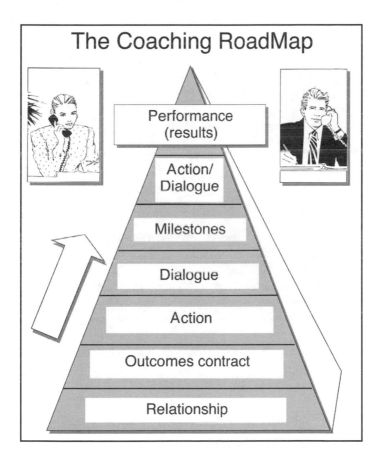

Figure A.1 excerpted from Chapter 3, *Coach Anyone About Anything*, Volume 1.

Performance (results): The outcomes of effective coaching are always specific, measureable results.

Action/Dialogue: Review of actions taken, what got done and what didn't, what's next?

Milestones: Meeting intended objectives and promises regularly. Fulfilling the coaching outcomes contract/making a new contract.

Dialogue: Permission to coach, conversations directed at closing the distance between the present level of results and intended outcomes. What would Thunderbolt! be for the player?

Actions from the future: Actions correlated to an articulated future. An absence of activity and excuses. Implementation of the 80/20 principle.

Outcomes contract: Ground rules. Measureable targets/outcomes in time. Expectations (the coach's, the player's)

Relationship: Build credibility and rapport (coaching biography). Share coaching philosophy.

Figure A.2, The Coaching Scope, is excerpted from Chapter 4, Coach Anyone About Anything, Volume 1.

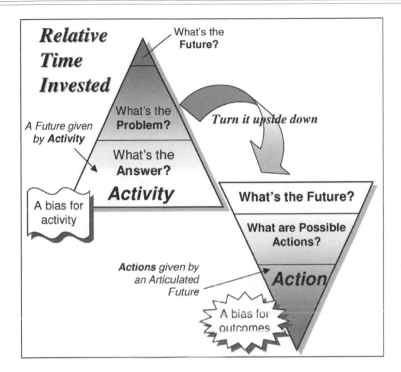

Figure A.3, The Activity Versus Action model, is excerpted from Chapter 2, Coach Anyone About Anything, Volume 1.

Actions are related to high-value, strategic outcomes; activities are not. *Activities* are low-value, reactionary, and associated with moment-to-moment urgencies rather than planned outcomes.

Worksheet

Coaching Outcomes Contract

Player/Client: _____ Date: ___/___/___

Purpose for the Coaching:

Scope of Work:

Measurable Outcomes:

Timeframe for the Work:

Expectations:

Ground Rules, Constraints:

Coaching Session Frequency & Format:

Financial Arrangements/Fees:

Cancellation Clause:

Figure A.4, Coaching Outcomes Contract, is excerpted from Chapter 3, Coach Anyone About Anything, Volume 1.

Ten Ways to Get the Most From Your Coach

(Excerpted from Chapter 5, Coach *Anyone About Anything*, Volume 1.)

1. Choose this coach to be your coach. (Coaching doesn't work otherwise).
2. Reread your Coaching Outcomes Contract before each coaching session, until you "become the contract."
3. Be certain about your goals and objectives.
4. Be open to your coach's questions, observations, and suggestions:
    a. Make yourself coachable, and be open to take coaching.
    b. See yourself as a novice-have a beginner's mind.
5. Communicate freely and candidly.
    a. Err on the side of overcommunicating. What constraints or obstacles do you face that your coach might assist you in designing creative ways forward?
    b. Don't be afraid to be contentious with your coach. Constructive contention breeds creativity. Just be sure it isn't your uncoachability doing the talking.
    c. Keep talking until you experience that your sales coach hears and understands you.
6. Tell the truth.
7. Do what you say you'll do, when you say you'll do it. Keep your word and contract agreements.
8. Use your coach as a resource, not the answer.
9. Come to each coaching session prepared to:
    a. List the outcomes you intend to accomplish in each coaching session.
    b. Do a fresh Dream**Makers** & Dream**Brakers** audit before each coaching session.
10. Make it your job to inspire your coach. To do that, you will have to be inspired yourself. At the end of each coaching session, tell your coach the things he or she did or said that you believe will make a real difference for you in achieving your objectives.

The DreamMakers & DreamBrakers Exercise
Part 1-Your Audit

Take a sheet of paper, and divide it into four quadrants (Figure A-5 offers a more graphic worksheet). Label the quadrants LIFT, WEIGHT, DRAG, and THRUST. Aeronautically speaking, these are the four forces of flight. These are forces one must manage in order to fly successfully. We use lift, weight, drag, and thrust here as a metaphor for the forces affecting you in accomplishing the intended outcomes of your project. (Your project may be your job, a particular accountability associated with your job, or an actual project.)

In each of the four quadrants, note elements or aspects associated with your project that remind you of the label or name for that quadrant. Said another way, translate your experience of the circumstances of your project into the four quadrants' names. Here are a few questions and suggestions to help you in this inquiry:

LIFT—DreamMakers

What do you find uplifting about your project? What inspires you about your project? What aspects of your project give you feelings of exhilaration, freedom, or joy? What makes your project worth doing? What makes your project fun? In this quadrant you might include people associated with your project who inspire you.

You may recall incidents of giving or receiving recognition during this project, or possible future acknowledgments that may be received upon the project's completion. Lift could be provided by visualizing the future state-your project completed and the benefits that you and others enjoy. Lift can be particular aspects of participating in your project that simply make you happy.

WEIGHT—DreamBrakers

What elements or aspects of your project do you experience as weighty? Are there things that dominate or oppress you? What parts of your project, when considered, leave you with a sense of burden, resignation, or the feeling of being bound? What obstacles seem immovable? What difficulties demoralize you? What takes the air out from under your wings? What thing wipes out your energy? What barriers occur for you as insurmountable? What parts of this project stop you cold?

Items of weight might be heavy obligations you wish you didn't have or deadlines that seem impossible to meet. Weight could be lingering guilt over things you should or should not have done. Weight might be resentments you have over unresolved issues or past events that seemed damaging or unfair. Weight could be a paralyzing fear about attempting something that must be done.

DRAG—DreamBrakers

What things about your project do you experience as a drag? What are some areas that hold you back a bit, impede your progress, or increase your frustration? What things about your project annoy you? Needless bureaucracy or cumbersome rules often make it into this quadrant. Fuzzy objectives can drag you down as you fritter away hours and days figuring out what you ought to be producing. Frivolous complaints, defensiveness, antagonism, petty conflicts, and negative interactions are aspects of projects that can drag us down. What things drain your energy-not all your energy, just a little? What things do you not like doing that must be done in this project?

THRUST—DreamMakers

Urgency can produce thrust. Urgency gets us into action. What things about your project provide urgency or add a jolt, spurring you to act swiftly and effectively? What things give you an energy boost? What things propel you to complete your project?

Completing something can create thrust. It's not just the sense of satisfaction from achieving what you set out to do, but there is also freedom available in acknowledging honestly what isn't done. Both are forms of completion and can provide thrust or energy. Being complete includes acknowledging what progress has been made, and it even includes acknowledging intended outcomes you've chosen to abandon-for the moment or forever.

Thrust can be produced by your being supported by others. Thrust is often generated by the experience of having the ability to make requests of others. New insights that grant fresh perspectives on issues you face in the project provide thrust. Exciting new possibilities for action provide energy. Thrust can even come from simply being respected and appreciated. Physical activity often provides thrust and energy.

Part 2-Your Adjustments

When you have completed this audit of the four forces of flight, you are ready to take a look at possibly making some changes to affect the balance of the quadrants (Figure A-6). Once you have more or less emptied your mind about your project into the four quadrants, step back and take a look: What elements of your project would you like to adjust in any of these quadrants?

First, look at WEIGHT. What is one thing you can do to reduce unwanted weight? Which element can you reduce, eliminate, or in some way alter so that its impact on you is diminished or even disappears?

Now look at how that single change might impact the other three quadrants. You may find that an action that eliminates weight simultaneously increases lift.

Continue looking. What can you do to increase LIFT? What about reducing DRAG? Look at the things that are a drag in your project. What pulls you off course or acts like wind resistance on your achievement fight path? What annoys you? Can you eliminate something there? Will its elimination allow you to add anything to the THRUST or LIFT quadrants?

The idea is not to eliminate all weight and all drag, nor is it to increase all lift and thrust. Small adjustments can produce dramatic results-just like when you fly an airplane. Look for the things you could change that would give you the most leverage. You may find some easy things to do right now that could accelerate your project quickly in the right direction.

Finally, look to see how these possible adjustments might shift the overall balance of the forces in your project.

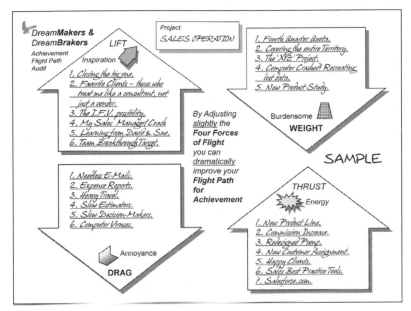

Figure A.5

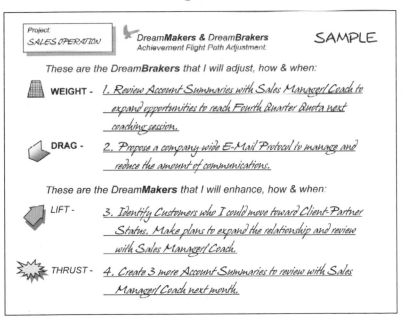

Figure A.6

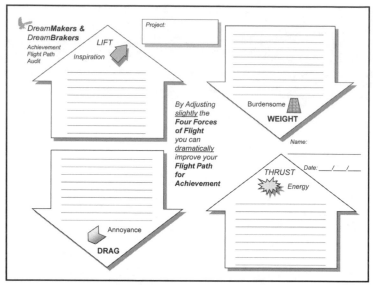

Figure A.7

Figure A.8

Coach Anyone About Anything, Volume 1, Chapter 13, contains a complete description of the DreamMakers & DreamBrakers tool with more examples.

INDEX

A

Accelerate, 95, 161, 175, 260
Accelerated learning, 169
Accomplishing, 12, 24, 25, 63, 78, 84,
    87, 93, 112, 116, 184, 258
Accomplishments, 66, 8, 187
Accountable, 4, 62, 117, 158, 165, 223
Acknowledging, 5, 185, 187, 259
Action Plan, 96, 98, 100, 103, 108,
    109, 110
Action/Dialogue, 29, 30, 31, 254
Activities, 31, 39, 40, 48, 66, 78, 83,
    87, 90, 92, 132, 145, 157, 198, 217,
    218, 229, 255
Activity, 24, 25, 26, 34, 43, 46, 48, 57,
    58, 84, 89, 91, 103, 142, 145, 217,
    253, 254, 255, 260
Activity Versus Action, 24, 48, 57, 58,
    217, 253, 255
Adjustments, 32, 110, 229, 240, 260
Advice, 2, 3, 4, 6, 7, 49, 124, 247
Always and never, 184
Ambiguity, 5
And/both, 82, 121
Answers, 5, 12, 17, 23, 74, 102, 199,
    212, 217, 244, 246
Appreciation, 153, 205, 206
Architecture, 97, 111, 112, 114, 120,
    121
Asking, 17, 22, 23, 25, 41, 49, 53, 74,
    80, 99, 100, 142, 152, 210, 213, 217,
    220, 223, 234
Athletic events, 89
Atmosphere, 18, 49, 52
Attributes, 11, 26, 121
Aucoin, Vickie, 5, 217
Audit Worksheet, 105, 107, 108, 109

Authentic, 6, 34, 183, 213, 222, 246
Awards, 43, 48, 49, 176, 225

B

Bad news, 23, 24, 90, 105
Bagyura, Susan, 221
Balcony people, 5, 13, 14
Barnes, Neal, 214
Behavior, 15, 27, 48, 49, 52, 75, 99,
    118, 217, 230, 235, 240
Believe or prove, 31, 44, 47, 49
Bernal, Christopher, 211
Best, Worst, Probable, 32, 143, 151,
    154
Bias for, 25
Bina, Shideh, 240
Borrow the will, 56
Business as usual, 35, 36, 123, 170
Business by accident, 95, 104, 110
Buy-in, 112, 119, 164, 170

C

Carefrontation, 223, 225
Case for action, 114
Celebrate, 62, 177, 187
Certification, 68, 115, 116, 120
Challenge, 90, 115, 123, 224, 211, 224,
    233, 238, 239, 240, 242, 248, 250, 251
Champion, 21, 114, 213, 224, 226,
Chaos, 57, 99, 163, 181, 182, 184, 185,
    187, 230, 246
Charter, 114, 150, 181, 178
Chatterbox, 27, 84, 86, 88
Cheerleading, 175
Chi-running, 119
Choice Panorama, 143, 155, 156

Closing the distance, 29, 254
Clutter, 51, 53, 54, 184
Coachability, 244
Coachable moment, 203. 204, 206, 209, 251
Coaching conversations, 29, 48, 57
Coaching culture, 110, 111, 112, 114, 116, 120, 121
Coaching definition, 3
Coaching Dialogue Process, 29, 41
Coaching Dynamics Matrix, 125, 126
Coaching elements, 122
Coaching factors, 123
Coaching levels, 122
Coaching methods, 124, 126
Coaching Outcomes Contract, 40, 226, 227, 253, 254, 256, 257
Coaching paradoxes, 200
Coaching philosophy, 28, 248, 254
Coaching practice, 40, 121, 126, 127, 128, 129, 204, 229
Coaching relationship, 30, 41, 247, 248
Coaching RoadMap, 29, 253
Coaching Scope, 2, 18, 21, 253, 254
Coaching session, 23, 31, 32, 37, 39, 40, 41, 123, 124, 136, 210, 217, 221, 222, 226, 227, 257
Coaching structure, 122
Coaching style, 21
CoachLab, 23, 24, 116, 227
Collegial, 123, 124
Colors, 16, 58, 59, 60
Commandments, 197, 201
Commitment, 3, 15, 18, 34, 39, 76, 110, 113, 117, 123, 151, 159, 173, 175, 178, 185, 186, 187, 197, 215, 220, 222, 225, 227
Communicating, 14, 23, 175, 196, 238, 239
Competence, 27, 144
Competent coaching, 120

Competition, 45, 47, 161, 172, 177, 224, 225, 231
Complacent, 15
Confidence, 4, 5, 51, 55, 118, 129, 144, 152, 153, 185, 211, 231
Confidentiality, 212
Consensus, 149, 150, 232
Consequences, 120, 122, 134, 238
Content-orientation, 21
Contest, 45, 46, 173, 207, 208
Context, 16, 17, 29, 73, 79, 80, 83, 108, 123, 197
Contract, 40, 110, 114, 123, 124, 135, 200, 204, 222, 226, 227, 237, 238, 239, 245, 248, 253, 254, 256
Contrast Coaching with Mentoring, 7, 8
Contrasting conversations, 37
Contribution, 89, 110, 148, 167, 208, 217
Conventional wisdom, 36
Coordinated Actions, 32, 48
Criteria, 146, 149, 156
Critical mass, 119, 120
Cultural change, 113, 117, 118, 121

D

Data & Observations, 31
Deadlines, 15, 76, 82, 217, 222, 259
Delivery categories, 125
Delivery media, 125
Delivery methods, 120, 124
Dependent, 17, 23
Design, 24, 26, 29, 45, 48, 58, 63, 85, 95, 97, 98, 99, 100, 104, 109, 110, 112, 115, 116, 121, 126, 144, 152, 159, 161, 164, 166, 169, 170, 171, 173, 74, 179, 186, 197, 200, 257
Design games, 169
Desktop background organizer, 127,

139, 140, 141
Developing people, 27, 120
Dialogue, 15, 26, 29, 30, 31, 37, 41, 47, 49, 86, 198, 212, 213, 254
Difference-making, 39, 115
Direct reports, 9, 23, 36, 49, 98, 114, 218, 232,
Discipline, 55, 56, 128
Disorganized, guilt-free, 179, 181, 188
Display, 70, 122, 124, 129, 133, 137, 141, 145, 164, 249
Dissatisfaction, 35, 36, 171
DreamMakers & DreamBrakers, 96, 228, 229, 253, 257, 258, 262
Duct tape, 128

E

Eagle's view, 54, 60, 61, 74, 90, 95-100, 110, 122, 127, 129, 132, 137, 139, 142, 161, 164-167, 181, 186-188, 196-197, 226
Eagle's View Inventory, 181, 187, 188, 196
Edwards, Angelo, 226
Either/or, 82, 121
Elevator speech, 199
Empower, 14, 17, 23, 142
Empowered, 23, 128, 162, 210
Encourage, 2, 4, 6, 100, 145, 170, 175, 186, 223, 248
Energy, 40, 46, 48, 53, 54, 59, 92, 98, 170, 181,187, 198, 219,220, 221, 259, 260
Enrolling, 8, 12, 120, 198, 200
Enthusiasm, 3, 7, 18, 26, 39, 45, 67, 116, 157, 175, 187, 197, 210
Environment, 51, 52, 53, 55-57, 59, 60, 63, 75, 83, 98, 100, 105, 109, 93, 106, 117, 135, 136, 137, 145, 113, 136, 152, 162, 231, 233

Evaluating Possibilities, 143, 145, 146, 148, 150
Excellence, 27, 151, 172
Expert, 4, 17, 21, 36, 37, 116, 117, 124, 150, 220

F

Face-to-face, 125, 126, 134, 135, 137, 216, 241
Facilitate, 18, 96, 116, 145, 149, 150, 197, 243
Facilitator, 17,163, 164
Facts, 21, 31,43, 44, 46, 47, 48, 49, 59, 110
False urgency, 48, 103
Fantasies, 182, 185, 186, 196
Farr, Cristin, 230
Feedback, 23, 24, 30, 227, 240
Feedforward, 23-26,62, 107, 174, 197, 234
Feng shui, 59
Fertile field, 33
First steps, 35, 36, 70
Formal, 2, 4, 122, 123, 124, 158
Formula for Change, 35, 41
Freedom, 86, 185, 259
Fun, 20, 71, 78, 81, 92, 161, 162, 167, 169, 172, 173, 183, 230, 231, 258
Fun, 20, 71, 78, 81, 92, 161, 162, 167, 169, 172, 173, 183, 230, 231, 258
Future, 8, 9, 12, 24, 25, 31, 35,36, 39, 81-85, 105, 108, 136, 148,150, 151, 152, 153, 162, 174, 184, 186, 197, 213, 214, 216, 221, 230, 237, 238, 240, 254, 258

G

Geography, 134, 136
Gordon, John, 247

Gossip, 34, 117
Group, 12, 23, 45, 69, 84, 108, 115,117,
    119, 123, 125, 139, 146, 150,151,
    157, 161-165, 167, 172, 177, 178,
    201, 241, 245, 246
Guilt, 40, 179, 181, 185, 186, 187, 196,
    259
Gutsy coaching moments, 203, 208,
    219, 251

H

Handwriting analysis, 209
Hat, 2, 9, 13
Hatfield, Iris, 7, 209
Hearing, 15, 44, 214
Henson, Try, 237
High-impact, 147
High-value, 25, 40, 87, 90, 142, 198,
    218, 255
Human resources, 68, 112, 214
Huiras, Dick, 228

I

Impatient, 19, 23, 224
Implementation, 112, 114, 144, 145,
    254
Impossible, 16, 18, 37, 145, 162, 184,
    219, 259
Incentives, 100, 102, 107, 108
Individual, 1, 30, 35, 99,108,111,117,
    121,123, 124, 145, 146, 151, 167,
    176, 178, 243
Informal, 120-124, 158
Inquiring, 75, 86, 109
Inquiry, 13, 31, 32, 62, 73, 78, 80,
    95-97, 100, 109, 122, 124, 126, 153,
    154, 258
Internal coaches, 114, 115
Internal dialogue, 26, 86

Interpretations, 31, 44, 46, 47, 48, 49,
    76, 80, 110
Intolerable, 36
Inventory, 86, 108, 146, 181, 187, 188,
    196
Investigation, 43, 46, 149, 213
Invisible designs, 99
Invitation, 33, 78, 115

K

Katrina, Hurricane, 226
Key influencers, 115
Know-it-all, 17, 235, 236

L

Landscape of possible roles, 17
Language, 28, 41, 68, 113, 218, 241,
    243
Lamb, Larry, 232
Launch, 6, 13, 45, 46, 111, 112, 114,
    115, 120, 121, 148, 150, 152, 169,
    174, 177
Law of gradual progress, 111, 119, 120
Leader, 2, 8, 9, 12-14, 69, 83, 97, 150,
    151, 207, 217, 221, 241
Leadership, 2, 4, 8, 9, 49, 97, 98, 107,
    110, 197, 201, 204, 211, 213, 221,
    223, 232, 238, 240, 241
Learning, 19, 23, 56, 119, 125, 145,
    169, 186, 222, 225, 230, 231, 244,
    249, 250, 251
Levels of conversations, 9
Lift, weight, drag, and thrust, 9, 258
Listening, 1-3, 9, 11-13, 15-17, 23, 24,
    26-28, 31, 44, 45, 54, 144, 151, 177,
    227, 236, 2505
Low-impact, 147
Low-value, 15, 31, 40, 87, 142, 149,
    198, 255

M

MacDonald, Machen, 223
Management, 2, 8, 9, 19, 36, 73, 78, 79, 82, 84, 86, 96-98, 100, 107, 109, 113, 115, 120, 124, 132, 137, 150, 171, 182, 204, 205, 209, 211, 232, 241, 249, 250
Manager, 6, 8, 9, 12-14, 21, 23, 27, 36, 49, 57, 58, 81, 97, 98, 111, 113, 120, 128, 134, 137, 138, 166, 169, 171, 173, 178, 198, 201, 209, 211, 214, 215, 217, 232-235, 242, 244
Managing, 9, 11, 12, 14, 51, 62, 78, 79, 110, 137, 140, 186, 215, 232, 245
Managing Complex Change, 96, 100
Mandate, 115, 150
Marathon, 84, 87
Measurable, 31, 112, 118, 120, 123, 124, 157, 178
Mentor, 4, 7, 13, 97, 124, 219
Mentoring, 2-7, 9, 14, 97, 109, 122, 204, 213
Mentors, 2-7, 9, 14
Metric, 178
Milestones, 9, 164, 175, 187, 254
Miscellaneous mission, 66
Missing, 35, 68, 101-105, 107-109, 144, 152, 199, 217, 229
Modern coaching paradigm, 37
Momentum, 169, 172, 175, 187, 198
Money, 17, 40, 49, 51, 74, 79, 86, 119, 128, 148, 156, 176, 207, 217
Moods, 59
Morale, 54, 179, 211, 213
Motivate, 45, 46, 108, 186
Motivating, 47, 89, 142, 171, 172
Motivation, 45-47, 98, 107, 171, 235
Myth, 67, 68

N

Near misses, 178, 179
Norway, 23, 59

O

Offshore Technology Conference, 249
Onboarding, 4
Open field, 33
Open-door policy, 232
Opening, 16, 28, 33, 73, 76-86, 248, 251
Opinions, 46, 47
Organizational culture, 4
Organized, 114, 140, 181, 184, 186
Over-communicating, 117
Ownership, 166, 167

P

Panorama Card Planning, 162, 163, 166, 167
Paradoxical, 28, 197, 201
Parents, 2, 5, 205
Passion, 219, 220, 230
Passionate, 126, 220
Pathways, 51, 60, 118, 165
Patience, 18, 20, 221
Perfect, 6, 12, 13, 17, 28, 44, 65, 67, 69, 71, 132, 133, 143-145, 171, 182, 185, 188, 206, 229, 251
Performance, 37, 59, 108, 125, 148, 176, 211-213, 217, 228, 232, 240
Personality-styles, 243
Planning, 25, 34, 61, 69, 97, 126, 127, 132, 133, 139, 142, 144, 153, 159, 161-163, 166, 167, 186, 217
Player's Preflight Checklist, 39, 40, 41
Polish, 143, 144, 145
Politics, 18, 43

Possibility, 18, 21, 23, 34, 35,51, 76, 78, 80, 83, 86, 126, 146-149, 156, 170, 196, 198, 212, 236, 250, 252
Powell, Jeff, 245
Power, 17, 19, 28, 41, 43, 54,67, 79, 87, 93, 95, 97, 126, 143, 181, 183, 246, 248
PowerPoint, 141, 166
Preflight checklist, 20, 39, 41
Preparation, 29, 40, 41, 154, 221
Prime Time, 134, 137
Prizes, 176, 177
Processes, 92, 95, 113, 142, 228, 245
Procrastination, 63, 65, 67, 71
Progress board, 61, 62, 63
Promised actions, 29, 31, 32
Protégés, 2, 4, 9
Public conversation, 63

Q

Questions, 12, 17, 20, 21, 23, 28, 31, 39, 44, 47, 49, 68, 69, 81, 110, 112, 113, 139, 143, 144, 151-154, 188, 198, 200, 209-211, 213, 220, 227, 233, 234, 243, 257, 258

R

R-A-C-I, 143, 157, 158
Ratios,128, 129
Recognition, 46, 108, 248, 258
Redesign, 96, 144, 150
Reengineering, 12
Referees, 170
Reject rate, 36, 37
Relationship, 4, 16, 30, 37, 41,73, 76, 81, 83, 119, 120, 136, 184, 211-213, 216, 232, 240, 243, 244, 246-248, 254
Repercussions, 115, 238

Report-outs, 115
Reputations, 205
Request, 12, 18, 34, 40, 61, 116, 117, 124, 140, 227, 229, 244, 245, 248, 249, 259
Resistance, 35, 36, 98, 99, 260
Resources, 40, 54, 67, 79, 83, 100, 103, 107, 108, 110, 112, 115, 120, 152, 214, 238, 243
Respect, 4, 7, 17, 115, 150, 219, 260
Responsibility, 1, 17-19, 157, 176, 214, 233, 243
Reward, 108, 170, 179, 216
Roles & Responsibilities, 143, 157
Routine actions, 66, 89, 90
Rules, 69, 111, 118, 170, 173, 174, 227, 254, 259

S

Safety, 107, 169, 178, 179, 213
Sales coaching, 126, 127
Sales Executive Council, 132
Sales managers, 23, 138, 171
Sales process, 128, 129, 140
Sales professionals, 132, 134, 137-139
Salespeople, 23, 46, 57, 69, 108, 128, 129, 132, 133, 136, 142, 157, 171
Saving time, 87, 88
Self-assessment, 181
Self-selected, 115
Self-talk, 55, 63
Selling, 127, 128, 129, 171
Selling Scorecard, 129, 142, 253
Shadowing, 116
Significance, 67-71, 219, 220
Significant, 41, 47, 66-71, 92, 198, 211, 216, 220, 228, 231
Silver bullet, 69
Skilled, 26, 27, 46, 48, 63, 107, 123

Skills, 3, 15, 23, 26, 95, 100, 102, 107, 125, 155, 156, 166
Solutions, 17, 18, 28, 198, 245
Spandex Story, 13
Speaking, 1, 2, 3, 6, 11, 12, 15-17, 21, 46, 118, 166, 207, 212, 243, 246, 258
Specific outcomes, 34, 48, 242
Speculation, 46, 47
Sponsor, 5, 114, 123, 249
Standing, 59, 60, 83, 105, 124, 171, 200, 215, 234
Stand-up files, 60
Stand-up meetings, 6
Status quo, 60, 61
Storytelling, 275
Strategic business initiative, 112, 120
Strategic partners, 17
Strategic thinking, 39
Strategic-thinking partner, 197
Strategy, 26, 96, 108, 109, 233
Stress, 51, 52, 57, 68, 81, 137, 186, 209, 230, 231
Stuff, 52, 53, 63, 66, 69, 78, 88, 146, 150, 184, 205, 220, 252
Synonyms, 67, 101, 104, 107, 108, 157

Tent-card reminders, 60
Think or know?, 31, 44, 47, 49
Think with, 7
Three Ps, 143, 144, 145, 159
Thunderbolt, 24, 41, 84, 89, 96, 136, 139, 254
Time as a constraint, 73, 75, 76, 78, 80, 81, 83, 84
Time as an opening, 73, 76, 77, 78, 79, 81, 82, 83, 84, 86
Time generator checklist, 87, 92
Time invested, 88, 162
Time Traditions, 87, 90, 92, 93
Time Transformation, 73, 78, 80, 86, 90
Time victims, 75, 89
Timetext, 80-82, 84
Trainer, 2, 19
Training, 2, 15, 84, 87, 113, 115, 116, 166, 199, 215, 226, 236, 242
Trust, 5, 6, 18, 118, 128, 150, 176, 211, 212, 240
Turnover, 102, 211, 213
Tutoring, 230, 231
Types of coaching, 30, 121, 122, 124, 126

T

Task, 55, 62, 63, 67, 68, 84, 85, 112, 114, 157, 161, 164, 165, 178, 182, 184, 210, 217
Teaching, 69, 116, 230, 250
Team leaders, 150, 151
Teamwork, 63, 176, 177
Technical Application, 123
Telephone, 46, 60, 88, 89, 109,125, 126, 129, 134, 223, 229
Tell versus ask, 21, 23
Telling, 21-23, 28, 89, 109, 139, 187, 201, 205, 236, 246

U

Ultimate Week, 132, 133, 134, 136, 137, 138, 138, 142, 253, 263
Unacceptable, 36
Unproductive, 48, 90
Unskilled, 26, 27
Upchurch, Doug, 62, 219
Urgency, 48, 67, 68, 103, 128, 259

V

Value drift, 41
Value proposition, 198, 199, 200
Velocity, 65

Victim, 18, 19, 34, 75, 78, 89, 92
Vision, 9, 12, 25, 35, 36, 82, 83, 100,
   101, 102, 104, 105, 152, 211, 240
Voluntary, 115

W

Walk the talk, 113
Wang, Paul, 249
Water-cooler coaching, 121, 122
Ways to Get the Most Out of Your
   Coach, 38, 40, 249, 253, 257
Weeds, 33, 34, 35
Win, 20, 41, 85, 108, 118, 153, 172,
   173, 175, 176, 177, 179, 201, 224,
   226, 231
Winners, 80, 175, 177
Winning, 20, 43, 80, 84, 132, 170,
172,
   174, 176, 177, 223, 224, 225, 230,
   247
Winter, Stacey, 242
Wires crossed conversation, 12
World-class, 110, 111, 112, 113, 120

BIOGRAPHIES

Germaine Porché and Jed Niederer have also co-authored *Coach Anyone About Anything: How to Help People Succeed in Business and Life, Volume 1*; the bestselling humor book series *Coaching Soup for the Cartoon Soul; The Power of Coaching: The Secrets of Achievement; The Power of Coaching: Managing the Time of Your Life*; and the CD series *Ask The Coaches*. They are the creators of CoachLab® and the Eagle's View® time-transformation and outcome-management workshops. Jed and Germaine serve as lecturers in the Practice of Executive Education, Jones Graduate School of Business, Rice University, Houston, TX.

Germaine enjoys running marathons, yoga, strength training, and cycling. She finds relaxation in reading, cooking all types of food, and spoiling her nieces and nephews. Jed enjoys, running, cartooning, reading, cycling, and appreciating classic automobiles. They love traveling together and volunteering for youth mentoring programs. Germaine and Jed have been married 21 years and reside in Houston, Texas, with their dogs Gus and Mitzi.

Germaine V. Porché, MSOD

Germaine is President of Eagle's View Consulting. She specializes in working with organizations to produce performance breakthroughs in productivity and leadership. Her 23 years of consulting experience is in the design and delivery of training programs that incorporate clients' specific developmental needs, such as Rapid Work Redesign™, productivity breakthroughs, employee engagement, coaching, and communication skills.

She coaches executives, individuals, and groups at all levels to deliver high-impact business results. Germaine is a resourceful and innovative designer and dynamic deliverer of consulting interventions. Her consulting work is multicultural, including work in Europe, Indonesia, Israel, and Canada. Some of the industries Germaine has consulted in are real estate, insurance, sales, forest products, law, manufacturing, mining, and energy. She has also worked with teams of labor and management personnel to produce breakthrough results.

Germaine holds a Master of Science degree in Organization Development from The American University in Washington, D.C., and the NTL Institute (National Training Laboratories). She was recognized as a *Top Ten Business Woman* for the American Business Women Association in 2006 and received the Federation of Professional Business Women's *Woman of Excellence* award in 2008.

Edward (Jed) Niederer, III

Jed is Vice President of Sales Effectiveness at National Oilwell Varco. He has coached executives, managers, teams, and entrepreneurs to break-through performance for 30 years. A skillful program developer and deliverer, Jed has created and led courses and workshops in personal effectiveness, communication, leadership, sales, and coaching for more than 100,000 people in the U.S., Canada, Europe, the Far East, the Middle East, South America, and Australia.

Jed's consulting and coaching career has included work in mining, manufacturing, energy, insurance, computer, forest products, and healthcare industries. He has successfully managed projects involving a wide range of large-scale change methodologies, including Rapid Work Redesign, high-impact work teams, and breakthrough process reengineering.

After earning a B.A. in Communications & Advertising from the University of Washington in Seattle, Jed entered the life insurance business and was a million-dollar producer his first year. At age 24 he was appointed the youngest-ever agency manager for Provident Mutual Life, eventually leading his associates to win the President's Trophy. Jed holds a Chartered Life Underwriter (CLU) degree from The American College, Bryn Mawr, Pennsylvania. He served as a Second Lieutenant and aviator in the U.S. Army Transportation Corps.